Theory and Practice of Dialogical Community Development

This book proposes that community development has been increasingly influenced and co-opted by a modernist, soulless, rational philosophy, reducing it to a shallow technique for 'solving community problems'. In contrast, this dialogical approach re-maps the ground of community development practice within a frame of dialogue, hospitality and depth.

For the first time community development practitioners are provided with an accessible understanding of dialogue and its relevance to their practice, exploring the contributions of internationally significant thinkers such as P. Freire, M. Buber, M. Gandhi, E. Levinas, D. Bohm and H.G. Gadamer, J. Derrida, G. Esteva and R. Sennett.

What makes the book distinctive is that, first, it identifies a dialogical tradition of community development and considers how such a tradition shapes practice within contemporary contexts and concerns – economic, social, political, cultural and ecological. Second, the book contrasts such an approach with technical and instrumental approaches to development that fail to take complex systems seriously. Third, the approach links theory to practice through a combination of storytelling and theory-reflection, ensuring that readers are drawn into a practice-theory that they feel increasingly confident has been 'tried and tested' in the world over the past 25 years.

Peter Westoby is a Senior Lecturer in Community Development (CD) within the CD Unit, Queensland University, Australia, and a Research Fellow with the Centre for Development Support, University of Free State, South Africa. He is also a Director/Consultant with the non-profit co-operative Community Praxis Co-op, which provides youth, community and organisational development services.

Gerard Dowling has 20 years of experience in various community development roles in Brisbane, Australia, including housing work with the Tenants' Union and collaborative community planning consultancies with Community Praxis Co-op. He currently manages a strategy unit for Brisbane City Council, working to make the city's programmes, services and facilities more inclusive.

Theory and Practice of Dialogical Community Development

International perspectives

Peter Westoby and Gerard Dowling

LONDON AND NEW YORK

This edition published 2013
by Routledge
2 Park Square, Milton Park, Abingdon, Oxon OX14 4RN

Simultaneously published in the USA and Canada
by Routledge
711 Third Avenue, New York, NY 10017

Routledge is an imprint of the Taylor & Francis Group, an informa business

The right of Peter Westoby and Gerard Dowling to be identified as authors of this work has been asserted by themselves in accordance with sections 77 and 78 of the Copyright, Designs and Patents Act 1988.

All rights reserved. No part of this book may be reprinted or reproduced or utilised in any form or by any electronic, mechanical, or other means, now known or hereafter invented, including photocopying and recording, or in any information storage or retrieval system, without permission in writing from the publishers.

Trademark notice: Product or corporate names may be trademarks or registered trademarks, and are used only for identification and explanation without intent to infringe.

British Library Cataloguing in Publication Data
A catalogue record for this book is available from the British Library

Library of Congress Cataloging-in-Publication Data
Westoby, Peter.
Theory and practice of dialogical community development : international perspectives / Peter Westoby and Gerard Dowling.
  pages cm
  Includes bibliographical references and index.
  1. Community development. 2. Interpersonal communication.
  3. Dialogue--Social aspects. I. Dowling, Gerard. II. Title.
  HN49.C6W474 2013
  307.1'4--dc23
  2012050410

ISBN13: 978-0-415-53788-9 (hbk)
ISBN13: 978-0-203-10994-6 (ebk)

Typeset in Times New Roman
by Bookcraft Ltd, Stroud, Gloucestershire

Printed and bound in the United States of America
by Edwards Brothers Malloy

Contents

About the authors vii
Acknowledgements viii
Preface x
Foreword xii
Abbreviations xvii

Introduction: a practice framework 1
International community development practice 2
Dialogical community development: a framework 4
Restoring depth: why dialogical community development? 10
Widening the framework 12
A reflection on theory and practice 17

1 Theoretical prelude: an introduction to dialogue for community development 20
 A normative perspective on dialogue 22
 A historical understanding of dialogue 29

2 Re-imagining community practice 32
 Awakening love 32
 Deepening participation 39
 Place-making 45
 Welcoming problems and shadow 52

3 Transformative community processes 61
 The discerning and gentling of method 61
 Widening analysis 68
 Careful conflicting 77
 Structuring not strangling 82

vi Contents

4 Analytical interlude: what weakens dialogue within community
   development   91
   Ideological positions 91
   Therapeutic culture 94
   Growing inequalities 95

5 Caring for different spheres of community life   99
   Caring for the ordinary 100
   Caring for the economy 102
   Caring for politics 110
   Caring for the cultural 118
   Earth care 121

6 Dialogue and training for transformation   128
   Space to re-imagine 131
   Stories for sparking re-imagination 133
   Methods and models for transformative training 138
   Inspiration and empowerment, not information 145
   The logic of wishing, willing and acting 150

   Conclusion   154
   A passion of not knowing 157
   Invitation to dialogue and dissent 157

   Notes   158
   References   159
   Index   171

About the authors

Peter Westoby

Peter originally hails from the UK but now loves living in Highgate Hill, Brisbane. He is currently a Senior Lecturer in Community Development within the University of Queensland, and a Research Fellow with the Centre for Development Support, the University of Free State, South Africa. He is also a director/consultant with Community Praxis Co-operative.

His experience includes work in South Africa, Papua New Guinea, the Philippines, India, Vanuatu and Australia. His interests are in refugee-related work, youth-work practice and community development. He is passionate about running, reading, good coffee, hanging out at his local AVID reader bookshop, bushwalking and travelling. His current greatest dilemma is how to align his love of travel with carbon emissions.

Gerard Dowling

Gerard was born in North Queensland, a descendant of Irish-English folk who came looking for gold in the 1870s and ended up scratching for tin and wrangling packhorses and cattle in the bush. From 1987 until 2011 he lived in the inner Brisbane suburb of West End, where he shared a home with Lyn, raised Ciaron and Jack, and (much to his surprise) fulfilled Ciaron's naive childhood dream of growing a rainforest in the backyard of a humble rented cottage on a little 16-perch block. He's done 20 years in various community development roles, including housing work with the Tenants' Union, prison work with the Catholics, youth development and social policy work with Brisbane City Council, and collaborative community planning consultancies with Community Praxis Co-operative. He loves the methodology described in this book because it gives all introverts an effective, easy way to work with a few others to change the world.

For those curious about the relationship between the authors, we recommend Michael Leunig's *The Curly Pyjama Letters* (2001). This delightful Australian allegory describes a dialogue between the insightful Vasco Pyjama, travelling the world on an intrepid voyage of discovery in the company of his direction-finding duck, and the affable Mr Curly at home in Curly Flat, a life of considered domestic contentment in the company of his teapot. You will soon know who is who.

Acknowledgements

As in our first book on this topic, we are keen to acknowledge the people with whom we have shared the journey. We are both attentive to process, and have learned much practice wisdom in living, working and playing alongside others. The approach to community development we are describing is not something we alone have made up – it is an approach that we have co-created and co-discovered with many others in multiple processes of dialogue over 25 years. This book is a reflection on the community, the work and the research that we have shared with many very different people. If you have been our companion, the chances are you may recognise your own insights here – if not in specific phrases, then in a familiarity with perspectives, values, principles and ideas that we have distilled from a shared history of practice.

Like any authors whose work is built on the shoulders of many, we want to thank everyone, but will inevitably leave out someone really important. Sorry to such people. However, we would like to acknowledge some of the many people who have made important contributions to our understanding of community and our practice of community development.

Fellow-travellers in the inner Brisbane neighbourhood of West End: Johnny Glover, Ruth and Chris Todd, Dave and Angie Andrews, Judy and Steve Collins-Haynes, Matthew Leggett, Greg Daley, Wendy Webster, Wendy Moore, Jim Dowling, Trevor and Theresa Jordan, Edmund Cocksedge, Bob Cunningham, Nigel and Sue Lewin, Carmel Rosella, Jennifer Alford, Jenny Nash, Michael O'Brien, Kimberley Williams, Faye Lovett and all the crew at the West End Reading and Writing Group.

Those who have journeyed with us, with refugees: Carlos and Roberto Monterosa, Dionisio and Oscar, John Kor Diew, Russell Eggins, Domingo Montenegro, Marco and Elvia Ramirez, Paula Peterson, Donata Rossi, Keithia Wilson, Renae Mann, Nermina (Nera) Komaric, Ally Wakefield, Lois Wiseman, Robyn Sheptooha, Danijel Kis, Saba Abrahams and Catalina Hernandez.

Colleagues who have shared, among many other things, the ongoing experiment that is Community Praxis Co-op: Jason McLeod, Chris Brown, Betty Chapelle, Noritta Morseu-Diop, Helen Beazley, Athena Lathouras, Lynda Shevellar, Ken Morris, Neil Barringham and Howard Buckley.

Brisbane colleagues we have learned from: Maria Tenant, Deirdre Coghlan, Janelle Scognamilglio, Erna Hayward, Juanita Phillips, Ian Schmidt, Julie Ling,

Maria Brennan, Morrie O'Connor, Paul Toon, Paul Donatiu, Bea Rogan, Fiona Caniglia, Anna Spencer, Colleen Kelly, Lisa Price, Anthony Esposito, Karen Walsh, Phil Crane, Mark Young, Jeremy Liyanage, Wally Dethlefs, Jon Eastgate, Liz Upham, Roberta Bonnin, Steve Capelin, Deanna Borland-Sentinella, Nina Bowbridge, Donna Bowe, Gabrielle Huggett, Rajendra Padhee, Ingrid Martonova, Pam Bourke and Ken Butler.

Some of those Peter has journeyed with from around the world:

South Africa: Sipho Sokhela, Verne and Kerry Harris, Mike and Pauline Cuthbert, Nick Lindner, Caroline Skinner, Mpume Zama, Treven Hendricks, Lucius Botes, Doreen Atkinson, Mark Ingle, Allan Kaplan, Sue Davidoff and Rubert Van Blerk.

Vanuatu: Anne Brown, Anna Nolan, Mark Love, Paul Jensen, Charles Vatu, Selwyn Garu and Dickinson.

Papua New Guinea: Landy, Joe and Louise.

Philippines: Therese, Digna, Jose, Stuart and the rest of the 'gang'.

Students who have taught us by challenging our practice: Denise Foley, Anna Strandring, Helen Abbott, San-Marie Esterhuysen, Tim Graham, Nina Sharpe, James Douglas, Nicholas Haines, Fiona Murray and Gabby Denning-Cotter.

Those who sat in the playground and imagined a vibrant community around our children at Buranda Primary School – for all those 'what if ...' conversations: Julie, Mark, Lyn, Lynne, Kath, Don, Miriam, Sue, Mark, Maaritt, Lynne, Carlos, John, Lynne, Ivy and Corena.

Gerard's colleagues from the early days of the Tenants' Union of Queensland: Janice Jordan, Lurline Comerford, Robyn Cochrane, Gary Penfold, Tim Seelig, Tim Wilson, Peter See, Louise Villanova, Lillian Lawson-Geddes and Rebecca Foote.

University teachers and colleagues: Allan Halladay, Ann Ingamells, Mary Graham, Lilla Watson, David Massey, Jayne Clapton, Patricia Harrison, Anthony Kelly, Polly Walker, Ingrid Burkett, John Owen, Lynda Shevellar, Serge Loode, Kristen Lyons, David Palmer and David Ip.

Our families: Iris, Michael, Lisa, Jim, Ella, Kaiya, Ross, Karen, Ciaron, Jack, Dot and Pat, Sharon, David, Marilyn, Ross, Tamma, Maurie, Dorothy and Peter. And of course as fellow-journeyers and also supporters in the writing task we would like to thank our partners: Larah Seivl-Keevers and Lyn Dowling.

Finally, we would like to acknowledge those who have given indispensable help with this book. Thanks to the five anonymous reviewers – their comments were invaluable. Thanks to Polly, John, Roland, Serge, David, Jacques, Sue, Allan and Lynda for strong feedback challenging our assumptions, and also for the people at Routledge-Earthscan, particularly Khanam Virjee, our commissioning editor, and Helena Hurd and Charlotte Russell, our editorial assistants.

We dedicate this book to three of our mentors: Dave Andrews, Ann Ingamells and Anthony Kelly.

Preface

This book is a reflection on our combined 50 years of shared and separate experience of community life and community development practice. These years have seen us live and work in our own Australian neighbourhoods and cities, work in several different countries (namely South Africa, Vanuatu, Papua New Guinea (PNG), the Philippines and India) and also conduct research in a range of other countries (such as Ecuador, the United Kingdom (UK), the United States of America (USA) and New Zealand). This book, as a reflection on international perspectives of dialogical community development theory and practice, is informed by our experiences and research into stories, practice and theory from this diverse set of places and contexts.

The main difference between this book and our previous book, *Dialogical Community Development: With Depth, Solidarity and Hospitality* (2009), is the extension of our reflections beyond practice within our own homeland of Australia. The gaze is broader, incorporating stories from all those countries and contexts named above. This book is also more cognisant of dialogue theory. Within the previous book theory was sub-textual, layered within the reflections on practice. Within this new writing we have surfaced theory more explicitly, providing a new 'theoretical prelude'.

In reflecting on our and others' community development practice, we have often struggled with questions such as: What is it that we see?; How do others experience it?; What are we trying to achieve?; What is it that we actually do?; and, What concepts help make sense of, or provide new ways of seeing, what we do? In answering those questions we have articulated the implicit method in our work – the practice that we have built on intuition, embodied experience, theory, reflection, and the integration of our selves into the community development practice. It has been a challenge to find words to express ways of thinking and acting that seem to come naturally, that we share easily, that we take for granted. Moments of agreement between us were a sure sign that we were articulating something significant for us that might also be of use to others.

A note on authorship

Peter is the primary author. The book has had various iterations. It started as *A Soulful Approach to Community Development* (1997), a paper written when he was living in South Africa, published by an organisation called OLIVE. Gerard has always been a fan of that paper, and was thrilled when Peter came to him in 2007 with a book-length expanded draft, saying 'While I'm overseas I'd like to leave this with you – to go through with a red pen, edit and give me critical feedback.' As we chatted Peter eventually made this invitation: 'If you really get into it, you could become a co-author and we could finalise it together.' We agreed that this was probably a reasonable thing, given the old 80/20 rule: that even though Peter had the heart of the book 80 per cent written, he had probably only done 20 per cent of the work needed to get it to press, and we could share the 80 per cent of work that would be required to finish it. That effort resulted in our book *Dialogical Community Development: With Depth, Solidarity and Hospitality* (2009), published by a good friend and colleague, Roland Lubett, at Tafina Press.

In writing this new book, *Theory and Practice of Dialogical Community Development: International Perspectives*, Gerard has again taken a co-author role, working as a critical friend, reflecting on shared experiences, questioning, developing a collaborative analysis, articulating a shared practice framework, and testing it against our shared and independent histories of practice. Gerard has also worked in dialogue with an evolving text: refining the expression, unpacking unfamiliar terminology, grounding it in practice, and relentlessly shortening and lightening sentences and paragraphs.

Foreword

Developing communion – one dialogue at a time …

I can truly say that I have been hoping and waiting for Peter's and Gerard's *Dialogical Community Development* to become more widely available ever since their first book on this topic appeared a few years ago. This is not because I don't believe in the importance and relevance of local writers writing for local people and certainly not because I find small presses rather useless (their first book was published by a local press). Indeed, the importance of writing with and about and for people in the place where one lives and practices, and of sharing it with them, cannot be overestimated. And without the small presses, where would those of us without the resonance of past publications and other accoutrements of fame find the encouragement and support – and risk taking – to share thoughts and experiences that are not promising best-seller fortunes for the publisher, mail-order giants and retailer bookshops?

No, apart from showcasing more globally some of the good thinking and practice that does happen in Australia (and in spite of many of its not so admirable facets), there are several quite important reasons why I think this book should be read more widely and why it deserves to become part of a more global set of ongoing and hopefully growing conversations and – indeed – 'dialogues'.

First, the two authors' own learnings have derived from dialogues in and with a number of countries and are therefore testimony of our growing willingness, capability – and need – to reciprocally learn from one another across cultures and beyond the artificially imposed boundaries of states and formal borders. And anyone working and thinking in the area of Community Development (or whatever other name is now given to our practice) will be well aware of our desperate need to grow beyond our respective provincialisms and the limits they impose on our creativity and bravery … indeed, we need to contribute to the growth of our global commons of knowledge and understanding and this book certainly does so convincingly.

Second, the imposition of rigid modes of thinking and of prescriptive practice modalities presumably leading to predetermined outcomes (associated with present forms of governance and funding a.k.a. economic rationalism or neo-liberalism) has reinforced the recipe-like approach to Community Development many of us have been critically rejecting for a long time, without much success, one may add. As well, savage cuts to tertiary and professional/vocational educational institutions and their increasingly reductionist approach to producing the 'human resources' and 'competencies' the 'labour market' now (presumably) asks for, have gradually robbed important concepts like empowerment or participation of their 'depth' meaning. They have resulted in attempts at imposing – presumably – relevant 'capacities' on to individuals, groups and communities who – also presumably – did not possess them or who were deemed deficient in other ways, thus systematically ignoring their strengths and capabilities while implicitly blaming them for their assumed absence.

The authors invite us to learn from 'other places' how resistance to such impositions can become effective and how good and deep thinking and good relational practices will offer communities as well as community development professionals a more promising avenue for positive social change – dialogically, indeed!

Third, the authors aspire to offer 'humanising attention to the kinds of relationship that enable creative transformation'. This is an absolutely essential contribution in an age where the dialectic of globalising consumerist egocentricity and an Orwellian drift towards the 'digital vertigo' (Keen 2012) leads us to the 'big dis-connect' (Slade 2012) and the loss of personal autonomy in the fake sociality of the 'social' media. These 'virtual' practices demand ever more information about who, what, how, why and where we are, all the time, but never allowing us to really relate and 'be' social. Peter and Gerard focusing on the relational condition of our lives – with others of our own species and with other species – thus join up with several recent attempts at filling the gap between the 'me' and the 'us'– such as Gergen (2009), Spretnak (2011), Thayer-Bacon (2003), a rather belated but vitally important reconnection with the work of Martin Buber, and with the re-appreciation of the essential nature of 'gifting' relationships, first by Mauss (1925/1990) and more recently by Liebersohn (2011).

Indeed, good company to be in!

Fourth, with the authors, it probably is about time to leave the rather unproductive – and often very superficial – debates about 'left' and 'right' and 'bottom-up' and 'top-down' and where Community Development 'sits' in this rather two-dimensional framework and whether it contributes to the preferred societal and ideological arrangements of the respective 'parties' in the 'debate'. As I recently wrote in a contribution in the *New Community Quarterly*, given that – at least in Australia – the 'left–right' distinction has become virtually inert in established politics, both major parties closely adhering to the neo-liberal agenda, we see:

> a curious amalgam of people meet in the 'middle' and remain 'true' believers in the capacity of community programs to achieve anything meaningful at all (even if they often are not sure what …). One will find believers in the small, local community and its capacity to create happy and safe havens against many evils; radical communards and anarchists; and, yes, lots of community and social workers, who, being paid to do the impossible and often seeing the conceptual and practical limits of individualised explanations of 'social' problems and 'deviance', try to serve two 'bosses'. They try not to 'bite the hand that feeds' (given that they are government employees

or employed by government-funded NGOs) and they try to make the people affected by the programs aware that all is not well with the ways in which those who control 'the system' treat them and their rights to livelihood and that the choice between acceptance of their 'fate' and resistance to it is not straightforward – and certainly not without dangers. Not to speak about the rather cavalier way in which the Universal Declaration of Human Rights is often used to justify about anything which comes to the mind of 'developers' of any persuasion!

(Boulet 2010: 27)

How refreshing and promising, therefore, is a book that invites practitioners and others interested to re-imagine community life and work, soul-fully, critically and with depth; an approach that focuses on transformation and care, rather than on offering a 'cure' for situations not of the community's making ... and certainly beyond the community's reach (in spite of the global and the local being 'one' and inter-penetrating). A book that does posit our personal and collective responsibility to the planet (and therefore is critical of the very concept of 'development', replacing it with hospitality) and evokes ways of being and working in solidarity with others and calls for humility rather than the well-worn phrase of 'leadership' and its – implicit – assumptions of superior skills and knowledge ...

Finally, fifth, the theoretical and philosophical strength of the book relies on a collection of teachers and writers who appeal and contribute to our reflective thinking and to the further development of our attitudes towards those we live and work with, two emphases that somehow feel counter-cultural to what is going on in the so-called 'mainstream'. When universities advertise their 'wares' by promising prospective students they will 'get there faster'; when funded programmes promise – or expect – fail-safe steps to achieve predetermined 'outcomes'; when leadership can be hired by the highest bidder for the required 'expertise'; Peter and Gerard present their dialogical approach to Community Development in a similar vein to what we came to call (in another time (the 1970s) and another working context (then West Germany)) a 'working principle of community work' (Boulet *et al.* 1980):

A working principle, consequently, implies that, like a working definition, the principle is not yet ready, not yet completely elaborated; it is continuously in the process of refinement, of redirection, of being enacted. As societal reality proceeds through human action and interaction, the working principle becomes part of that process, is dialectically related to it; it is preliminary and yet orients and directs action and is simultaneously changed by it. While working with or 'imbued' by the principle, it will prove its truth, its validity; it will be reflected upon, transformed and further verified as it develops in the relational practice it is applied to. Hence, a working principle of community development ... is a general maxim, which assists in orienting professional (or 'service delivery' or policy-based) action(s) or practices in and across the most differentiated fields of practice. A working principle thus should offer integrating power in several ways. It should assist in integrating theory and practice, different methodical/technical approaches, diverse (social) scientific disciplines and the 'ongoing-ness' of daily living of those we relate with in the course of our work ...

And so, dear reader, is the call of Dialogical Community Development ... it invites to experiment, to allow community to emerge and our solidarity to become embodied and 'real'. I hereby warmly recommend the book to you for reading, reflecting on and for adding your own practice wisdom to ... in further dialogue with all who strive to contribute to 'the wealth of (a new local and global) commons, a world beyond market and state' (Bollier and Helfrich 2012), which we desperately need to work towards, if 'only' to assure our very survival on this planet ...

Jacques Boulet
Director, Borderlands Cooperative
December 2012

Abbreviations

ABCD	assets-based community development
ACPACS	Australian Centre for Peace and Conflict Studies
ADHD	attention deficit hyperactivity disorder
ASBOs	anti-social behaviour orders
AusAID	Australian Agency for International Development
BALLE	Business Alliance for Local Living Economies (USA)
BLP	Better Life Options Programme
CBO	community-based organisation
CCE	Community Capacity Enhancement
CCTV	closed-circuit television
CDRA	Community Development Resource Association (South Africa)
CEPAUR	Centre for Development Alternatives (Chile)
CIRA	Community Initiatives Resource Association (Australia)
CSA	community-supported agriculture
DECOIN	Defensa y Conservacion Ecologica de Intag (Ecuador)
DFID	Department for International Development (UK)
GNP	gross national product
HIV	human immunodeficiency virus
INGO	international non-government organisation
LETS	local economic trading schemes
LGCDP	Local Governance and Community Development Programme (Nepal)
NGO	non-government organisation
NMF	Nelson Mandela Foundation (South Africa)
PAR	participatory action research
PLA	participatory learning and action
PNG	Papua New Guinea
PTSD	post-traumatic stress disorder
QPASTT	Queensland Programme of Assistance to Survivors of Torture and Trauma
SEQICF	South East Queensland Intercultural Cities Forum
SEWA	Self-Employed Women's Association (India)
SLA	Sustainable Livelihoods Approach
UK	United Kingdom
UNDP	United Nations Development Programme
USA	United States of America

Introduction
A practice framework

We love community work. Both of us have spent many years trying to live as citizens with a community orientation in our own neighbourhoods and workplaces, while also working professionally as practitioners of community development elsewhere. During that time we have learned much about community life and community practice – understood by us as both a citizen and professional project. Our lives have been deeply enriched as a result of this private, personal and public work. We have had the privilege of working with amazing people, been a part of creative community processes, and lived in sometimes challenging and often beautiful places. In reflecting on those years we find there is much to celebrate.

When starting out as practitioners in the late 1980s, we were introduced to several traces of what can be understood as a tradition of community development. Colleagues such as Ann Ingamells, Dave Andrews, Morrie O'Connor and Anthony Kelly introduced us to authors such as Martin Buber, Paulo Freire and Mahatma Gandhi. Their work has seeped deeply into our bones. In the past few years we have been attempting to distil how we might name our approach. We have called it *dialogical community development.* In naming this approach we are cognisant of many diverse approaches and traditions. We therefore consider it useful, before discussing what is meant by dialogical community development, to locate our thinking within the broad array of traditions and approaches being articulated internationally.

Before doing this we would like to say something about 'voice' within the text. Readers will find the book elastic and shifting in voice – between the more personal and the acutely academic. The book makes use of personal stories, researched case studies, theoretical writing and reflective essays. The shape is somewhat dialogic, at times meandering and at other times written with careful ordered precision. Often the first person *we* is used – and it is important for us to state we are unapologetic about this. It is not a mere case of genre, but reflects a philosophical position. As will become clear within our reflections on theory and practice, we do not write this book with any position of objectivity – if we had removed all references to *we* or *us*, they would have simply been submerged under the text. So we have 'come clean' with the reader – there is often *us*, wanting unapologetically to make ourselves explicit within the text. As novelist and intellectual Siri Hustvedt (2012: xi) expresses it, we do not want to hide behind the 'conventions of an academic paper' (albeit the book is written with an academic rigour). With this behind us, let us move on.

A useful starting point is from the observation of our Australian colleague Jim Ife that, '[e]very community worker will conceptualise practice in a different way, and will build a different practice framework that will develop and change with experience' (Ife 2002: 265). Ife recognises that community development cannot be objectivised – and is far more than a set of propositions or principles. Coming to an understanding of community development requires practice, constant effort and reflection based in a person's own experience and context.

While many community workers learn 'on the job' so to speak, from mentors, friends or colleagues, some also draw on institutionally or organisationally diffused or academically published community development frameworks. These frameworks provide a starting point for guiding their work by articulating propositions and principles about practice (Healy 2005). Then over time, with experience, people reinterpret or shift their relationship to this set of propositions and principles to bring them more into line with their own worldview, their various experiences, their awareness of recurring practice dilemmas and their understanding of social, cultural, political, economic and organisational contexts of practice. This is a reflective and reflexive effort requiring discipline. In many ways it is the process we have engaged in to write this book.

International community development practice: traditions and frameworks

Because of this reflective/reflexive phenomenon that is fundamental to disciplined work, there are many different traditions and practice frameworks (and we use the notions of 'framework' and 'approach' interchangeably) being accessed by community development workers around the world.

Previous research has synthesised the literature into three broad ways of thinking: identifying geographical, methodological and intellectual traditions of community development, albeit cognisant of Jacques Derrida's notion of the 'trace' to signpost the limitations and dangers of the idea of tradition (Westoby and Hope-Simpson 2010). Within that synthesis there are traces of tradition aligned to geography, for example the Nova Scotia tradition or the Irish tradition; then there are methodological traditions such as the Alinsky, the Freirean, the Settlement House, or the social planning and so forth; and then there are intellectual traditions, broadly categorised into the social learning, social mobilisation and social guidance (Campfens 1997) or more narrowly linked to ideas such as the communitarian, anarchist or critical traditions.

Alongside such traditions are also approaches or frameworks. For example, several are currently being institutionally or organisationally diffused around the world (see Pawar 2010). These include:

- Community-driven or -led development, as championed particularly by the World Bank (Everatt and Gwagwa 2005) and various governments, for example, within the UK and New Zealand (Inspiring Communities 2010).

- Rights-based community development (Ackerman 2005), which is being diffused by numerous international non-government organisations (INGOs), for example Action Aid and some United Nations Programmes.
- Assets-based community development (ABCD), which is researched and internationalised by the Coady Institute and the work of Kretzmann and McKnight (1993) and Mathie and Cunningham (2008), and which has most recently been articulated by the International Association of Community Development and the Carnegie UK Trust (O'Leary *et al.* 2011).
- The Sustainable Livelihoods Approach (SLA), as diffused by the UK Department for International Development (DFID) and others such as the African regionally oriented NGO Khanya-accid, drawing on the research and writing of Robert Chambers (1997).
- A people-centred capacity building approach, as articulated by Deborah Eade (1997) and diffused through the work of Oxfam International.

Other well-known frameworks being used internationally would include the South African *Training for Transformation* (Hope and Timmel 1984), grounded in a Freirean approach to development practice, being diffused through the work of the Grail Centre and authors Anne Hope and Sally Timmel. Another is the developmental approach articulated by the Community Development Resource Association (CDRA) and best articulated in Allan Kaplan's *The Development Practitioners' Handbook* (1996). From Australia the narrative approach (Denborough 2008) is being diffused through the international work of the Dulwich Centre and various iterations of a relational approach through the Centre for Social Response and Community Praxis Co-operative.

Many practitioners are more cognisant of frameworks developed, articulated and diffused by academics. Examples include: 'human rights from below' (Ife 2009), a networking approach (Gilchrist 2004), a critical approach (Ledwith 2005; Butcher *et al.* 2007; Rawsthorne and Howard 2011), a neighbourhood-based approach (Henderson and Thomas 2005; Twelvetrees 2008), radical empowerment (Craig and Mayo 1995), community organising (Alinsky 1969, 1971; Deacon *et al.*1985), non-directive approaches (Batten and Batten 1967), community-building approaches (Kelly and Sewell 1988; Andrews 2007), human-scale development (Max-Neef 1991) and so forth.

It is within this understanding of the plethora of traditions and frameworks that we articulate a dialogical approach to community development. It needs to be understood as *one approach* among many. In a sense dialogue is implicit within most of the frameworks named above. For example, Jim Ife's 'rights from below' (2009) articulates a way of thinking about human rights that requires discussion within communities, starting with people's understanding of lives lived and the accompanying rights they would like to enjoy. Dialogue then becomes the means by which people make sense of their own lives and construct the rights they would like to experience. In the same way, the ABCD approach, while focusing community discussions on assets, is still reliant on those discussions – easily construed as dialogue – to map, analyse and assess what assets they have and/or would like to have. So while acknowledging that dialogue is in no way new to people drawing on any of the above approaches and frameworks, our approach makes the dialogue theory and practice more explicit and central. In some ways we are highlighting what we understand to be, like the participatory turn of the 1980s, the dialogical or narrative turn that is now transforming applied social science.

Dialogical community development: a framework

During our combined 50 years of community development experience we have often found ourselves coming back to basics: How do people experience community?; When we enter into conversations with people, how do we make sense of the complex dialogue at play?; and, When we use the metaphor of development what are we trying to articulate? This section provides a brief insight into how our thinking about these cornerstone concepts of dialogue, community and development has been shaped by an international literature on these topics, and weaves the thinking into a broader practice framework.

We have broken the discussion into three parts. The first is a brief introduction to dialogue as other-oriented, humanising attention to the kinds of relationships that enable creative transformation. This part also articulates an understanding of our second cornerstone: rethinking community as hospitality, as *communitas*, as ethical space and as collective practice; and the third cornerstone pointing the reader in the direction of post-development imagination. The second part centres our framework with the notion of depth – orienting people to a philosophical approach to community development. Finally, within the third part we widen the framework by exploring six other dimensions of practice.

Introducing dialogue

As young community development practitioners we immersed ourselves in the works of Martin Buber, Paulo Freire and Mahatma Gandhi with an appreciation of their focus on dialogue. Over the years we have travelled further into the worlds of David Bohm, Hans-Georg Gadamer, M.M. Bakhtin and Michael Foucault, and learned from their perspectives on the theory and practice of dialogue. Our understanding of the interplay between theory and practice has been enriched by holding both what can be observed – dialogue as something describable, as an object of study to be researched within a historical and cultural context; and what is aspired to – dialogue as a constructed and contextual normative ideal, as an idea that has a long tradition of thought within moral philosophy (Maranhão 1990: 5). We have therefore come to draw on normative and historical perspectives for understanding dialogue within our practice.

A caveat

We have wanted to resist articulating anything that can easily be reduced to an ahistorical and decontextualised definition, because in many ways such definition, while providing clarity for some people, closes thought and reduces possibilities for others. So instead, and from a dialogical perspective, we simply offer

Introduction: a practice framework 5

a Freirean 'code' (Freire 1974: 38), which is an attempt to integrate some of our thinking into the limits of words that we hope triggers further thought about what dialogue within community development might mean for the reader.

A code

With this caveat in mind, we then understand dialogue normatively as a deep, challenging, responsive, enriching, disruptive encounter and conversation-in-context; and also a mutual and critical process of building shared understanding, meaning and creative action. Furthermore, dialogue is understood historically[1] as the interplay of social forces that shape the life we now live individually and collectively. Those social forces at times attest to the power of domination that arrests dialogue, but also at times attest to groups of people in dialogue encountering the other as profoundly different – which opens new possibilities for social transformation.[2]

To unpack this 'code' readers can turn to the next chapter, 'A theoretical prelude', which engages with the theory of dialogue in relation to community development in more depth. That chapter is a little heavy going at times and you might want to skip it all together, or return to it later! If you do wade in you will be rewarded with an introduction to international theorists offering profound insights that have shaped our work and provide conceptual rigour to our framework. We now turn to discussions on community and development.

Rethinking community

At the centre of our understanding of community is an understanding of 'community as dialogue', which is discussed within Chapter 1. However, we also understand community in four other distinct but interconnected ways: community as hospitality, as *communitas*, as ethical space and as collective practice, each now considered in turn.

Community as hospitality

In the early days of our community work we learned about the practice of hospitality from our friend Dave Andrews (1992, 2007, 2012), our compatriots at a local 'hospitality house' of the Catholic Workers, and from reading the likes of Canadian humanitarian Jean Vanier (1979) and Dutch priest Henri Nouwen (1975). These authors invited us to reflect on collective spiritual life. However, it has been more recent reading of the Mexican 'de-professionalised intellectual' Gustavo Esteva (1987) and French philosopher Jacques Derrida (1997) that has enabled us to identify hospitality as central to our framework of community development. Hospitality orients towards relationship that is welcoming of the other. Strangers and intruders are welcome into the kind of community that we advocate.

Re-imagining community as hospitality also involves considering the way in which ends and means are enfolded within one another – as destinations, and as processes of moving towards those destinations. For Buber 'community is dialogue', whereas for Derrida 'community is hospitality'. The term community describes the ends being worked towards – the kind of community dreamed of and yearned for. Community is a space where people have created a climate and culture of hospitality. When people close themselves, their groups, their spaces from others, then they are no longer experiencing a Derridean community, but some other kind of closed collectivity.

Hospitality as means invites practitioners to consider the experience of community along the journey – the process and social practice of building community within the work. Hospitality refers to the practices of welcoming other people, other ideas, and other ways of thinking about community life – living together, naming and solving community problems. It is an orientation that ensures people do not close minds, souls and hearts to the other.

From a Mexican perspective Gustavo Esteva shares insight on post-development as hospitality, arguing that hospitality orients towards the principle of non-intervention and 'co-motion'. The in-hospitable and instrumental practices of intervention and 'pro-motion' tend to mean that many professional development practitioners have predetermined what they are going to do with and for people or communities (Esteva 1987: 149). In a spirit similar to Esteva's, North American authors Margaret Wheatley and Deborah Frieze (2011: 161ff.) articulate a community development approach that advocates for friendship as opposed to intervention. Such an approach calls for an opening up of spaces with people and to be part of the people, not only with them but among them. This kind of hospitality involves the creative regeneration of spaces where people can interact and find common ground.

These insights lead to a deeper understanding of community, and of the role of hospitality as crucial within a dialogical approach to community development. In re-imagining community as hospitality, we recognise that dialogue, community and hospitality are holistically enfolded within one another.

In no way could such practice be considered easy, especially within the current context of modernity. The Italian political philosopher Roberto Esposito, more than anyone else, has helped us recognise the difficulties that we ourselves experience in attempting to extend hospitality. In his challenging book *Communitas: The Origin and Destiny of Community* (2010), Esposito reminds us that at the heart of community is the notion of *munus*, which entails a gifting and obligation. We gift one another, extended as hospitality, but this comes with obligation. Yet the problem for most 'modern' people is that they do not want obligations. There is often hostility to obligations. The whole socio-economic system is geared towards individual life-projects, free of obligations. Richard Kearney and Kascha Semonovitch's meditation on *Phenomenologies of the Stranger: Between Hostility and Hospitality* (2011) echo much of Esposito's thought. They remind us of the ongoing universal dilemmas of welcoming strangers and recognise it as having an ongoing 'edge character' where there can be no 'infallible guide to action' (Casey 2011: 48). They argue that people can at least maintain openness to strangers and awareness of the subtle complexities at work in every new encounter despite the unknown challenges and potential obligations.

Also, of significance to our framework is the shift in Derrida's thinking towards the end of his life, when he started to extend his understanding of hospitality beyond people, focusing on ethical concerns towards animals. His thoughts resonate with our reading of Deborah Bird Rose – a scholar working with indigenous Australian communities. She explores aspects of the indigenous worldview in which the notion of community involves a cross-species understanding of kinship. In *Wild Dog Dreaming: Love and Extinction* (2011) she argues that humans are destroying animals at a rate that should be understood as an act of suicide. The logic behind this is that we live as humans-in-context, not just humans, and if we kill the context we are actually killing ourselves. From this perspective, theorising community as hospitality that is inclusive of animals and other elements of the biosphere sharpens a practice that leads to sustaining our humanity and ourselves.

Community as ethical space

Alluding to Derrida's ethical concerns, other recent theorists explore a notion of community as ethical space as opposed to common space. For example, community economists Katherine Gibson and Julie Graham (2006) (writing as J.K Gibson-Graham) draw on the work of French philosopher Jean-Luc Nancy (1991) and North American feminist Iris Marian Young (1990) to argue that 'we need to liberate community from its traditional recourse to common being ... a commonality of being, an idea of sameness ...' (Gibson-Graham 2006: 85–6). In a similar vein, Italian political philosopher Giorgio Agamben (1993: 19) argues for an 'inessential commonality, a solidarity that in no way concerns an essence'.

Gibson and Graham therefore understand community in a different way, as signifying 'ethical coordinates for a political practice, not a model or plan' (2006: 88). From this perspective community can be re-imagined as a geographical or symbolic site of decision and ethical praxis that attempts to re-socialise development. This purposefully weaves a connection between dialogue, community and development, signposting the need for dialogical skills enabling ethical decision-making about the process and trajectory of development people choose. There is no one fantasy of development – but there is the need for multiple spaces where people can discuss, deliberate and decide on their vision together.

Community as communitas

Avoiding a single vision of development and providing space for multiple viewpoints requires a more nuanced understanding of community than is commonplace. Helping us explore such a nuanced view, a colleague and friend David Denborough (2008) from the Adelaide-based Dulwich Centre, introduced the idea of *communitas*, developed by the British anthropologist Victor Turner. Turner was attempting to describe the phenomena of community in a way that communicated a shared sense of unity among individuals that also preserved their individual distinctiveness (Turner 1969). He found the idea of community inadequate, dominated as it was by structural ways of thinking, and instead adopted the concept of *communitas*. In many ways Turner's ideas are similar to his colleague Anthony Cohen's symbolic notion of community (Cohen 1985) – and *communitas* represents an experience whereby people 'evoke' the symbol of community that expresses unity.

The idea echoes Paulo Freire's notion of 'the invention of unity in diversity' (1994: 57) and also the importance of not colluding with the kind of fantasy in which 'community' depends on an in-group versus out-group. Conceptually, *communitas* is therefore not synonymous with community – it can be understood as a moment, an experience where people encounter one another, and 'see each other and [their] place in the world unencumbered by [their] history' (Beavitt 2012: 2). As Beavitt observes, *communitas* 'helps us to sustain the tension that arises around [people's] differences for long enough that [they] can share in a collective imagining of the future different from the present' (ibid.: 28). Turner acknowledges that this will rarely be a sustained space – the experience of *communitas* will pass and relationships will soon tend to acquiesce into being determined by structures that tend to eschew the humanising possibilities (Turner 1969).

Community as collective practice

Finally, and working on the assumption that people can maintain trust for some time, we also recognise that, within community development theory and practice, community usually signifies *collective* processes of social change. For us community, emergent through people's efforts in dialogue (accounting for difference) and extending hospitality (to other), becomes the platform for collective social change efforts.[3] It is the collective approach that differentiates community development from many other approaches to social change. People work co-operatively together (Henderson and Thomas 2005) and in choosing to trust one another then hold each other accountable (through mutual obligations), working together to bring their strategies and tactics to bear for social change.

Collective practices have received renewed interest since Nobel Prize winner Elinor Ostrom and her colleagues' seminal work, represented by such publications as *Working Together: Collective Action, the Commons, and Multiple Methods in Practice* (Poteete *et al.* 2010). Their research shows how, under certain conditions, people are able to work co-operatively, particularly as user groups in relation to managing commons. Within community development theory and practice, 'community' also signifies this collective process, while 'development' signifies the vision for the social change desired. This is explored below as the third cornerstone of a framework for dialogical community development.

Re-imagining development

Development is a troublesome notion. Sometimes we want to ditch the word altogether. Like sociologist Phil McMichael, we sense that 'development is not only in crisis but is at a significant turning point in its short history as a master concept of (Western-based) social science and cultural life' (2012: 2). We have been involved in initiatives that we have purposefully called 'community animators' or 'community building', simply to avoid the complexity of the term 'development'. Like Swiss scholar Gilbert Rist (2011), we are aware of the devastating histories and practices of development. Like Indian ecologist Debal Deb (2009), we are cognisant of the colonising mind-set of 'developmentality'. Like Columbian-American anthropologist Arturo Escobar (2010), we constantly grapple with the ongoing traction of assumptions and paradigms that underpin developmentalist practices. However, as we locate ourselves within the citizen and professional project of community development there is no escape from the concept. We have to make sense of it and at this historical moment continue to use it.

Furthermore, in our experience, the idea of development can be very useful for sharpening critical analysis. For example, in Peter's work in Vanuatu, even though customary chiefs often deride development as something brought by outsiders and done to them, focusing a conversation around what kinds of development have been helpful and unhelpful has enabled those same chiefs to deconstruct the concept themselves. They have been able to 'contest development' (McMichael 2010) and create their own definitions based on their own visions of the good life.

In reflecting on the theory and practice of development our primary response is to re-imagine development in two ways. First, development can be understood as a metaphor signifying a qualitative change (Kaplan 1996, 2002; Escobar 2010) that can be contrasted with the quantitatively oriented metaphor of growth still underpinning most practices and mind-sets. It is a qualitative change that focuses on people-centred processes rather than growth-centred outcomes. Qualitative questions also focus practitioners on some of the most pertinent 'development'-related challenges of our times, such as:

- How do we ensure all people on the planet have a decent quality of life, without being hostage to the current model of economic growth that is so fossil fuel reliant?
- How do we direct resources to women's literacy, enabling individual women to make more decisions about their lives – and from a planetary perspective reduce population pressures?
- How do we reduce consumerism among those of us who are wealthy in a global context, thereby reducing both the planetary footprint and social inequalities?
- How do we, as community practitioners, position ourselves in the context of a war of paradigms – between an industrial and indigenous paradigm (Guardiola-Rivera 2010), with the industrial paradigm representing unfettered expansion of modernity, 'globalisation from above' and rampant surplus accumulation?

This final point begs the question of whether community development becomes a tool of modernity's impulse and trajectory, aligned to an industrial paradigm, or alternatively, whether community development can be guided by an indigenous or decolonising paradigm. In this latter paradigm it would potentially contribute to more radical and robust practices of resistance to [some] aspects of modernity, reconnection to nature/mother earth and revitalisation of the commons.

Second, development is re-imagined as within the post-development and post-structural tradition (McMichael 2012). By this we mean that there is what Arturo Escobar identifies as the:

> possibility of visualising an era where development ceased to be the central principle of social life ... The post, succinctly, means a de-centering of capitalism as the definition of the economy, of liberalism in the definition of society and polity, and of state forms of power as the defining matrix of social organisation. This does not mean that capitalism, liberalism and state forms cease to exist; it means that their discursive and social centrality have been displaced somewhat.
>
> (2010: 12)

To align ourselves with the post-development tradition then is to be consistent in our reflections on practice. We see many diverse practices aligned to different visions of the good life, different 'competing political visions ... of the ideal society' (McMichael 2012: 3) or different 'life-projects' (Blaser *et al.* 2004) – that is, different visions of 'development'. When we observe dialogical forms of community development practice we see an alternative pluralistic vision for development whereby people collectively, associatively, co-operatively and individually can have control over decisions that impact on their lives – so determining their own futures. The Vanuatu chiefs provide one example. There are many more.

Restoring depth: why dialogical community development?

Over 25 years of experience one of our observations is that community development, like its big sister 'development', is increasingly being co-opted by a hegemonic, Euro-centrist, modernist approach to philosophy and life which leads to a technical orientation to practice. Such an orientation is underpinned by a reductionist and instrumental worldview, which in turn is shaped by 'an episteme ... of market calculus' (McMichael 2010: 3). In common with the ideas of Jacques Ellul (1965), Hans-Georg Gadamer (1998) and Ivan Illich (1977), we argue that to some extent community development has been captured by this modernist and market-oriented worldview. In doing this it has lost something of its depth and potential soul, and therefore its capacity both for genuine solidarity with the marginalised and also for contributing to a post-development, post-liberal and post-capitalist world (Escobar 2010). In losing that capacity, we propose that community development could lose its basis for legitimacy among progressive citizens and professionals.

At a fundamental level our worldview directly influences our practice. It is our contention that a Euro-centrist modernist paradigm is underpinned by an epistemological worldview that is reductionist, 'wilful' and instrumental. Solutions are reduced to the technical, and technique becomes the 'instrument' of social change, whether that change is 'attacking' oppressive structures or 'becoming' self-sufficient, depending on where one sits on the ideological continuum. Such a worldview applied to technique-oriented community development understands practice in terms of interventions comprised of inputs, time-lines, outputs, impacts and measurable indicators. The assumption is that the 'will' for intervention, supported by the technologies of modernity and markets (experts, money, technology, coordination and effective management), affects social change that benefits the marginalised.

This Euro-centric modernist paradigm often accompanies colonial and neo-colonial processes of 'aid and development', or 'scaled-up programmes'. The assumption is that a supposed 'universal' model of community development technique, aligned to a universal model of development, can be imported and exported anywhere in the world – transferred through capacity-building initiatives and train-the-trainer courses. It is with such an analysis in mind that we were motivated to articulate a dialogical approach to community development.

It is worth saying at this point that our critique of modernist community development is in no way meant to imply that techniques are unimportant. On the contrary, techniques are essential; but they must be put in their right context. Any use of technique must be informed by an understanding of the intellectual, methodological and geographically shaped traditions that provide a deeper reading of community development work (Westoby and Hope-Simpson 2010).

Embracing depth as a philosophical orientation

One useful way of imagining the loss that comes with an overemphasis on technique is to imagine it is as a 'shallow-ing' approach to community development. This shallowness is contrasted with the idea of depth articulated in Manfred Max-Neef's (1992) ground-breaking book *From the Outside Looking In*. The Chilean economist and environmentalist argues that development 'requires a study in depth; a penetration of the hidden relationships of existence' (ibid.: 12). He goes on to observe that, 'the person who can really help in the solution of even such apparently strictly material problems as economic development, is therefore the philosopher rather than the mere specialist and technician' (ibid.). In the same vein one of our key propositions is that community work practitioners require depth, that is, a philosophical orientation.

We therefore use depth as a metaphor that calls for a movement beyond oversimplified instrumental and shallow approaches to community development. It orients practitioners towards the philosophical – our way of understanding 'a theoretical attitude', discussed below. Our world can be characterised as complex (Rihani 2002) and full of uncertainty (Rose 2011). Any approach to community development that is not cognisant of such complexity and uncertainty in our experience is bound to do harm.

A depth approach to dialogical community development invites workers to bring philosophy, theory and attentiveness to the practice. It challenges practitioners to learn how to observe and 'read' the complex patterns that both foreground and background complex social phenomena (Kaplan 2002). It requires a resistance to the shallow-ing of practice, the product of an age of speed, spin, quick fixes and amnesia. Since our initiation into community development work, we have constantly been told 'it takes time', 'slow down', 'first watch, and then listen and learn'. Such mantras invite a depth approach that opens up the possibilities of counter-cultural practice.

Widening the framework

With depth at the heart of our framework, and dialogue, community and development as the cornerstones, we then widen the framework by identifying six other dimensions that complete the conceptual structure of our approach to dialogical community development:

- enfolding community development within a commitment to social solidarity;
- infusing practice with a soulful orientation;
- contextualising practice as vocational professionals;
- reconstituting community work as a social practice;
- reading our work with an ecological sensibility; and
- opening ourselves up to deconstructive movements.

Each of these dimensions is explored below.

Enfolding community development within a commitment to social solidarity

The idea of solidarity is informed by the likes of nineteenth-century European mutual aid philosophers such as Peter Kropotkin (1902) and Pierre Joseph Proudhon (1902), and by the twentieth-century injunction of southern hemisphere liberation theologies towards a 'preferential option for the poor'. Such a preferential option emphasises relating to *everyone* with hospitality, but with a primary orientation towards what we prefer to think of as the marginalised.[4]

A dialogical approach involves entering into particular kinds of committed relationship with the marginalised, exemplified by Paulo Freire, who observed that 'this solidarity is born only when leaders witness to it by their humble, loving and courageous encounter with the people' (1972: 100). Such solidarity requires movement out of comfort zones, and engagement not only with the universal 'other' but with those particular 'others' who are marginalised in societies. Solidarity requires entering into dialogue with those people, listening to them, and learning about their social, political, economic, ecological, cultural and spiritual realities. In our experience solidarity, infused with dialogic ethos and practice, often disrupts naive intentions to 'help the poor' and usually requires significant reflexive capacities to challenge previous assumptions (Land 2011).

The work of community development enfolded within social solidarity is also committed to the principles and practices of mutual aid, and to a tradition of 'associationism' (Sennett 2012: 42) that fosters people's associations and citizen co-operative structures. This social tradition is historically manifest in organised activity such as Settlement Houses in England and the United States; the Hampton and Tuskegee educational institutes in Alabama and Virginia; the Nada and Kobe consumer co-operatives in Japan; mutual benefit and friendly societies offering health protection in Australia; Canadian agricultural co-operatives; Brazil's peasant leagues and landless workers' movement; the Mondragon co-operatives in the Basque region of Spain; and the Grameen Bank of Bangladesh.

It should also be noted that within our previous book on dialogical community development our consideration of solidarity started with reference to the Polish union movement Solidarity, but subsequent reflections, particularly of North American sociologist Richard Sennett's interpretation of solidarity, has helped us differentiate between the two traditions of social and political solidarity – the former as solidarity from below, more localised; and the latter 'from above' (ibid.: 40ff.). As community workers we are more aligned to the 'from below' tradition of social solidarity.

Infusing practice with a soulful orientation

For us solidarity is not enough. There is also a need for soul. A genealogy of soul would require a book in itself, but for the moment we are content to begin with the singer Ray Charles, who calls soulfulness 'the ability to respond from our deepest place' (Cousineau 1998: xxvii). North American psychotherapist Thomas Moore (1992) also helps us think about soul, proposing it as a quality, a dimension and a movement towards experiencing life in a way that adds depth, value, relatedness, heart and substance to community development practice. In this sense a soulful orientation invites hospitality towards other people and places and other ways of being, doing and imagining. It requires community practitioners to be both attentive to and engaged with community in 'another' way, one that demands heart, emotion and will. In a sense soul can be contrasted with spirit, with a spirited practice focused on vision, ideas, exchange and ethical imperatives. In contrast a soulful practice is focused on slowness, intimacy, ordinariness and memory.

While Ray Charles and Thomas Moore invite us to bring a soulful and imaginative gaze to our lives and work, the writings of Nobel Prize-winning Bengali poet and educationist Rabindranath Tagore focus that attention on how people relate to one another. Martha Nussbaum's recent reflection on Tagore and soul states it perfectly:

> [T]he word 'soul' has religious connotations for many people, and I neither insist on these nor reject them. Each person may hear them or ignore them. What I do insist on, however, is what ... Tagore ... meant by the word: the faculties of thought and imagination that make us human and make our relationships rich human relationships, rather than relationships of mere use and manipulation. When we meet in society, if we have not learned to see both self and other in that way, imagining in one another inner faculties of thought and emotion, democracy is bound to fail, because democracy is built upon respect and concern, and these in turn are built upon the ability to see other people as human beings, not simply as objects.
>
> (2010: 6)

Tagore's understanding of soul echoes Buber's notion of dialogue. Their work reorients towards a particular kind of 'community' within community development – focusing on the humanising dimensions of social relations rather than the instrumental. Our soul dimension always attempts to foreground this humanising requirement in an era of rationality.

Contextualising practice as vocational professionals

Such soulful practice is even more challenging for those of us engaged in community development as a professional project from which we earn a living. It is one thing to have a normative framework of how we want to practise; it is often another to step into a workplace and find the workplace itself to be the most challenging part of the job. Organisational practices themselves are part and parcel of the historical forces shaping society and human life. Some of these practices arrest dialogue, adding to the weight of domination and rationalisation as globalising processes of social policy formation lead to proliferation of regulation, compliance, corporatisation and new public management. These instrumental and technical pressures can feel immense. They impact directly on the capacity to implement processes of dialogical community development.

Reflection on our own practice has led us to consider three crucial responses to organisational context, understood as redefining professionalism, working creatively and becoming agents of organisational change, each now discussed.

Australian ethicist Peter Isaacs (1993) argues that it is more appropriate to see a profession as a calling rather than a career – with primary obligations to the people they are working with, the societies that sanction a level of autonomy in their practice, and the profession as a body of colleagues and practice that go beyond their obligations to their employer. Those primary obligations in turn have ethical, educational and political dimensions; an ethical commitment to use one's skills and knowledge for the society's well-being; a commitment to ongoing professional development; and a political commitment to address socio-economic and structural issues impacting the people we work with. We find that holding these obligations firmly in view can 'steady' a wavering practice orientation.

North American thinkers such as Peter Senge (1990) have also helped us understand the importance of working creatively to ensure that, in a globalised world, organisations can still thrive. Our experience is that a dialogical engagement with complex community and organisational dynamics generates creative possibilities and new opportunities that organisations need to augment their ongoing relevance. Dialogical community development will rarely be the core business of an organisation – it is more likely to be 5 per cent of the work, at worst tolerated and at best encouraged because it takes the organisation into new territory that is seen as innovative and responsive, both qualities valued by some decision-makers who fund the work.

We also understand that, while our dialogical practices might be shaped by the organisational context, it is not necessarily one way, and that dialogical practices can also [re]shape the organisational context. In our experience there is almost always space, particularly if joining with others, to create dialogical spaces

Introduction: a practice framework 15

which in turn can shift the culture, structures and traditions of an organisation. To the extent possible given these dynamics, we attempt to facilitate developmental, dialogical processes that build community within the organisational context – with our managers, among our colleagues, and with the members and constituents. By redefining professionalism, working creatively and supporting change we give our organisational contexts opportunities to benefit from our dialogical approach, while being true to our calling within the workplace and the community.

Reconstituting community work as a social practice

A social practice signifies a movement towards reclaiming the world and organisational contexts as a social world. From our perspective solutions to human problems will be primarily social and only secondarily technical. Social practice therefore means reconstituting 'development work' in terms of social agency and political contestation. From this perspective community development as social practice: (1) fosters social relationships; (2) invokes agency not just in private and personal relationships, but also in collectively oriented public relationships; and (3) strives to reclaim and re-inhabit places as spaces of social activity rather than speculative economic activity or technique-oriented development. We learned to value this tradition of the social through two beautiful, simple volumes of homegrown community development case studies from Australia – *People Working Together, Volumes II and III* (Kelly and Sewell 1986; Kelly et al. 1997).

This idea of community development as social practice will recur throughout the book. Freire (1972) has most clearly articulated such a social practice in the context of literacy programmes. He argued that literacy programmes cannot be just technical processes of enabling people to understand the word. They also need to embody a social practice in enabling people to transform their world, through dialogue with others and co-investigation. In the same way community work cannot be simply reduced to a mechanistic process such as 'toolkits' for community consultation and recipes for 'building social capital', but must hold instead the social practice of solidarity and political contestation.

Reading our work with an ecological sensibility

Another way we have found helpful to make sense of our practice is to read it with an ecological sensibility. By this we mean a sensibility that makes a constant effort to see and understand connections and relations between people, groups, networks, organisations, ideas and perspectives. British quantum physicist David Bohm's work around *Wholeness and the Implicate Order* (Bohm 1980) informs our understanding of the role of dialogue within such a framework, providing a lens that reveals an often hidden wholeness behind the visible component parts.

More recently we have also been inspired by the work and wisdom of Utah-based Margaret Wheatley from the Berkana Institute and Allan Kaplan from the Proteus Initiative in Cape Town. For both Wheatley and Kaplan one of the challenges of development practice is the use of a paradigm that is reductionist and technical. Within such a paradigm complexities and uncertainties are reduced to measurable component parts and simplifications. The reader by now would be aware of our problem with such a worldview. Community development, as a social practice, is not a practice of 'solving a puzzle' or 'using instructions to make sense of a machine' (Kaplan 2002: xv). Instead, social systems are a complex dynamic process of interacting parts (individual, group, organisation) and multiple contexts (policies, plans, culture and so forth). An alternative lens is an ecological or organic understanding of social systems (Midgley 2000) – bringing to the foreground the interacting dynamics that underlie collective efforts.

We have often found ourselves grounding such an ecological understanding through the metaphor of a web. When we observe and interact with a group of people who are part of a community development process we 'see' a web of connections, some strong, others frayed, still others knotted or even broken (Peile 1990). Our 'reading' of this web informs our analysis of potential ways forward, both as a practitioner in co-motion with the people, and also as a collective entity (Dethlefs and Kelly 1988). There is no point forging forward with collective action if the relationships between people are overstrained. Any further stress will potentially undermine the group's cohesion and sustainability. John-Paul Lederach's images of web-weaving (Lederach 2005; Westoby and Owen 2010) have also been helpful in thinking about how to strengthen nodes, how to increase resilience and so on.

Wheatley and Frieze's (2011: 220ff.) memes of 'look for the patterns that connect' and 'start anywhere, follow it everywhere' are indicative of social practice that flows from such an understanding. The wisdom of this ecological approach is to *not* start with the toughest problem, for example the 'root' cause of social disintegration within a community, but to start with what people are ready and able to do, based on the strong connections that already exist. Viewed through an ecological lens there is a trust that changes in one small part of a social system will flow on to impact and influence other parts of the system.

Opening ourselves up to deconstructive movements

Finally, the idea of deconstructive movements provides an opportunity to remain open to complexity, refusing to practise the tyranny of simplifying 'readings' of a situation. The notion of deconstructive movement also invites pulling apart or destabilising simplistic ways of thinking that are usually expressed through dualisms such as us–them, centre–periphery, top–bottom, landlord–tenant and rich–poor. It ensures that our thinking about community development is more nuanced by an awareness of the complexity of human relations and transformative processes.

The idea of deconstructive movement also marks the importance of always challenging given assumptions; ensuring that people remain open, humble and uncertain social beings; and therefore ensuring that people remain hospitable to the other (Levinas 1999; Kapuscinski 2008). When referring to the other we are drawing on a social science tradition that alludes to the 'stranger' that disrupts our world in some way. A particularly common practice in today's world is to think of strangers as 'difficult and dangerous classes' (Young 1999: 59). In contrast, for us 'other' is not about the difficult or dangerous, but simply about the disruptive – with all the positive as well as negative implications.

In many ways this book represents an attempt to destabilise some dominant current discourses of community development that are technique-oriented, and to reconstruct them in the light of an approach to being, living and working that brings a different attention, awareness and imagination to our social lives and social practice. This deconstructive movement requires what some interpreters of Derrida call 'alterity' (Smith 2005: 13), a focus on the other – not the obvious, the surface, the given, the assumed, but an-other way of thinking and imagining community life and community development work.

Summing up the framework

This conceptual framework holds at its heart a depth, or philosophical approach to community development, that centres a particular understanding of dialogue. The framework then draws on the cornerstones of: community as hospitality, as *communitas*, as ethical space and as collective practice; and an alternative pluralistic vision for development whereby people collectively, associatively and co-operatively can have control over decisions that impact on their lives. The framework is then widened through exploring six other dimensions of practice: a commitment to solidarity, a soulful orientation, working as vocational professionals, reconstituting community work as a social practice, an ecological sensibility and opening ourselves to deconstructive movements.

A reflection on theory and practice

We have approached this book with a view to exploring a theory and practice of dialogical community development and now pause to consider what is meant by theory and practice. Aligned to the dialogical tradition our task of theorising, researching and writing is understood as hermeneutical. This is understood as a 'sense-making' process of critical dialogue with one another, with colleagues and with an international literature that also holds a historical consciousness of the traditions, the perspectives and biases located within them.

We have not set out to use any universal scientific method to examine or research dialogical community development. Instead we bring a theoretical attitude (Gadamer 1998: xxix) towards the idea of 'dialogical community development' as a whole, trying to make sense of our experience and observation of it, but also recognising that 'making sense of' requires a philosophical and historical approach. Our theorising refers to Gadamer's notion of 'bearing witness to' practices of dialogical community development, combined with the equivalent of contemplation (ibid.: 21). We theorise 'dialogical community development' through getting close to ourselves and others, doing it, and writing intimately about it. Yet we also distance ourselves, requiring a pause, understood as contemplation.

We then bring attention to practice. Practice in its most obvious form is what people do – but we like to think of it as 'skilful means'.[5] It is not just what people do but what *thoughtful* and *empathic* people using community development theory reflectively and reflexively do in subtle and skilful ways. Practice for us is also a social and ecological process that is primarily oriented towards relationality. Therefore practice becomes the ability to 'skilfully dance the dance of relationship, being present and responsive to other and context' – but also to be intuitive, empathic, careful, thoughtful, creative, playful and disciplined.

As stated above, practice, drawing on theory, is both reflective and reflexive. It is reflective in the sense that a practitioner is able to pause and contemplatively check as to whether what they are doing is what they intend to do. Questions can be asked: Is the practice dialogical? Is space opening up for diversity and plurality? But practice that integrates a theoretical attitude is also reflexive practice, understood as going that one step further beyond theory-practice congruency (a question of intention and reflective capacity), to questioning theoretical assumptions. Reflexive thinking pushes, or orients, practitioners towards uncertainty and recognition of complexity.[6] In this flow between practice and theory we hope this book offers insights that are both conceptually sharp and also practically useful.

An overview of the book

This introduction has articulated a framework for dialogical community development that provides a conceptual way forward for practitioners. Chapter 1 considers the traces of theory that we draw upon to shape our understanding of dialogue within community development. The remainder of the book is an exploration of how this theory relates to everyday challenges of practice in our own experience and in various international contexts. Within the whole book we hope there is a flowing interplay between theory and practice; however, occasionally we tell stories in depth or give account of particular case studies in detail. These stories and case studies are easily identifiable as they are indented.

Chapter 2, 'Re-imagining community practice', aims to support community workers to re-imagine community and our work within it. In re-imagining community as the context for our work, we begin to deconstruct contemporary community work, and to explore alternative approaches that are soulful and social, have a critical edge, and draw us into the depths of our professional and life experience.

Chapter 3, 'Transformative community processes', explores how community can become a vehicle for social change in which people find their own paths towards development.

Chapter 4, 'Analytical interlude: what weakens dialogue within community development', examines three of the most significant trends that weaken the possibility of dialogue within community development practice.

Chapter 5, 'Caring for different spheres of community life', suggests that our role as community development workers changes remarkably if we think about it as ongoing care rather than the modernist quest for a cure. We identify *caring* as a core imperative of dialogical community development, with a focus on the ordinary, economic, political, cultural and ecological spheres of community life.

Chapter 6, 'Dialogue and training for transformation', reflects on our experience that one of the keys to community development is the quality and creativity of the people who dream of a better community. This chapter considers how skilled practitioners can facilitate particular types of training spaces where people can learn transformational skills and strategies.

The Conclusion weaves together the ideas central to the book, inviting readers to test the theory developed within the book. Finally it invites an ongoing attitude of humility undergirded by a 'passion for non-knowing' (Caputo 1997b: 338).

Invitation to dialogue

We hope this book will engage readers in a dialogue and invite them into a dialogue, informed by both Buber and Freire, each of whom leads to a different tone that readers will sense within the text of the book. On one hand there is a tradition of dialogue as per Buber, creating a tone that constantly seeks the building of connection with the reader. Within this tone there is an invitation to 'dialogue' in the sense that we as authors hold our positions somewhat lightly, and follow the Gandhian sentiment that we are 'experimenting with truth' (Gandhi 1940). However, our commitment to dialogue is also informed by the Freirean tradition, one that is more critical and at times brings with it a more forceful and 'opinionated' tone.

Holding both is the trick. We invite dialogue, but not at the expense of solidarity or hospitality. One could say that we are open, we are in dialogue with the reader, but we are also trying to persuade. In that spirit we hope you take to this text with a vigorous pen that captures your own reflections, questions and critiques. We hope that those who reject parts of our analysis will not dismiss the whole book – but instead take up an engaged critical dialogue. We would love to hear from you!

1 Theoretical prelude

An introduction to dialogue for community development

This chapter discusses the first cornerstone of our framework of dialogical community development, that is, the idea and practice of dialogue. We start by restating the perspectives we apply to understanding dialogue, while also introducing other possible lenses we could have used. Readers are reminded of the code and caveat from the previous chapter. The core of the chapter is then a relatively systematic exposition of key theorists' contributions to dialogue theory, and also a meandering invitation to meditate on the relevance of that theory to community development practice.

Introduction

As stated within the introductory chapter, we have come to draw on normative and historical perspectives to focus our understanding of dialogue for community development practice. We say 'perspective' to simply signpost that there are many ways through which dialogue can be seen, each focusing on different aspects and implications of this multidimensional, dynamic and subtle concept.

For example, other ways of thinking about dialogue could be through linguistic-structural, phenomenological, dramaturgical and deconstructive perspectives (Flecha *et al.* 2003). The linguistic-structural perspective would focus on understanding dialogue in *relation to another idea* – something considered non-dialogical. Dialogue, as a linguistic device, is thereby considered meaningless outside the structural relationship of another idea. Readers will be able to discern such thinking in this chapter, as for example when we contrast dialogical with agnostic and antagonistic politics in Chapter 5. From a phenomenological perspective dialogue is understood as an 'ideal type' of practice, that is, practice *given meaning* through practitioner consciousness and their making it conscious in conversation with others. Some of the theorists' views of dialogue explored below are clearly phenomenological. A dramaturgical perspective would focus on the performance of dialogue – how practitioners embody dialogue in particular settings and contexts, also with awareness of settings and contexts whereby such dialogical performance is probably difficult, if not impossible. Many stories told within the book imply such a performative understanding of dialogue. Finally, a deconstructive perspective would ask: What does the word dialogue do? Within

Theoretical prelude: on dialogue 21

this frame this is no metaphysical presence of meaning to the word dialogue; it is the language itself that creates the presence of dialogue. Such a deconstructive 'reading' of dialogue within community development would also look for cracks in what is inevitably set up as a binary of dialogical versus non-dialogical. It would ask about the silences within our book – the tough stuff, or grey areas usually overlooked.

However, returning to the primary perspectives applied in this book, the notion of normative is used to discuss how some theorists argue dialogue 'should be' – their perspective of an ethical imperative. Yet even our understanding of this is informed by a decision about whether to subscribe to what we call a shallow as opposed to deep normativity. Shallow normativity is a way of thinking about dialogue and community development in terms of a limited normative set of principles or orthodoxies. The discourse of such approaches would be something like: 'dialogue is *always* ...'. Within this approach the norms and customs, that is, normativity, of such dialogue thinking-practice, is considered shallow because there is no discussion of where these norms come from. They are discussed as being self-evident and are usually framed ahistorically.

Alternatively, deep normativity is a way of rethinking dialogue and community development in terms of diverse sets of norms and customs that are situated within diverse cultural, literary or historical traditions – hence from the beginning our use of the language of 'tradition'. The norms and customs of practice, also potentially discussed in terms of principles, ethics and orthodoxies, do not claim to determine what dialogue is but rather to describe what a *particular tradition* or genre of dialogue is. There is depth to the norms, because they are grounded in historical and other dimensions that are particular and that have stood the test of time. For this reason we are careful to identify the author/theorist informing the discussion, also locating their discipline of thought and the geographical 'home' that we contend infuses and informs their way of understanding dialogue.

And also a reminder: we want to resist articulating anything that can be easily 'lifted from the text' so to speak, reduced to an ahistorical and decontextualised definition. So instead, and from a dialogical perspective, as mentioned in the Introduction, we offer a Freirean code that hopefully triggers further consideration about what dialogue within community development might mean.

With this caveat in mind, and at risk of repetition, we then understand dialogue normatively as a deep, challenging, responsive, enriching, disruptive encounter and conversation-in-context; and also a mutual and critical process of building shared understanding, meaning and creative action. Furthermore, dialogue is understood historically as the interplay of social forces that shape the life now lived individually and collectively. Those social forces at times attest to the power of domination that arrests dialogue, but also at times attest to groups of people in dialogue encountering the other as profoundly different – which opens new possibilities for social transformation.[1]

To unpack this code we now trace some theorist perspectives on dialogue, while also beginning to explore implications for dialogical community development.

A normative perspective on dialogue

Our normative perspective on understanding dialogue draws together the work of leading thinkers from different places and disciplines: Hans-Georg Gadamer, Martin Buber, David Bohm, Paulo Freire and Mikhail Bakhtin. Each contributes insights that enhance our approach to community development.

An orientation: turning to the other – reaching for understanding

Our understanding of dialogue at its very core is informed by the seminal work of German phenomenological philosopher Hans-Georg Gadamer (1975), who articulated the need for people to engage one another in dialogue by *turning to the other* and *reaching for understanding* (Maranhão 1990: 4).

Community development is a people-centred practice grounded in particular kinds of relationship between people. We draw on Gadamer to highlight that, from a dialogical perspective, the kind of relationship within community development is other-oriented, whereby people disrupt self-orientation and instead 'turn to the other', and in that other-orientation there are attempts to reach for mutual understanding of the other. Turning to the other and reaching for mutual understanding requires engaging with other perspectives, or what Gadamer calls 'horizons'.

Drawing on the work of Gadamer, anthropologist Vincent Crapanzano asserts that such turning to the other requires a reaching to understand the other that is 'immediate, open and authentic' (1990: 272). This reaching for understanding invites each party within the dialogue to be aware of their own prejudices, their horizon so to speak, but also being open to the other parties' questions and claims, allowing themselves 'to be conducted by the object' of conversation (Gadamer 1975: 33). Furthermore there is recognition that there will inevitably only be a *provisional* mutual understanding, recognising that any understanding can only be fleeting, because people, perspective and context change.

For Canadian philosopher Charles Taylor, reflecting on Gadamer's contribution to the human sciences, such turning to the other also requires openness. This implies openness to shifting our own views and, more significantly, our own identity. For example, he argues that, '[t]aking in the other will involve an identity shift in us' (Taylor 2002: 141). Taylor goes on to assert that, '[t]his is why it is so often resisted and rejected. We have a deep identity investment in the distorted images we cherish of others' (ibid.), and it could be added, ourselves. Dialogue in community development then requires a stance of intention to understand, but also of provisionality and uncertainty, recognising that any attachment to beliefs, ideas, identity-constructions and so forth will undermine capacities for dialogue.

As community practitioners intrigued by dialogue we have observed that it is often the kinds of relationship that honour difference (perspectives, traditions, claims) while searching for mutual understanding that create both an openness and solidarity. These are important ingredients for collective practice. This is not to suggest it is easy to forge such relations. Many practitioners stay attached to their own prejudgements and find it very difficult to remain open and therefore forge solidarity. For Gadamer the imperative to ensure such dialogue is possible is tolerance and openness to one another's perspectives. This in turn requires a willingness to enter the uncertainty of different perspectives and acknowledge the provisionality of any mutual understanding that might be forged (Gadamer 1998: 84ff.). Without such tolerance dialogue becomes very difficult, signposting the limits of a dialogical approach to community development and the value of focusing on other approaches in some circumstances.

A paradox: 'community as dialogue' and strategic dialogue

Building on Gadamer's notions of 'turning towards the other' and 'reaching for understanding' we turn to the Jewish philosopher Martin Buber, who offers wisdom around what we identify as a central paradox of dialogue within community development (discussed below). Buber has been used extensively within philosophy, communication, educational theory and other fields. Inspired by and drawing on the work of one of our Australian colleagues Anthony Kelly (2008), we have attempted to make sense of what Buber's philosophy of dialogue might mean for community development.

The paradox that Buber alerts us to is that within dialogical community development people are invited to turn towards each other with an attitude of authentic encounter, being open to what we refer to as an experience of 'community as dialogue'. A the same time there is the need also to be conscious of the strategic element of dialogue as a conscious intention to connect and communicate in a particular way named by Buber as 'technical dialogue'. To unpack this paradox we start with Buber's understanding of community as dialogue. In this sense, community is an experience of dialogue, both in everyday practices of being present to one another, and also in extraordinary moments when people experience 'deep presence' with one another (Buber 1947/2002, 1958). For Buber this is ultimately an unconscious experience – to be in dialogue with someone is to be *not* conscious of the dialogue per se, which would undo the presence and instead focus on the dialogue. People are aware of having had this kind of encounter only after the encounter is over. Siri Hustvedt puts it beautifully, arguing that for Buber, 'the ideal relation between human beings resulted in "a change from communication to communion, that is, in the embodiment of the word dialogue"' (2012: 201). This dialogical moment is experienced as an 'in-between' space, emerging from the dialectic between what Buber understood as I and Thou. It is a third space where neither party to the dialogue gives up their own point of view and yet both experience one another as whole.

This perspective of community has profound implications for dialogical community development. For Buber the dialogic attitude cuts through a worldview that is founded on separateness, which has clear distinctions between subject-knowers, and objects-known. That is, the world is not to be seized and reduced to manipulable formulae (Cohen 1957: 48ff.). While avoiding some of Buber's more mystical orientation (deeply influenced by Judaism) we draw on his humanising vision with a secular sensibility and also acknowledge the contribution of his spiritual impulse towards holism.

24 Theoretical prelude: on dialogue

This humanising vision and holistic focus puts the emphasis within community development on a particular understanding of 'community', or more accurately 'communion', rather than 'development'. In fact we often think about our work as 'developing community' rather than 'community development', or at least hold both ideas in tension. Reflecting on the question, 'How does community originate?' in 1930, Buber argued, 'nothing but remnants are left nowadays, because everywhere the aim is to rationalise life instead of humanise it' (Glatzer and Mendes-Flohr 1991: 41). He understood community as a humanising experience (with people not treating one another as objects) that was under assault in his lifetime. However, his ongoing reflections invite a process of re-humanisation and resistance to such rationalising assault. Like Buber, we propose that human community, as dialogue, is still possible.

However, and returning to the issue of paradox within dialogical community development practice, our reading of Buber also offers up the idea of not only holding the humanising process of community as dialogue, but also holding the strategic element, articulated by Buber as 'technical dialogue' (Arnett *et al.* 2009: 83). While community as dialogue is an embodied attitude and experience, technical dialogue is a conscious intention within community development to connect and communicate in a particular way.

Acknowledging Anthony Kelly's (2008) work in interpreting Buber's ideas for the purposes of community development, we consider this element of dialogue practice through the idea of the movements in working relationally with people (Buber 1947/2002; Kelly and Burkett 2008; Westoby and Owen 2010; Owen and Westoby 2012). Relational community work focuses on the subtle, dynamic *and* at times *conscious* processes of valuing and nurturing relationships between people. Within community work this valuing and nurturing invites an orientation towards the triad of:

- Connection – building relationships of care.
- Communication that is oriented towards learning – which requires, 'withholding the impulse to tell until one understands the context, topic, and the persons' (Arnett *et al.* 2009: xiii).
- Commitment – acknowledging the need for people to work together for change.

Community development practice informed by technical dialogue and this triad engages people with a commitment to *the practitioner's own* agenda of both community and development, but holds that agenda lightly while intentionally listening to people's stories, attempting to understand their concerns and perspectives and therefore engaging *with their* agendas. This engagement requires adeptness in dialogue – an ability to engage text and sub-text while accounting for context. In other words it requires us to be cognisant of what is said, what is potentially meant and what shapes the meaning. There is the need for skilful listening, not merely responding to people's abstractions and generalisations, but purposefully attending to specific words and sentences. It is through artful, careful listening and purposeful response that the movements of dialogue are sustained and connection is co-created (Kelly 2008; Owen and Westoby 2012).

This dialogical process creates the possibility of what is often discussed within community development practice as 'a common agenda'. There is a fundamental tension here. While dialogic practice reaches for understanding and coherence, community development theory and practice requires something else. People need to not only connect and understand one another while also reaching for coherence; they also need to reach some *mutual agreement* to propel joint action. However, dialogic practices tend not to seek agreement – they seek understanding. Agreement is usually the realm of dialectic conversations where people reach between thesis and antithesis, seeking synthesis (Kelly and Sewell 1988; Sennett 2012). It seems prudent therefore to acknowledge that embedded within dialogical community development there are both dialogic and dialectic logics – and an awareness of when each is at work is crucial to skilful practice.

A reaching: for collective coherence and a participatory consciousness

Building on this challenge of finding a 'common agenda', we turn to the North American physicist David Bohm, whose seminal work on dialogue invites consideration of the importance of reaching for collective coherence (Bohm 1996). His work is particularly pertinent for the group processes that are often central to community development. Recognising that people can get stuck within their own presuppositions and perspectives, Bohm suggests it is only through genuine group dialogue that people can disrupt their individually oriented, entrenched thought. He identifies ways in which a new collective coherence can emerge from the flow of meaning that happens when defensiveness is reduced and many perspectives are shared within a group.

Bohm's understanding of coherence is illuminated by his physicist's comparison of normal diffused light with focused laser light. For Bohm, coherence (importantly for our purposes this is not necessarily agreement) signifies focused analysis, insight and thought. Bohm's idea of thought as a complex system (Bohm 1994) is significant because, within his understanding of dialogue, to mistake your own thinking with thought is to be unaware that individual thinking is located (or constructed) within a larger 'structure' of thought emergent from society, tradition and history. To become conscious of this structure or system is a step forward, and requires a letting go of attachment to one's own thinking.

Community development workers are often accompanying people, usually within groups or community-based people's organisations, attempting to solve entrenched social or community problems. Therefore the need to reach imaginatively for collective coherence is crucial. In a nutshell, Bohm's contribution is that dialogue within groups can shed real light on difficult issues. Sometimes within our practice we refer to such collective coherence as a 'narrative thread' emerging from the interplay of centrifugal forces (diffusing diverse ideas and perspectives) and centripetal forces (drawing together of ideas and perspectives). The idea of collective coherence and narrative thread recognises that the 'truth of the matter', an analysis of what could be done, rarely emerges from one person, truth or perspective, but from the flow of meaning-making emergent from deep listening and attention to the collective meaning-making possibilities.

Furthermore, Bohm's work signposts the importance of thinking holistically. Our earlier critique of modernist, reductionist ways of thinking and working in community work is echoed in Bohm's insights into the fields of scientific thinking and working. However, with that critique he offered an alternative – that of dialogue and holism (Bohm 1980). His idea of 'taking part in the truth' recognises that there is always a broader complexity within the work than any one person can understand. He acknowledges therefore the need to think holistically, but also argues that people can never 'see the whole' because 'the whole is too much' (Bohm 1996: xii). Instead he offered the idea of a *participatory consciousness* emergent through dialogue with one another, whereby '[e]verything can move between us. Each person is participating, is partaking of the whole meaning of the group and also taking part in it' (ibid.: 31). In this dialogical space people are not trying to convince or persuade each other of 'their truth', but are reaching for a common coherence.

Again, within the space of community development such practice is not easy. People rarely come to a group with the stance of reaching for such coherence, but rather tend to be habitually attached to their own ideas and perspectives. Hence, dialogue requires community workers to clearly present and model new ways of practising, ways that disrupt the habitual tendencies to be self-oriented rather than other-oriented, and coherence-oriented rather than persuasion-oriented.

An intention: transformation and questioning

Gadamer, Buber and Bohm argue that dialogue, as they describe it, requires transformation. If someone genuinely turns towards the other, opens themselves to the flow of conversation and difference, then there will be a disruption to their perspective and experience of the world. This is personally transformative, and is hopefully experienced in many people's everyday life through conversation. However, for us it is the Brazilian Paulo Freire who best articulates the role of dialogue as a catalyst for social and structural transformation. Freire, best known as an educationalist, has deeply influenced many fields of inquiry and practice, including community development. Contemporary examples of that application to community development would be Anne Hope and Sally Timmel's *Training for Transformation: A Handbook for Community Workers* (1984) and Margaret Ledwith's *Community Development: A Critical Approach* (2005).

From a Freirean perspective dialogue very deliberately and carefully fosters a critical and transformational space. Within such a space people set out to do what Freire (1972) calls 'naming the word and the world', thereby being able to ask strategic questions and challenge dehumanising social relations. From Freire's perspective dialogical practice is not only about 'turning to the other', listening, connecting, learning and finding collective coherence and potentially shared agendas. Applied to community development it is also about practitioners eliciting a mandate from the people they are engaging with. This is a mandate to do

Theoretical prelude: on dialogue 27

critical analysis together, pushing the boundaries of how people together interpret the shared world, and then creating 'other' spaces of awareness and possible action. For liberation psychologists Mary Watkins and Helene Shulman (2008), what is crucial about Freire's contribution to dialogue is his emphasis on context. For them, Freire's work emphasises 'coming to understand the context one is in, gaining voice to address this context, and being able to creatively engage in efforts to transform it' (ibid.: 192). Contemporary initiatives such as REFLECT groups (Archer and Cottingham 2012) exemplify this understanding of transformational dialogue focused on context.

For Freire dialogue therefore requires a process of careful and critical questioning. This is a crucial contribution to our understanding of dialogical community development, albeit his understanding of dialogue is shaped by dialectic logics. Freire's idea of dialogue involves careful and critical questioning, not only by community development practitioners to community members, but between the two, understood as *mutual* critical questioning. A dialogue oriented towards the critical but also inviting mutuality requires practitioners to understand the 'delicate relationship' (Bell *et al.* 1990) that they are engaged in within transformational practice. It requires exercising some authority as an 'expert' in dialogue (guiding a process) but not allowing a drift towards authoritarianism (ibid.: 61). Skilled practitioners offer their own perspective and questions lightly, and are receptive to the perspectives and questions of others. As Watkins and Shulman put it, 'the animator [practitioner] co-creates with the group participants a space in which dialogue becomes possible' (2008: 193). This critical dialogue can only occur when people no longer see the given world as normal or natural (as Freire put it), but instead understand the world as emerging from historical and cultural processes that are open-ended, open to questioning, and able to be to transformed.

We now step back briefly. Freire importantly sees the world as historically and culturally constructed to be understood through questioning. Is Freire arguing that his notion of dialogue is ahistorical? To pause and reflect on that question we turn to the work of Russian literary theorist Mikhail Bakhtin (1981), considered by some to be the first to coin the word 'dialogic' (Sennett 2012: 19).

A reflective pause: genres and culture

One of Bakhtin's contributions to thinking about dialogue is that there are many genres of spoken and written communication – each with different implications for dialogue. By 'genre' we mean a particular style of communication, with characteristics that 'fit' that style. Alasdair MacIntyre (1984) adds to this, arguing that real understanding might only occur in dialogue when people correctly identify a conversation to be in a particular genre. Bakhtin himself wrote that, 'we choose words according to the generic specifications' (1986: 87). Within dialogue there is the particular conversation at play between two or more parties, but the 'rules' or characteristics of that conversation are contextualised by the genre, which is in turn historically and culturally constructed. Remember our introductory comments!

Returning to Freire, clearly his notion of dialogue as careful, critical and mutual questioning represents a particular genre of dialogue, different to that previously discussed in relation to, say, Gadamer and Buber. For example, as already mentioned, Freire's genre of dialogue would have been powerfully shaped by the rules of Marxist dialectics. This insight of Bakhtin's is very helpful for community workers, ensuring that they not only partake in dialogue, being open to encountering the other, but that they also attempt to understand the genre of dialogue that they are a part of. Genres or the 'rules of dialogue' can be very subtle, varying within and across cultures, and often it requires painstaking efforts to learn about the situation at hand.

For example, our Western Australian colleague David Palmer shared with us how in the Kimberley desert indigenous people have a cultural practice of 'sideways talking'. This refers to the idea that it is often considered rude to come straight out and tell someone something directly, particularly if it has to do with their lack of knowledge or a mistake. Instead people often tell stories about a fictional third person, for example, 'I know this other bloke who came up and did this thing once ... he didn't know it but he was really causing offence.' For the astute person who is open to, and understanding of, the local rules of dialogue, the story initiates space for the person to reconsider their actions. Awareness of such rules, or more often awareness that we do not know the rules, alerts us also to the illusionary hope of complete understanding.

Positionality: a responsive dance

Continuing this examination of how notions of dialogue relate to community development, we turn to a second idea elicited from Bakhtin's work – that of the community practitioner's awareness of their own *positionality*. In the Introduction we described community development *practice* as 'skilful means', understood particularly as an ability to skilfully dance the dance of relationship, being present and responsive to the other and the moment.

This idea has been crystallised through further reflection on Bakhtin's dialogics by New York-based sociologist Richard Sennett. Central to Sennett's interpretation of Bakhtin's work is the idea of dialogic, whereby 'no shared agreements may be reached, [but] through the process of exchange people may become more aware of their own views and expand their understanding of one another' (Sennett 2012: 19). From this idea Bakhtin developed the concept of 'knitted together but divergent exchange' (ibid.), perhaps more easily imagined the way Sennett explains it, likened to musicians playing jazz, each bouncing off one another, eliciting nuanced responses as complexity flourishes (ibid.). Within this bouncing and responding something happens.

Two useful ideas can be pinpointed from this wisdom. The first is that Bakhtin's work suggests a skilled practitioner needs to be conscious of self in relation to the practice *and* relationships formed within the practice. This is the jazzy exchange – conscious of self as musician/practitioner and also conscious of the exchange with others in creating the jazz piece. Second, we find it helpful to understand

Theoretical prelude: on dialogue 29

this particular exchange as an *embodied dialogue* and to imagine it metaphorically as a responsive dance.

Understanding this particular exchange as embodied dialogue foregrounds the idea that, while practitioners need to learn the faculties and skills of dialogue or exercise their dialogical muscles so to speak, there is a sense in which the faculties and skills eventually inhabit the practitioner.[2] As when playing jazz, a musician has to become technically proficient, but that alone does not make a good jazz player. The skills get inside the jazz player and are drawn out or evoked in a context of resonant exchange.

In a similar way practice as a responsive dance requires the technical proficiency of the dance moves, but also requires a letting go of the focus on skills only, and instead becoming aware of a dancer's own movement in relation to the other dancer. A responsive dancer gets into the flow of dance. Jungian depth psychologist James Hollis also alludes to this when reflecting on the idea of practice, arguing that, 'one has to learn the rules and master the techniques, so as to transcend them in one's practice' (2001: 93). Community practitioners, embodying dialogue, are then not so much conscious of dialogue but are in a state of responsivity and flow, attentive to a diverse ecology of relationships.

Having considered some of the theory relevant to the normative understandings of dialogue and applied it to dialogical community development, we now turn to a historical perspective on dialogue.

A historical understanding of dialogue

The second component of our code focuses on a historical perspective of dialogue, one that we are gradually coming to understand as having profound implications for dialogical community development. Some of our thoughts on this perspective are drawn from French social theorist Michel Foucault, but we rely heavily on the interpretation of his work by Australian philosopher Chris Falzon.

In *Foucault and Social Dialogue* (1998) Chris Falzon identifies what he calls 'thin dialogue' as both an 'encounter with the other' (ibid.: 33) and the 'reciprocal, two-sided character of the encounter between ourselves and other' (ibid.: 39). It might sound similar to Gadamer or Buber, however the difference is that for Foucault such dialogue is both an ethical practice and also a *historical process*.

Falzon, in interpreting Foucault, is clear that, as an ethical practice, dialogue requires a genuine encounter with difference in which no parties to dialogue yield to the other. He argues that such an encounter is both a 'conceptual requirement and a palpable experience' (ibid.: 33). Certainty has gone, and any quest for certainty rests on nostalgic hopes for solid foundations that no longer exist in this historical moment. Despite the potential anxiety and disturbance that accompanies uncertainty, such dialogue can be 'stimulating and revitalising' (ibid.: 34). Engaging or encountering people who are different enables parties to dialogue to rethink ideas and perspectives, and to dance the dance of renewing change.

Falzon also provides the useful insight that our 'current forms of life ... are the particular historical products of human activity, having arisen out of the play of dialogue' (ibid.: 13). Such an approach to understanding historical processes echoes North American literary critic Fredric Jameson's reflections on Marx and Bakhtin, whereby Jameson argues that 'class discourse ... is essentially dialogical in structure' (1983: 69). Drawing again on Bakhtin, Jameson argues that 'the dialogue of class struggle is one in which two opposing discourses fight it out within the general unity of a shared code' (ibid.: 70). From this perspective, dialogue then can not only be understood as an ethical practice but also 'serves as a general account of our being-in-the-world' (Falzon 1998: 39). It is one of the forces giving shape to our ways of living as historical processes unfold through the interplay of forces for dialogue and domination.

The perspective offered from Falzon's interpretation of Foucault, and Jameson's interpretation of Marx and Bakhtin, orients us to re-imagine community development as both an ethical practice (as per many of our normative reflections) and also as a 'social and political project' that can be a purposeful force for change within historical processes whereby the dynamics of dialogue, domination and de/re-humanisation unfold. If we see dialogue as constitutive of being-in-the-world and of history itself (that is, as a constant social process of people acting and being acted upon within the social field of life), then dialogical community development can be understood as an account of embodied concrete collective practices that foster 'creative transgression' (ibid.: 41). However, understood relationally and historically, what must be foregrounded is that community development can only be constituted as dialogical if it understands collective efforts of social groups in relation to other groups – that is, through the lens of social antagonisms and conflicts. Dialogical community development can be observed and made explicit or conscious as a social and political force within the unfolding process of history, a force accompanying those on the margins in their resistance against domination, opening up new spaces for alternative social innovation.

Adding to this, what is clear is that people encounter resistances in the social world as an inevitable experience of engaging difference (the other who will not yield to sameness). How people experience these resistances will determine in many ways their ability (potentially as community practitioners or community members), to *join* with one another in ways that foster the kind of collective action that is informed by multiple viewpoints, without glossing over the real social antagonisms that constitute capitalist societies. From this perspective it is important that people *be open*, despite uncertainty, with anticipation of learning and appreciation of new perspectives. We can therefore rethink dialogical community development as an ethical and political practice for progressive innovative social change in which people can choose to 'adopt different attitudes towards the other, attitudes of openness towards the other which are opposed to domination, and which are instrumental in promoting ongoing resistance, creative transgression, dialogue and transformation' (ibid.: 57).

This project of dialogical community development then is one humble contributor to social change – part of the myriad of social forces *for* transgression, for destabilisation of forces of domination that constantly attempt to 'arrest dialogue' (ibid.: 48) and in turn close history into ossified patterns of social arrangement and order. Dialogical community development is a particular ethical collective practice, oriented towards openness to the other, which contributes to social innovation. Such social innovation is understood as new ways of organising social arrangements – clearly oriented, for us as practitioners, towards progressive values of justice, equality and ecological sustainability.

Summing up

This prelude has considered traces of dialogue theory relevant to community development. We began with Gadamer's orientation of turning to the other and reaching for understanding, Buber's paradoxical understanding of community as dialogue but also the potential for strategic dialogue, and Bohm's insights into collective coherence and participatory consciousness. We then considered Freire's articulation of dialogue as a catalyst for social and structural transformation, triggered through careful, critical and respectful questioning, and paused to reflect on Bakhtin's understanding that genres of dialogue are culturally constructed. Our normative understanding is rounded out with Bakhtin's understanding of positionality and its implications for dialogue imagined metaphorically as a responsive dance. Finally, we examined implications of Foucault's understanding of dialogue as a historical inevitability within which forces of domination and [re-]humanisation are played out.

As per our comments within the opening paragraph of this chapter, we have not attempted any systematic comparative or critical analysis of these authors. We are not trying to build an overarching theory of dialogue for community development. Instead the chapter has been laid out as a systematic yet meandering wander through the crucial work on dialogue that we have concluded is relevant to community development theory and practice. With this in mind we now turn to Chapter 2 – exploring some of the implications for community practice.

2 Re-imagining community practice

This chapter supports practitioners to re-imagine community practice – discussed through the concepts of love, participation, place and social problems. These concepts have been chosen as representing core ideas that are important to rethink in the light of a dialogical community development framework. We therefore grapple with their meaning and implication for practice in both citizen-oriented and professional practice.

In re-imagining our work in the light of our understanding of these concepts, we also begin to deconstruct technically oriented community work and to explore alternative approaches that are soulful and social, have a critical edge, and draw practitioners into the depths of their professional and life experience. With this in mind we start with a reflection on love within contemporary community work, focusing on the quality of relationships central to good practice.

Awakening love

Anyone who has lost someone they loved dearly has reflected on sayings such as '[i]t is better to have loved and lost, than never to have loved at all' (Tennyson 1850: 27). Such a saying is infused with emotions of fear, anxiety, grief, hope, relief, wonder and delight. Tennyson evokes generative words – love, risk, obligation and fear – describing things that are central to community life. They cannot be avoided in community work.

An invitation to reclaim love in our practice

Love is not a fashionable idea in the contexts of community work. A few years ago Peter was asked to remove the word 'love' from an academic journal article he had written about community development. For many it is too closely associated with Hollywood or Bollywood and with romance, with shallow 'new age' personal development, or with abuse and misuse of trust in professional or pastoral relationships. However, while acknowledging the concerns, it is our argument that love needs to be reclaimed within our re-imagining of community practice.

In 2007 Peter was travelling in India. He decided to use some of that time to reread Paulo Freire's seminal book *Pedagogy of the Oppressed* (1972). The reading reminded him of a critique, analysis and method of work that is still highly relevant to community development practitioners. But the striking feature of this rereading was Freire's constant and unembarrassed use of the word 'love' in relation to his work, and more particularly in relation to dialogue. For example, he states:

> Dialogue cannot exist however, in the absence of a profound love for the world and men. The naming of the world, which is an act of creation and re-creation, is not possible if it is not infused with love. Love is at the same time the foundation of dialogue and dialogue itself.
>
> (ibid.: 62)

In this statement Freire not only articulates a powerful method of social change, but also reveals he understood soulful practice infused by a profound understanding of humanity and the need for humanising processes. Freire drew heavily on the works of Eric Fromm and their dialogue gives valuable insight into the place of love within community work.

Cultivating a capacity for love

Love, as described by the likes of Freire, is transformative. Community work without love can become technical, routinised, shallow and exploitative. While Freire reminds practitioners of the significance of reclaiming love, it is the humanist Eric Fromm (1957) who provides an invitation to relearn the art, ethics and practice of love. There is no point in reclaiming it without relearning to practise it.

For Fromm, learning the art of love requires engagement in the challenge of overcoming egocentricity, and moving towards a position where the needs of the other become as important as our own. It echoes Gadamer's idea of community as an orientation towards the other. Here is a central point in arguing for the reclamation of love – people move towards a position of *mutuality* whereby their legitimate needs as a human being are levelled alongside awareness and attention to other people's needs. Without this mutual consideration of one another's needs, community as dialogue or hospitality is impossible.

As psychotherapist David Yalom (1980: 371), drawing on Fromm's work, points out, people can then move from a state of needing to be loved to that of loving as an 'effective potent state'. For Fromm, love is an active state of being that requires giving. Yalom argues that mature love implies other practices: concern, responsiveness, respect and knowledge. His contribution is to show that to reclaim love as an integral part of community life, people can foster the attitudes within themselves and one another that ensure an attitude of concern about others, are responsive to the needs of others, and are respectful of the uniqueness of the other. For Fromm, 'true knowledge of the other is possible only when one transcends one's self-concern and sees the other person in the other's own terms' (ibid.: 372). To engage people in this way, with such knowledge and attitude, is to reach a more effective, ethical and potent state.

In a dialogical approach to community development, it is suggested that practitioners could more consciously awaken such love. This requires a fundamental, counter-cultural shift towards the other. Much of the way people live is now based on fear and risk aversion – building fences and gated communities, retreating from public spaces and public transport, and relating only to others of similar class, race, education, sexuality and sub-culture. There is a kind of 'bunkering down', a closed collectivity of passive hostility that is anti-hospitality. Even if encountering other people, more often than not we merely pass the time in superficial chatter – a process of making a point, providing our perspective, rehearsing our opinion. In short, people get stuck in their own story. By reclaiming love such trends can be destabilised.

Community as dialogue and hospitality infused with such love invites movement out of the bunker, movement into public spaces, engagement with people who are different, and movement away from the habit of chatter. Instead it cultivates a commitment to the other person's story. It is easy to live a shallow life that never takes the time to enter the world of those around us. It is easy to find oneself with people but failing to take the time to ask, What is your story? Where do you come from? How did you get to be here? What are the deep concerns in your life? or What are your passions and hopes? To take the time to hear someone's story means responsibly gaining knowledge about them, their lives and their concerns. It is the respectful willingness to be responsive to such stories that is a crucial movement in community as dialogue and community as hospitality.

The profoundly humanising process of co-creation

Martin Buber (1947/2002, 1958) can provide further guidance in this awakening and practice of love. As already alluded to in Chapter 1, Buber talks of the experience of community as requiring a shift between two people from what he described as an *I–It* encounter, crudely understood as a subject–object kind of relationship, to an *I–Thou* encounter, understood as a subject–subject kind of relationship. This shift is crucial to experiencing a dialogical or hospitable community. The shift can be illustrated by the following story from Peter:

> I was recently teaching some Master of Development Practice students from Vietnam. They were telling me how they felt 'tortured' by a feeling that their four years of work on a large AusAID-funded[1] project in Northern Vietnam had failed. Independent evaluations had shown how the local indigenous people had hardly gained anything from the multimillion dollar initiative. In talking with the students about their sense of failure, we started to reflect on how the project workers had engaged the villagers.
>
> After some discussion, one of the Vietnamese students had an 'aha!' moment and shared it with the class. She realised that, 'what we did wrong is that we didn't really approach these villagers as people equal to us; we didn't go and sit with them around their village fires, hear their stories and understand their world. We didn't create the project together'. I asked her what

they did do. She thought about the question for some time and then reflected back to us how the project workers would turn up in four-wheel drives, facilitate meetings, talk about the importance of participation, empowerment and natural resource management, then draw up a list of activities and actions for local people, and leave.

Peter then introduced Buber's contrast between I–It and I–Thou to reflect on the workers' unintentional but disastrous process and the sad story's sad outcome. The student realised that the project workers as subjects (that is, as active agents making decisions, using their creativity, resources, relationship and intelligence) related to the villagers only as objects – in a sense the villagers become people to whom a project could be done *to* or *for* rather than *with* or *among*. There was no sense of the villagers as equal participants in a process of dialogue and co-creation.

The student's 'aha!' moment also incorporated a renewed vision of what awakening love could offer to such a project. She recognised that awakening love could reorient everyone towards subject–subject and co-creative kinds of relationship – an I–Thou relationship in which a space for relationship building, for storytelling, for deep listening, and for building a shared commitment to change could be activated. As Peter went around the class reflecting on this student's analysis, others started to realise that many of their failed attempts at development work came down to this failure to truly love the people they were working with. There was a recognition that this failure to love blinded them to the possibility of dialogue and therefore to the profoundly humanising process of co-creation and co-motion within development work.

Some challenges in developing a practice built on love

For many people such I–Thou kinds of relationship are not easy to imagine in contemporary society. The analysis within the above reflection could be challenged by arguing that it is unreasonable to expect such project workers to take the time to build loving relationships with the villagers. It could be argued that there are simply too many villagers or that the project schedule itself would not allow for it. In the same vein, some people could argue that contemporary life is too fast, relationships are too many and there are too many needs. However, the irony is that, while for many there is a sense of 'too fast, too many', there is also a sense that relationships are lacking in deep connection, solidarity and meaning. Many people are so overloaded with diverse kinds of relationships that they have lost their capacity to discern a moment of true, genuine encounter with the other (characterised by I–Thou qualities); or if such an encounter is discerned, people move on so fast that they fail to cherish or celebrate it, and then build on it. The opportunity for a more meaningful sociality, which is a foundation for dialogical community development, is missed.

But there is a fallacy in arguing that I–Thou relationships take too much time. Love develops from the very beginning of an encounter; and if community workers are going to spend minutes, hours or days with someone, then surely they invest in the quality of relationship for those minutes, hours or days. However, while it does not take more time to be loving, it does take more attentiveness. Rebuilding dialogical and hospitable community may require a reorientation towards 'slow and less' (which might in the above story mean working with fewer villages), and in most of our lives this would mean fewer connections, but deeper ones.

Those that are on a journey from I–It to I–Thou often encounter a central paradox. To make the shift towards others requires a reflexive journey in which the depth of their own capacity for hospitality not only towards other people but also towards themselves needs exploring – the complexity associated with 'I'. While it implies a movement away from egocentricity, I–Thou in no way means a movement away from the self. It may require a confrontation, or put more gently, a dialogue with the ego; it might require the painful suffering of re-socialisation; it most certainly does require an ongoing encounter with the complex and dynamic self. This encounter requires movement away from egocentricity towards other-orientedness. It requires reskilling not only in interpersonal relations, but intrapersonal relations.

Building on this importance of the individual, a dialogical approach to community development can in no way move to simply a *collectively oriented* consciousness devoid of love for people. This is what is often disastrous about revolutions – they inspire collective action devoid of love. People are sacrificed for collective ideologies. While being concerned about community, dialogical community development is also acutely aware of, and concerned with, individuals. The notion of dialogical community is a way of signifying the enfolded nature of individuals as mutual participants within a relational world – denying neither individuality nor relationality.

Buber (1947/2002) articulates such an enfolded perspective, carefully arguing that collectivity is in many ways the antithesis of community. Community is the space 'in between' collectivity and individuality. For Buber, 'collectivity is based on an organised atrophy of personal existence ... it is a flight from community's testing and consecration of the personal, a flight from the vital dialogue, demanding the staking of the self, which is at the heart of the world' (ibid.: 37). In contrast community is where community happens. Community is a 'dynamic facing of the other, a flowing from *I* to *Thou*' (ibid.) – in other words, a dynamic of awakened love invoked through a soulful movement that takes the mutuality of I and other very seriously.

Transformation of the ordinary into the extraordinary

In exploring the place of love in community life and work, it would be easy to simply dismiss romantic love or *eros* as irrelevant and to focus more on the place of love as ethics as described by the likes of Fromm, Freire and Buber. However, in arguing for the reclamation of love, we propose that the erotic can also teach practitioners something important about community. Deborah Bird Rose reminds us pertinently that love requires both 'ethics and *eros*' (2011: 118).

Plato called the *eros* kind of love 'divine madness'. He recognised the archetypal worlds lying deep within people's psyches that are unlocked when 'in love'. When people 'fall in love' they are usually transformed by such archetypes. It can be seen in the dreamy eyes, the music that is played and the way people in love float around the house or the office. This transformation can be said to bring both a kind of new life and a new death – even if for only a short period of time. There is a new aliveness that emerges due to the encounter with the archetypes, and a death to the pragmatic, rational world where so many of our waking but unawakened lives are spent. When in love, people are animated; the world is full of a whole new sense of wonder, meaning and beauty. At the same time love's dark sides are encountered anew, with complexities of fears, wounds and pains. Many of the concerns and efforts that previously claimed energies – at work, in homes, and even ideals – suddenly shrink from the centre to the periphery. A new dance is being danced!

Some observers of such love interpret it as *not* so much about relationships (a huge concern of modern society when thinking of love) but as about soul (Moore 1992). Romantic love is often an initiation into soul. It is a grand opportunity to enter life's inner dramas and mysteries; it is an invitation to explore those inner parts that have remained dormant, quiet and asleep. It is often the first opportunity to encounter other dimensions of our selves in all their grandeur and complexity – as well as to encounter the 'other' person.

This kind of love can also illuminate the process of re-imagining community work, as it transforms the ordinary into something other and potentially extraordinary. Awakening love as *eros* alongside love as ethics can introduce people to a soulful orientation. With this erotic as well as ethical orientation people bring a new awareness, attention and imagination to their lives, to others and to the world around them.

Let us look deeper into this argument. Rose argues that the erotic self is always seeking connection (2011: 121) and it is this seeking that intrigues us. North American novelist and intellectual Siri Hustvedt adds to this intrigue when discussing the significance of 'desire' within human imagination (2012: 5). She says it would appear that, while animals have 'needs', humans move beyond needs to 'desires' and there is something about this that is linked to imagination. Desire includes an ability to hold an object in the mind – an imaginative process – and for us, the wisdom here is that desire can therefore unlock imaginative capacity within community life. A soulful and erotic orientation has huge potential to transform imaginations and therefore energise community practice.

In *The Re-enchantment of Everyday Life* (1996), North American Thomas Moore goes even further and argues that, to reclaim erotic love into community life, the world needs to be re-sexualised. His analysis is that *eros* has been banished to either the bedroom or to the pornographic underground and the results (among other things) are that branded advertising and ugly architecture dominate public spaces, and discussions about sexuality are vulgar, moralistic or fearful. Moore argues that people need to rediscover *eros* in community life and culture – in the context of real everyday relationships. This can be imagined through life-giving carnival, festival and other rituals, through beautiful and provocative architecture, through public art and performance that expresses creativity, through a reintroduction of life-giving, pulsating love into everyday social lives. People might no longer literally make love in the fields as a way of invoking the gods to provide a plentiful harvest, but the equivalent kind of erotic attention to community hopes and desires can be sparked through new kinds of ritual and action.

This potential transformation from the ordinary to the extraordinary is the daily concern of dialogical community work infused with soul and awakened by love. It is this transformation of awareness, attention and imagination that animates community as dialogue. A dialogical approach to community work therefore requires an attention to people in a way that pays attention to detail, an orientation to openness and people's stories, and an awakening of different kinds of love. Here is an example from Gerard's practice:

> Every day of my working life is filled with conversations. Many are important, but most are superficial. They don't touch either of us, the group is not moved; there is no sense of the extraordinary. However, I know when I am having an intimate conversation with someone – my heart rate changes, the pores of my skin open, I am holding their eyes. I know when I am being hospitable – I am alert to every nuance, I listen deeply and in silence, and my body language communicates a profound respect for the moment and the other. All these things are familiar to me ever since I was about ten and in love for the first time!
>
> I vividly remember one interagency network meeting among the dozens I have attended in recent years. There was the usual exchange of information, some fun personal disclosure, and the gentle ribbing that builds collegiality in Australia (where no one is allowed to take themselves too seriously). Then one of our colleagues strayed into a personal reflection on the recent tragic deaths in a police car chase of two young men whom many in the network had worked with. Others told the stories about what had happened, the agenda was suspended, and for twenty extraordinary minutes the network became an intimate space and the nature of the relationships between us was transformed – we experienced extraordinary community as dialogue and hospitality.

We do not want to pretend that this is easy. Freire admonishes people who engage in work for social change without love, and his warning is a daily challenge to our own community work practice. What we do know is that we want to live, work and play in communities where people are alive, in love with life and skilled in this animated dance called community as dialogue and hospitality. And we want to work with colleagues who are alive – the kinds of fools who continually fall in love with life, and who are alert to the potential transformation of the ordinary to the extraordinary that is the daily concern of soulful community work.

Having considered the significance of love in community work we now turn to a second important concept, participation, inviting people into a deeper practice.

Deepening participation

For many involved in community work, there is awareness that participation is crucial to development 'success' (Craig and Mayo 1995; Botes and Rensburg 2000). Authors such as Robert Chambers (2005), Somesh Kumar (2002) and Amartya Sen (1999) have helpfully emphasised the importance of people exercising their own social agency – articulating the importance of participation both as a means to, and an end of, development work.

The limitations of disembedded participation

Conversely, countless evaluations point out the failure of many activities, projects, programmes and plans due to a lack of participation (Hickey and Mohan 2004; Cornwall 2011). Many community workers have seen buildings sitting in impoverished communities, a potential resource, but empty, unused, wasted. Some workers have also seen well-funded programmes, filled with participation, achieve little or nothing. Often participation becomes 'a politically attractive slogan', or 'economically, an appealing proposition' (Rahnema 2010: 128). We share Iranian development scholar Majid Rahnema's analysis that, like 'Karl Polanyi's description of the modern economy, participation has come to be "disembedded" from the socio-cultural roots which had always kept it alive' (ibid.: 132). In this sense the ideas and practices of participation can easily be co-opted by instrumental reason and the economic *episteme*. People simply become an object of actions and interventions that others construe as 'participatory development'.

Clearly there has been a response to such critiques, with many practitioners advocating for a more popular form of participation – one more aligned to 'dialogical methods', such as action research, action learning, and participatory action research (PAR). However, from the perspective of our approach to dialogical community development many of these forms and practices of popular participation are still outsider-led and instrumentally oriented interventions captive to a modernist paradigm. There is little space for notions of development as hospitality and co-motion, ensuring that participation is embedded within the socio-cultural roots of people. Our response to this malaise is the idea of *deepening participation*, the title of this reflection. We have distilled the elements of deepening participation and now discuss each one in turn.

Enabling creativity

Central to our understanding of deepened participation is the notion of creativity, defined beautifully by English academic Rob Hope in *Creativity: Theory, History, Practice* (2005: xvi) as, 'the capacity to make, do or become something fresh and valuable with respect to others as well as ourselves'. Community activist Mary Lou Cook's famous quote is also apt, arguing that 'creativity is inventing, experimenting, growing, taking risks, breaking rules, making mistakes and having fun' (Masters and Wallace 2011: 241). Participation can be deepened within community development practice when practitioners bring a sustained attention to enabling creativity. There is something significant about the process of 'making' or 'becoming' as per the first definition. Our sense is that unless spaces are supported within community practice for people, in groups, to make, or become (that is, to create), then all the problems of disembedded participatory *technique* surface. Unless people are given the space to create in the ways Mary Lou Cook articulates, that is, being free to invent, experiment, risk, break rules and so forth, then there is little chance that they will be able to do what Edward de Bono understands as 'breaking out of the established patterns in order to look at things in a different way' (Gogatz and Mondejar 2005: 10).

Drawing on Rahnema again, this kind of deepened participation, which takes creativity seriously, has both an inner and outer dimension (2010: 139). The inner dimension refers to creativity in the sense that people individually recover their own sense of freedom and imagination, as Freire put it, 'never accept[ing] their minds being bureaucratised' (Bell *et al.* 1990: 37). The outer dimension refers to creativity in the sense that people animate themselves *collectively*, that is, in relation to one another, in social change movements. Both processes require people to respect their own knowledge and imagination, individually and collectively. In many ways the opposite of creativity can be understood as stuck-ness, whereby there is a lack of energy and the bureaucratised or modernist mind is ossified. A deepened participation requires processes that unlock energies and remove stuck-ness, enabling people to trust their creative capacities.

While creativity is the work people must do themselves, we still see community workers as having a role, hence the inclusion of 'enabling' within the title of this sub-section. Rahnema again has something to contribute here, and he focuses particularly on the Indian stories of the Gandhian, the Chipko and the Swadhyaya movements as examples whereby being 'very sensitive animators, able to listen to their own people, to the world at large, and to the roots of their common culture, has enabled them to cultivate the possibilities of action and self-discovery dormant' (2010: 140). It has not necessarily been well-trained professional change-agents, but instead practitioners who, rooted in place, culture and love, have been able to trigger alchemic processes of creativity. This is illustrated with Margaret Wheatley and Deborah Frieze's account of a practice story from the *favelas* of Brazil. They recount how:

'More than 150 people have arrived already ... at our meeting place ... and are itching to start playing the Oasis Game. The game will take two days to play, and there is excitement in the air' (Wheatley and Frieze 2011: 57). The game has been organised and hosted by an organisation called the Elos Institute based in Santos, Brazil. Their philosophy of change is one of 'serious play' (ibid.: 53) and they describe their work as 'helping people recover their ability to dream and find the will to realise their dreams with others ... They believe that everyone wants to-and can-transform the world. And that we can do it voluntarily, cooperatively and joyfully' (ibid.: 53). The Elos Institute's practice involves a team of sensitive outsiders partnering and entering a community and animating collective wisdom for action. This is done through community conversation and co-operative games informed by a spirit of play. Their experience has shown that creativity is unlocked through play, stating that, '[i]t's like we've discovered a gift inside ourselves, something that we already had'.

(ibid.: 71)

From the story we highlight both the creativity that is unlocked, in this case study, through playful processes; and also the significance of the 'sensitive outsiders' who took the time to become embedded in the local place and culture. Finally, the last statement says it all – 'discovering something we already had'. The Elos Institute's experience is similar to ours – deepened participation is a process of unlocking this kind of self and collective creativity – ultimately a process of discovery!

Story-ing and participation

In our experience people open themselves up to such deep participation when they feel as though there is genuine space for their stories to be told and heard. They create narrative threads that locate themselves in relation to the topic at hand in a way that is relevant to 'where they are at'. In articulating and sharing their stories people can come to a new awareness of the nature of the world, of their personal place in it, and of the potential for collective efforts to make a difference. Referring to our previous reflection on creativity, there is the real possibility of people becoming 'unstuck'. North American planner John Forester calls this experience 'human flourishing' (1999), described by Wendy Sarkissian and Dianna Hurford, as:

> [C]reating spaces of trust for different kinds of stories to emerge and for people to express themselves in their own vocabularies. It also means listening deliberately to these stories and applying them to collective and participatory actions. Only then can we act in an imaginative dialogue, flourishing our hearts and minds within the capacity and nourishment of our environments.
>
> (2010: 13)

Australian academic Leonie Sandercock (2003: 26) has observed, 'when stories work as catalysts for change, it is partly by inspirational example, and partly by shaping a new imagination of alternatives'. This kind of story-ing is constitutive – it 'shapes community, character and culture' (ibid.: 20). Story-ing can be done in ways that lead to a deepening of participation as people together work with the stories that emerge. Finally, people experience a particular resonance with one another as they find connections within and between their stories and begin to weave them together. We explore these dynamics below.

Resonance and deep participation

A core enabler of both creativity and story-ing is not only a good understanding of practitioner dialogue as we have theorised it, but the capacity to also discard or carefully adapt outsider-designed plans, techniques and methodologies. More of this will be discussed in the next chapter, but at this point it is worth pointing out that creativity is often unlocked and people share stories when there is cultural resonance within a process of discovery. The Oasis Game mentioned in the previous story is an example.

Popular spiritualist A.T. Mann reminds us that resonance can be understood as, '"Being on the same wave length" as someone else, as when we sense the presence of someone we perceive as familiar across a room full of strangers ... Resonance enriches the significance of things and evokes spontaneous, deep, emotional experiences' (2010: 8). James Hollis argues 'the principle of resonance suggests that "like summons like"' (2001: 61). From our perspective deepened participation occurs when people are: 'on the same wave length', when there is an inner and outer connection to the concern/s at hand, when the process has been created by the people animating their creativity, and the process unlocks a vision for action. It could be said that there is a resonance between the people, concern, process of discovery and analysis for action – a vibrating energy that feels like an almighty shared 'aha!' moment.

Often plans, methodologies or techniques designed from outside a social group are not culturally resonant and therefore they block creativity and potent action. They are disembedded from people's socio-cultural roots. People's energies are transferred towards the assimilative or adaptive process of trying to make sense of the tool or technique. There is no or little energy left for creativity. And this takes us to the heart of dialogical community development and deepening participation. Unless the process of dialogue is rooted in local genres oriented towards the other (their culture, traditions, spirituality) then there is little chance of unlocking people's capacities for dreaming and action. This is illustrated in an extraordinary weekend Peter helped set up at the Nungeena Indigenous Women's Healing Centre near Brisbane:

> Several years ago I was involved in a wonderful initiative that brought together indigenous women and women from refugee backgrounds over a long weekend to share stories and overcome their misconceptions of the other. The initiative emerged out of a 'dialogue in healing' project whereby indigenous people and people from refugee backgrounds realised they knew little about one another. Their perceptions of the other were dominated by media images and 'politician-speak'. The outcome of the dialogue was an agreement that a group of refugee women from various African nations, El Salvador, Columbia and Vietnam, would spend a weekend at the Nungeena Indigenous Women's Healing Centre at Mount Beerwah – one of the Glasshouse Mountains in the Sunshine Coast area of Australia.
>
> Prior to the weekend those of us planning and hosting the initiative spent many hours in conversation thinking about the best platforms and processes for dialogue. During the event the women shared stories of losing country, both indigenous and refugee, their suffering and their journeys of healing. They cried and laughed but the real work started when they started cooking together. A new energy was accessed and while cooking the women decided to share recipes with one another.

The sharing of food and cooking together seemed to resonate between the women in a way that no planned participatory process would have enabled.

The poetic and intimacy

Continuing with our reflection on how to enhance a deepened participation, we not only re-imagine participation through the lens of creativity, story-ing and resonance, but also through the bard's notion of the poetic. Such an idea can be visited through Tagore's understanding that, 'it is the poetic that rescues people from the *ennui* which is the desert haze of inactive imagination' (Gupta 2006: 26). Tagore's proposal, that the poetic is a key to thwarting people's *ennui*, is infused with an idea that poetry is profoundly intimate – it invites people to explore their deepest fears, hopes, longings, vulnerabilities and sufferings. Poetry infused with such intimacy has a way of transcending a certain shallowness that is characteristic of a purely rational world.

We propose that if social and community participation can be infused with this kind of intimacy, an unfolding power will emerge that is grounded in strong community ties and a sense of respectful co-motion. This poetic resource of intimacy would pay the dividends of deep connections and correspondingly creative ideas (Bachelard 1994). In such spaces people start to envisage new worlds of possibility in their midst. People start to dream again. When they feel alone, many people hardly dare to dream – they are surviving; but when they are experiencing intimacy with others they sometimes find themselves living into a dawning awareness that 'maybe we can dream together'. People together recover what Paulo Freire (1972) called literary imagination. Here is a story illustrating the role of intimacy in practice from some work we did in Caboolture, a satellite city north of Brisbane on the east coast of Australia:

> Kate was a resident in a public housing estate where we were doing some community-based training. Along with about twelve other residents she attended a weekly three-hour dialogue discussing the kinds of communities people wanted to live in, the barriers to building those kinds of communities and some ways forward in building community. People shared their hopes and sadness about the decline of community. The intimacy of the group, created through people's vulnerabilities, created a safe space where ideas could be generated, experiments could be considered. Kate started to regain a sense that something could be different in the street where she lived. For years she had felt like a lone voice in her neighbourhood, but through the dialogical process of the community training, she realised she could be creative in trying to change the situation. Others in the group encouraged her.
>
> At the same time as the training course was running, the Government had set up a community reference group in the neighbourhood to consider actions for renewing the community. Kate was a member of this group but was disheartened by the lack of involvement of other local people. When she asked other locals why they didn't get involved, they told her it was too

formal, they couldn't understand the 'government speak' and they didn't want to look stupid asking for clarification all the time.

Kate had an idea. She decided to open her home for a morning tea, inviting residents in her street and letting them know what was happening at the community reference group. At first a couple of people turned up and they had a discussion about their experience of ordinary, everyday, working-class issues in their neighbourhood. The morning tea became a regular event and it grew as more people wanted a safe space to discuss their issues and to hear about the initiatives of the 'government group'. It wasn't long until Kate's Cuppa, as it became named, had more people involved than the formal group! For a time Kate become a conduit for people to share their concerns, but she encouraged others and soon they felt more confident to attend the formal meetings as well. The experiment to connect with others through a simple means of having a cuppa together in her own flat had not only become an expression of 'community as hospitality' but also gave voice to people who were not being heard.

The story of 'Kate's Cuppa' illustrates several crucial points about deepening participation. First, it was the intimacy triggered by the mutual sharing of vulnerabilities that created a context for Kate to discover a dream of making change. She felt safe to be human with others and to share previous failed efforts in creating community. Second, the intimacy also provided a context for risk-taking, a prerequisite to being creative. In the context of the emergent group Kate felt able to take a risk in trying something new. Third, Kate created her own participatory process – the 'cuppa' mechanism, and on top of that conducted it in her own home. It was not an outsider-imported plan, method or technique. It was hers and became a shared space with a genuine working-class resonance for her neighbours. People from the neighbourhood, distrustful and distant from the formal government reference group, were able to enter this participatory process comfortable they were not being manipulated, targeted or developed. They felt welcome by Kate and co-created a new learning, deliberative and decision-making space.

Within such a space people were animating their vision of life, what their neighbourhoods could look like and what authorities could contribute to that vision. Ordinary people were participating as co-creators of dialogical community, soulful people awakened by love in a context of resonance and intimacy. This is the kind of deep participation we want to see facilitated by skilled practitioners who invite people into an intimate engagement of their creative imaginations, with hospitality towards one another's ideas and perspectives, giving attention and care to building a shared analysis of ways forward.

A final caveat: widening participation

In advocating for deepening participation we also recognise the need for a second movement of widening participation in response to the reality that 'where people are at' can be very different in the contemporary world. Community practitioners cannot afford to make the mistake of trying to understand people's socio-cultural roots without taking into account the broader socio-cultural condition of postmodernity. By this we refer to the condition whereby people often experience the world in more fragmented ways than in the past and are faced with multiple calls to participate in many different causes.

As Australian community development academic Jim Ife reminds us, 'people are members of multiple communities' and 'have neither the time nor the energy to engage in serious "participation" in them all' (2012: 6). Ife argues that we therefore need to look at participation differently, recognising two forms – what he calls 'high-level short-term' and 'low-level long-term' participation. Within the former people 'will become actively and heavily engaged for a relatively short period of time' and in the latter 'people have a long-term engagement at a relatively superficial level' (ibid.).

From our perspective what is crucial is to recognise that participation is triggered and sustained when people are engaged in a way or form that recognises the uniqueness of each person's story, and the space provided harnesses what energy and creativity people can bring to the table. Our call for depth is not a call for uniformity, but recognition that depth requires the soulful attention to particularity while summoning people to individually and collectively step beyond the familiar and safe.

Place-making

It is commonplace to think about community primarily in terms of geographical place, as per many of the stories told in the previous reflections. This is an important perspective in people's everyday social lives. As people think about their community they often think about relating to family, friends, shopkeepers and neighbours in significant ways that have a particular resonance with place. However, an understanding of community that is too focused on a geographical sense of place can provide a rationale for superficial, technical and depoliticised notions of community development. Within such perspectives the 'community' can become objectified as merely a space, site or territory, targeted by professionally designed and driven interventions, usually to deal with perceived deficiencies or problems going on in that particular locality. From this perspective 'community as place' becomes an object to observe in a detached way and think about as something separate from the broader socio-political context. Also, when community workers inadvertently find themselves co-opted into this perspective, they tend to see themselves not as part of the social relations that make up community, but as separate to 'the community' – and hospitality becomes difficult.

Place-making as emplacement

An alternative, re-imagined approach can see dialogical community as a process of ongoing *emplacement* that requires attention to people's daily creative endeavours in purposefully inhabiting space. David Turton (2005), an anthropologist who has worked for many years in the Horn of Africa, drew our attention to Kiisa Malkki's (1995) naming of this social process as 'emplacement'. Within dialogical community development, part of the challenge is to awaken people's consciousness and release their creative juices so that they can actively engage in the processes of emplacing. The stories below illustrate how emplacement can play out in very different contexts around the world.

The North American author Kurt Vonnegut wrote his delightful final book *A Man Without Country* (2005) at the age of 84. Within the book he included the following story illustrating the importance of everyday emplacement for him on his New York streets:

> Not long ago, I used to type. And, after I had about twenty pages, I would mark them up with pencil, making corrections. Then I would call Carol Atkins, who was a typist ... we would chat away, and finally I say 'Hey, you know I got some pages. Are you still typing?' And she sure is. And I know it will be so neat, it will look like it was done by a computer. And I say, 'I hope it doesn't get lost in the mail.' And she says, 'Nothing ever gets lost in the mail' ...
>
> Anyway ... I go downstairs to take off ... and this is on 48th Street in New York City between Second Avenue and Third, and I go out to this newsstand across the street where they sell magazines and lottery tickets and stationery. And I know their stock very well, and so I get an envelope, a manila envelope. It is as though whoever made that envelope knew what size of paper I'm using. I get in line because there are people buying lottery tickets, candy, and that sort of thing, and I chat with them. I say 'Do you know anybody who ever won the lottery?' And, 'What happened to your foot?' Finally I get up to the head of the line. The people who own this store are Hindus. The woman behind the counter has a jewel between her eyes. Now isn't that worth the trip? I ask her, 'Have there been any big lottery winners lately?' Then I pay for the envelope. I take the manuscript and put it inside.
>
> I go next to the postal convenience center down the block at the corner of 47th Street and Second Avenue. This is very close to the United Nations, so there are funny looking people from all over the world. I go in there and we are all lined up again. I'm secretly in love with the woman behind the counter. She doesn't know it. My wife knows it. I am not about to do anything about it. She is so nice. All I have ever seen of her is from the waist up because she is always behind the counter. But every day she will do something with herself above her waist to cheer us up. Sometimes her hair will be all frizzy. Sometimes she will have ironed it flat ...
>
> So I wait in line, and I say, 'Hey what was the language you were talking? Was it Urdu?' I have nice chats. Sometimes not. There is also, 'If you don't like it here, why don't you go back to your tinhorn dictatorship where you came from?' One time I had my pocket picked there and got to meet a cop and tell him about it. Anyway, I finally get up to the head of the line. I don't reveal to her that I love her. I keep poker-faced. She might as well be looking at a cantaloupe, there is so little information in my face, but my heart is beating. And I give her the envelope, and she weighs it ...

> Then I go outside and there is a mailbox ... And I go home. And I have had one hell of a good time.
>
> (ibid.: 57ff.)

The story reinforces a perspective on emplacement, highlighting the importance of everyday social activity. It is as people walk their streets, engage in conversations, give attention to others and participate in local commerce that place is created.

Emplacement entails not only everyday social activity as per Vonnegut's story, but is often a socially and politically charged process. For example, in our home city of Brisbane we have been involved in a process whereby new groups of refugees and migrants are emplacing a neighbourhood (Storey *et al.* 2010), which brings particular challenges:

> In one of our Brisbane neighbourhoods called Moorooka there has been a substantial recent change to the demography. There has been a significant influx of African migrants and refugees into the area, both as residents and as business people. The local shopping streetscape is now dominated by Sudanese, Egyptian, Eritrean, Ethiopian and Somali shop-fronts. They call it 'our little Morocco'. Many older residents – both multigenerational Australians and the previous wave of refugees (Serbian, Croatian, Bosnian, Polish) are struggling to deal with this change process. There is a sense of displacement and disorientation.
>
> Peter has worked with the city council's community relation workers to rethink how to engage dialogically with people in this neighbourhood, so as to foster hospitality towards one another and re-imagine a sense of place. The way forward required moving from a focus on displacement and disorientation towards creating new processes of emplacement. The idea of Moorooka/Morocco becoming an African precinct in the city – a particular neighbourhood full of street life, music, diverse foods, colours, and languages – could revitalise the place and bring people back to the streets. The focus of the work became the process of imagining new ways of consciously and creatively inhabiting the place to build a new sense of place.

The New York-based cultural anthropologist Arjun Appadurai reminds us that 'locality is an inherently fragile social achievement' (1996: 179). He goes on to argue that the work of locality production is always and everywhere a constant struggle to keep at bay 'an endemic sense of anxiety and instability in social life' (ibid.). The social production of place is often a fragile thing, as the story of Moorooka illustrates. Anxiety and instability threaten to undo people's creative energies and shrink their imaginative capacity. Place-making can easily become captive to racisms and other forms of exclusion and violence. From our perspective, to counter such processes communities need people who give attention to the processes of place-making within a dialogical and hospitable frame, while also being conscious of the socio-political dynamics at play.

Place-making: not just belonging, but also becoming and resisting

As per the above discussion, more often than not in the jostling of geography and place-making particular kinds of groups or place-based constituencies mobilise themselves as 'community' on the basis of their own forms of belonging (Block 2008). This mobilisation is often 'for' their own belonging, and also 'against' others – usually those who have less ability, within a market-based economic system, to mobilise themselves. So, for example, migrants, refugees or young people are made not welcome in a neighbourhood as people with entrenched interests mobilise themselves as 'community' against those groups. Community as place-making is then framed through the politics of belonging – 'we belong, you don't'. Instead a more promising approach to place-making could be understood through the lens of *becoming*.

We summarise parts of a powerful case study provided by Cornell University scholar Gayatri Menon to illustrate the point:

> Within the city of Mumbai, India, many of the urban poor find themselves living as pavement dwellers. Their home is the street. Within the frame of the state and Mumbai's urban elites these pavement dwellers do not belong – they are invisible; non-citizens left to daily negotiate a home within the city. For Menon, 'not only do the urban poor not have a place to be, but they are denied a place to become; that is, to engage the world proactively, as historical subjects' (2010: 151).
>
> However, within Mumbai an alliance of three organisations – *Mahila Milan*, the National Slum Dwellers' Federation, and the Society for the Promotion of Area Resource Centres – is working to make change. Their work supports pavement dwellers organising through the formation of micro-credit groups, understood as a 'space for the recovery and affirmation of self, a space for bodies exposed to dehumanising violence and degradation on a daily basis' (ibid.: 155). The work of building micro-credit groups has led to many pavement dwellers getting to know their neighbours for the first time and to create a 'homeplace' for those abandoned by the market economy. The processes of contributing to micro-credit groups facilitate a movement of emplacement as neighbourhood is created – people are 'apprehended as one of inclusion rather than of exile' (ibid.: 157).
>
> These micro-credit groups are then linked together into federated structures that enable the previously disenfranchised to organise themselves to be visible. For example, the pavement dwellers have, through their organising efforts, conducted a census of themselves, therefore rendering themselves visible. This census data has then been used to engage with public officials to link services and resources to their needs.

This understanding of place-making as becoming rather than belonging is a basis of creating 'communities of resistance' (hooks 1990: 42) to the status quo – a status quo that excludes and exiles millions if not billions of marginalised people. North American grass-roots activist bel hooks (1990, 1994, 2003) and others (Watkins and Shulman 2008) have articulated how communities of resistance are also created as place-making occurs among people previously exiled (refugees and convicted criminals), rendered invisible (the homeless as per the above story) or excluded (groups of young people).

Building on this idea of communities of resistance, one of the crucial contemporary challenges of community development is contesting the efforts of those who continue the processes of enclosing what many people have called 'the commons' (Polanyi 1944; Shiva 2005; Patel 2009). A dialogical approach to community development is engaged with powerful dynamics: not only struggling against global capital's weapons of profit, not only struggling for significant issues such as affordable housing, but also struggling for soulful places with strong identities and deep connections. Contemporary community development as social practice is therefore politically purposeful in that it is oriented to supporting people to create communities of resistance to inhabit and transform places that are also being shaped destructively by the 'project of globalisation' and its accompanying flows of capital (Harvey 2011). Where there are creative and dialogical social processes of place-making, the soulful parts of selves are awakened. People feel motivated to engage in difficult struggles. They fight for something they love – a place where they have invested something of themselves. There are some delightful examples of this from around the world:

> Knitta is an international 'knit graffiti' movement that started with a small group in Houston, Texas in 2005. They spark re-imagination of urban environments by wrapping the objects of modernity that pervade public space (like parking meters, signs and poles and signs) in colourful, playful and intriguing hand-knitted or crocheted material.
>
> Parking day is another international movement to reclaim space from cars, by transforming car parking spaces into human habitats for the day – installing grass, swings, tables and chairs, sandpits and occupying the space with people, picnics and play for the day instead of abandoning it to cars.

Such an understanding of place-making as a crucial practice within dialogical community development invites practitioners to be attentive to the multiple geographies of a place, to the diverse populations seeking a home, jostling to be subjects of change rather than objects of development.

Place-making as ongoing dialogue with the living earth

We now push the dialogical and hospitable frame of reference further and in a different direction – one less politically, but more soulfully sensitised. Our efforts in bringing the kind of attention advocated above to the fore have been enhanced by working in more traditional societies. That work has revealed how place-making can be enhanced by dialogue with the living earth. For example, Peter has learned that within Vanuatu:

On the island of Pentecost each village is centred by a local *nakamal* – a meeting house as a hub of social activity. The *nakamal* is upon or close to sacred ground called the *nasara*. The *nasara* is a key place for rituals that continue to revitalise the web of relationships between those presently alive, and also between them and the ancestors. Without the ongoing rituals, the web of relationships, the order to community life and the land itself would suffer. Attention is given to this soulful, sacred social process of ongoing place-making in which place is alive, infused with the need to be danced upon, sung to, and toiled within.

These insights from Vanuatu echo those of Rose's co-authored book *Country of the Heart* (Rose et al. 2002), a story of homeland in Australian indigenous communities. She articulates the creative dialogical processes of place-making within indigenous social life, which involve people relating to country and also listening to country as it relates to them. Many indigenous worldviews illuminate this mutual process of place-making – people creating place in country and country 'singing it up' to people. This is a profound process of weaving webs of relationship between people, the cosmos, other creatures, and ancestors. It is a community as hospitality that stretches far beyond many Western conceptions of community.

One lesson from these indigenous worldviews is the genuinely dialogical nature of the process of place-making. While dialogue for Buber entails transformation of social encounters from I–It (subject–object) to I–Thou (subject–subject) kinds of relationships, indigenous worldviews remind us that I–Thou kinds of relationship can also be forged between people *and* places. The ground can also be a subject, rather than just an object that we act upon and try to control. Places can become subjects that are related to dialogically, with which people develop a profound relationship characterised by love, care, attention, deep listening and mutual learning. There are many beautiful examples of this from around the world in *Dialogues with the Living Earth* (1996), in which US environmental psychologist James Swan and his designer wife Roberta Swan argue that each place on earth has its own voice and spirit. Dialogical community development invites this kind of place-making.

If place-making can be dialogical, or more simply, if places can talk to people, it should also be possible to listen to the language of the streets. In the classic book *A Pattern Language* (Alexander et al. 1977), Christopher Alexander and his urban design colleagues provide insights into place-making processes for those of us living within modern urban contexts. They articulate the ways in which strong identity and deep connections can be reinforced by archetypal patterns of place-design. Christopher Day, in *Places of the Soul* (1990), specifically addresses the importance of architecture and environmental design in place-making processes. More recently Alain de Botton's *The Architecture of Happiness* (2007) reflects on people's relationships to things, objects and particularly buildings. His thesis is that buildings speak to people, but they only speak to those who listen – again, a quality of soul and a practice of dialogue not only with people, but also with 'things'. In being attentive to the way buildings, streets, streetscapes, parks, sculptures, shops and cafés speak to them, people can engage in more creative dialogical processes of place-making. These authors are delighted that people who are attentive to their environment, a quality of soulful awakening, can understand the languages of built form and urban design.

Brokering space and structures for creative emergence within places

In this dialogical process of place-making, community development practice often intersects with the work of spatial design and planning professionals – architects, urban designers and land use planners. Within this intersecting space we have come to see the community development practice as brokering, understood as a process whereby a community worker can stand at the interface between professional and non-professional, 'translating' between different logics, languages and actions.

Returning to our introductory comments in the chapter, most spatial design and planning professionals tend to adopt a modernist paradigm, viewing both place and community as objects for professional interventions. But there are alternative views within these professions, the more interesting of which take a more nuanced dialogical (Forester 1999) or enabling (Hamdi and Goethert 1997: 27) approach. This approach to community planning is still designed and managed by professionals, and even the most progressive tend to see process as a matter of cleverer technique (ibid.: 65), but in our experience there are still opportunities for skilled community workers to broker space for their communities' participation in these processes.

In England, Nick Wates (2000; Wates and Knevitt 1987) has articulated professional approaches on the understanding that, 'the built environment works better if the people who use it are directly and actively involved in its creation and management' (Wates and Knevitt 1987: preface). A community planning meme that is full of wisdom might be, 'If you want to know how the shoe fits, ask the person who is wearing it, not the one who made it' (Wates 2000: i). Taking this further, in the USA, 'new urbanism' (Calthorpe 1993; Duany *et al.* 2000) is a movement among professionals, 'committed to re-establishing the relationship between the art of building and the making of community, through citizen-based participatory planning and design' (Congress for the New Urbanism 2001: 1). Clare Cooper Marcus at Berkeley led the way with seminal works *Housing As If People Mattered* (Cooper Marcus and Sarkissian 1988) and *People Places: Design Guidelines for Urban Open Space* (Cooper Marcus and Francis 1998).

John Forester's *The Deliberative Practitioner* reframed planning as, 'people working with others to attempt to remake their common future' (1999: ix). He particularly encouraged the profession to take risks, eliciting diverse citizens' voices and community mobilisation, working creatively as mediators, fostering opportunities for 'transformative learning and participatory action research', while also facilitating 'deliberative consensus-building processes' (ibid.: 5–11). This approach could be understood as nothing short of 'an attempt to reshape planning as a practice of deliberative democracy' (Sandercock 2003:23), one that aligns very well with a dialogical approach to community development.

While agreeing with this attempt to reshape planning as deliberative democracy, we would like to see it go beyond processes of communication and deliberation to also embrace what pioneer in participatory planning Nabeel Hamdi (2010: xvii) identifies as a potent creativity that can emerge when place-making practices are 'held' by community structures. There are some great stories of local community efforts that exemplify the importance of structures and creative emergence in place-making. For example, in Christchurch, New Zealand, a local grass-roots initiative emerged from community efforts following the earthquakes that devastated the city in 2010 and 2011:

> Gap Filler is a creative urban regeneration initiative started in response to the September 4, 2010 Canterbury earthquake, and revised and expanded in light of the more destructive February 22, 2011 quake. The small charitable trust works to temporarily activate vacant sites within Christchurch with creative, people-centred projects for community benefit, to make for a more interesting, dynamic and vibrant city. The grass-roots initiative works with local community groups, artists, architects, landowners, librarians, designers, students, engineers and dancers – 'anyone with an idea and initiative!'
>
> Gap Filler projects pop up as spaces become available around the city. With smaller-scale temporary projects, the community gets to try out new ideas and create a dynamic for experimentation. Gap Filler gives everyday people a way to contribute to the city's regeneration instead of passively waiting for the professionals to do the job. Site-specific projects can help us celebrate, mourn and criticise all that we've lost; can help us play, experiment and toy with ideas for the future'.
>
> (Gap Filler 2012)

This story is an example of a structure that can emerge within places where spaces are created for people to come together, deliberate, reach for new ideas and experiment. It is within such spaces and structures that tensions can be held and emergent creativity can be mobilised. As Voula Mega observes, 'creativity can be contagious, it can create a climate for mobilising more creative potential' (1999: 6).

One key ingredient for unleashing such creative potential is viewing social problems in a nuanced way, which we explore in the next reflection.

Welcoming problems and shadow

The philosopher Michel Foucault's analysis of how populations came to be talked about in different ways through history has prompted us to reconsider how to think about community and social problems. Foucault's thesis is that, with the emergence of modern bureaucracy, populations increasingly came to be acted upon as objects (Faubion 1994: 215). In the same way that populations were acted upon, so place-based problems were also to *be fixed* by these modern bureaucracies. A science developed in which the collection of data and the manipulation of sectors of population became central. The population, with its accompanying problems, is seen as 'out there' to be acted upon as object, rather than being something 'we' are a part of. In *Powers of Freedom* (1999), Nikolas Rose, drawing on the analysis of Foucault, has called this a process of *territorialisation*.

For many professionals, the people are no longer subjects of their own transformation dealing with their local problems, but objects to be acted upon. Following this kind of logic, reductionist techniques of community development engage in territorialising processes such as mapping a community, targeting groups, collecting data, designing initiatives to solve problems and eliciting shallow-participation. Such a technocratic framework of community development gives ample opportunities for contractors and consultants, all given particular tasks from the above list and a brief to 'go, do and deliver'. This type of framework can indeed provide useful data and, occasionally, good processes and projects. However, the fundamental assumptions behind such a paradigm are open to serious question. This reflection asks the questions, and explores some ideas that might provide renewed wisdom.

Community problems as potential gifts

A dialogical approach to community development is a process that concerns itself not so much with 'fixing' particular problems as with attending to the details of social life and discerning where the energy and connections are that can sustain change. From our perspective a focus on particular problems can reflect an inability to imagine community with depth. We suggest that social problems can be imagined as voices calling people back, or summoning people to a renewed dialogue. Community workers are then invited to look with depth beneath the obvious manifestations of problems in particular places, and open a new dialogue starting with questions such as, What are the manifest problems really saying? What do these problems articulate about the condition of our places? How do we understand the particular problem within a holistic frame? What possibilities are summoned by the community problem? Within dialogical community development the 'problems' are symptoms, but also gifts, calling people to look deeper into themselves as individuals and groups. They are an invitation into what James Smith (2005: 13) understands as Jacques Derrida's call to alterity, another, often hidden, dimension of social life that could be considered.

A soulful orientation will see a problem as a potential gift that offers a quality or dimension of life in a way that adds value, relatedness, heart and substance. Practitioners may be tempted to see their role as that of an exterminator attempting to eradicate particular problems, or alternatively may easily collude with other people who themselves want to see a problem exterminated. But they would be passing up a gift, or an opportunity to develop an approach that gives back what is problematic to 'people as community' in a way that uncovers its value and invites people to give it appreciative attention within a broader sense of the whole.

One very clear example of this is the way government authorities around the world are responding to youth gangs. Clearly perceived to be a problem that needs eliminating, many adopt strong police-led interventions or 'crack-downs'.

However, in Barcelona, due mainly to the ground-breaking work of anthropologist Carlos Feixa (1998/2008), there has been a different approach. For Feixa the gang 'is an organisation for solidarity and mutual help' (Burke 2006) – it provides an opportunity to organise a civic movement among what in that city are mainly Latin American immigrants. Here is an existing social structure that the authorities can work with. Similar ways of working with gangs have been developed by David Brotherton (2007) and Lois Barrios (2007) in New York City.

Hospitality towards our problems

Paulo Freire's explicit critique of community development was that it often focused on a particular problem without understanding the whole social context. He made the case that this produced a *focalised* view of problems, which disconnected the community development workers' analysis from the *totality* of the situation (Freire 1972: 111). One of the most significant dysfunctions of technically oriented community development work is its continued focus on particular problems and even particular places. In this focus on fragments, a possible reading of the whole is lost.

Conversely, when people in places and social relationships begin to observe the ways in which problems are manifesting themselves, they can be enriched rather than impoverished. They can receive back what is theirs – the very things that they assumed were so horrible and thought they needed to be rid of. It follows that a dialogical approach to community requires practitioners to develop a new approach towards problems with a view to 'reading' the whole and then trying to discern a narrative thread that provides a way forward (Kaplan 2002, 2005). When regarding social problems holistically, with an open mind, people begin to find the messages that lie within the apparent social sickness, the corrections that are prompted by remorse and other uncomfortable feelings, and the necessary changes demanded by violence and intolerance. Here is a story of thinking holistically:

> For some time, part of Peter's practice has been training youth and community workers in intercultural youth work practice in settings around the world as diverse as Brisbane, Durban and PNG. In many workshops the challenge of working with 'problem youth' kept coming up. Initial discussions usually focused on these young people as the problem – criticising and problematising some of their ways of being and interacting, particularly the way they would hang around in groups, which was perceived by the wider community as anti-social behaviour. Eventually the heat would dissipate and the discussions would start to move in another direction. Questions would start to arise along the lines of 'Why are we thinking of these young people as a problem?' There was then often a gradual recognition that these problems are much more complex – sometimes tied up with young people being excluded from school and work opportunities; or with perceptions of race and ethnicity in relation to refugee, migrant, Muslim or indigenous young people. Sometimes the issues involved other people's perceptions of their legitimate uses of contested public space.

Participants started to recognise that the problem was one of inhospitality – the setting up of many dynamics of antagonism that are damaging personally, interpersonally, culturally and socially and reflect local, national and international dynamics and contexts. At this point, people started to realise the value of an open mind and a dialogical engagement with the issues. With fresh perspectives and the many questions that arose, they started teasing out some of the threads of their complex social situations.

In our experience, when asked the question, 'Is your picture of a healthy, well-developed neighbourhood simply one that has no problems?', most people's answer is an emphatic 'No!' Most people do not want to live shallow lives in a sanitised place. They welcome the rough and tumble of challenging social life, recognising that a community is much more than simply the absence of problems (Andrews 2012).

From a dialogical perspective a community is more likely to come alive where people together are able to remain open and hospitable towards their perceived problems. From a perspective informed by depth and soul, problems are signposts that invite people to reconsider the whole. If a particular group is perceived to be dysfunctional, then from a dialogical perspective this problem group simply highlights critical contradictions in the configuration of social relations in that place or society. Problems viewed this way ensure community workers remain attentive to the whole and that they keep on working towards transformation. Any attempts to remove a 'problem group' without a consideration of the whole usually indicates the choice of a pathway oriented towards sanitation rather than soul, towards further injustice rather than love and justice.

'Start anywhere – go everywhere'

Linking the discussion on how community practitioners view problems to the previous one on place, we have turned to the work of community practitioners Wheatley and Frieze. Within their book *Walk Out Walk On: A Journey into Communities Daring to Live the Future Now* (2011) they tell a delightful story of how focusing on community rather than problems helps shift the perspective for community development:

> Joubert Park in the Central Business District of Johannesburg, South Africa, is a place experiencing the legacies of apartheid. From a problem-oriented perspective the place is experiencing the epidemic of HIV; crimes such as murder, rape, robbery and assault; unemployment (closing in on 30 per cent); poverty; teen violence and so forth (ibid.: 83). Technical approaches to community development would focus on one of these problems – maybe the one perceived easiest to solve, or perhaps the one deemed the 'root cause'. Professionals would provide an analysis and then design an intervention. But as Wheatley and Frieze point out, such interventions 'often have little to do with the people who live in the community: they have to do with the professionals who come to solve the community's

problems. The citizens become the clients, needy people who are acted upon by wiser outsiders' (ibid.: 84).

In contrast an appreciative community development process works with the adage 'start anywhere and follow it everywhere' (ibid.: 91). Within Joubert Park this process was sparked by an invitation by some local residents to a community worker to 'fix up' their part of the park. The worker skilfully accepted the invitation while not buying into its problematising impetus, and instead got them to sit together, share their stories, dreams, resources and ideas and 'create learning relationships together', 'emphatic that the local community would have to discover its own path' (ibid.: 93). Such an understanding takes the uniqueness of each place seriously and ensures that the creativity needed to unlock social change is anchored in the 'native ecology'.
(ibid.)

For Wheatley and Frieze such an approach appreciates and explicitly values the unique independent web of relationships in any place. The focus becomes this web of relationships, rather than a particular problem. Community development, then, involves a creative process of people working within that web of relationships and disturbing it through new initiatives. Problems simply offer an opportunity to activate this already existing web and animate the life that may lie dormant within it. In many ways it does not matter what the starting point is; the process is about engaging the people in exploring its implications for the whole. We wish to explore this kind of holistic practice more carefully by drawing on the work of Carl Jung – particularly his idea of the shadow.

Going deeper – understanding problems as shadow

Our understanding is that, within the field of psychology, shadow simply means that issues not consciously acknowledged and dealt with will be pushed into the shadow or unconscious realm, only to manifest themselves at a later stage – usually in a more destructive way than the original problem. A similar pattern of behaviour can be seen in the social, interpersonal realm. For example, our own ambivalence towards some particular 'others' may eventually be manifest in that other group expressing a learned intolerance back towards us, perhaps even more violently than our own initial dismissiveness would seem to warrant. To the extent that communities refuse to acknowledge a particular social problem and understand its deeper implications for the whole, there is the risk of being left open to a greater destructive social dynamic. Hostile race relations and chronic unemployment are ignored in the suburbs of Paris, London and Sydney, and boom! there are riots. We argue that the task is to acknowledge and understand individual and collective shadows, to welcome all our shadow selves into soulful communities, and to learn to dance with them.

A dialogical approach to community development invites acknowledgement of the shadow (such as destructive race relations) both personally and collectively. Such an approach requires the courage to face ourselves and our society, warts and all – full of racism, sexism, greed, homophobia, guilt and violence.

Soulfulness and depth require openness as a starting point for creative intervention and transformation. Such acknowledgement of personal and collective shadow leads to a humility that crosses barriers of class, education, sexuality, gender, disability and race. People can then start working with shadow symptoms in neighbourhoods by working on the shadow in themselves, rather than looking straight away for the problem 'out there'.

Shifting the starting place can lead to a different ethos, strategy and outcome. For example, imagine that, while working in a community, a practitioner identifies a major problem as young people damaging public property. A typical response would be simply to mobilise resources to remove the young people from the community and clean up the mess. The traders and power-brokers would put pressure on the police and courts to take tougher action against young people now labelled as delinquents or vandals. A conventional community development approach would hopefully be more progressive, in that it would engage in a process of relationship building and participation to develop a programme that channelled the potentially destructive energy into creative energies of art, recreation, education and employment.

However, a dialogical approach would go a step further and work with other stakeholders within the community to develop a sense of solidarity with the young people. It would facilitate a soulful acknowledgement of how individual and collective compulsions and fears have caused young people to lose hope and feel marginalised from their families and in society. Within awareness of 'shadow' lies the possibility of an imaginative, long-term process of generating transformation together – not just among the young people (maybe through projects of art, recreation, education and job creation), but also among everyone else (through spending less time in compulsive work and giving time to children, less time in front of the TV and more time eating a meal together or playing football in the local park).

There are many people within neighbourhoods who pretend there are no problems, doing their best to remove or conceal the symptoms. Rhetoric develops: 'We do not have homeless youth in our neighbourhood' or 'We are not racist.' Of course there are good reasons why such rhetoric develops; people do not wish tourists to be afraid, or do not wish investors to leave the area. However, these good reasons do not legitimise a mythology that is colluding with shadow. Gerard reflects on one of his experiences:

> A school with an investment in the claim that 'we do not have bullying in our school' creates a myth of well-being that at a superficial level may be enjoyed by most students, parents and teachers. But what of the student who experiences what she thinks is bullying? She is not likely to find a sympathetic ear. She may encounter otherwise good people who, in not listening, are acting out of their own investment in the myth – their own desire to preserve or defend what they see as the good in their school community. In their determination to stay deaf and blind, they collude with a small injustice and create a much bigger injustice: a student who feels not only bullied by a fellow student but also by an uncompromising administration. She may feel forced to leave the school, depriving it of the ongoing benefit of her sensitivity.

In the long term the rhetoric and repression may lead to a shadow problem that explodes with much greater destructive impact than could have been previously imagined; or it may simply push the shadow into some other place. The ethics of this 'nimbyism'[2] are highly questionable.

Shadows as possibilities that have not yet been realised

Jung identified two kinds of shadow. The first as already discussed is shadow as repressed, negative, destructive energy. The second kind consists of possibilities that have not yet been realised – gifts locked deep within shadow compartments of our psyches. In our experience, similar gifts can be found in the hidden shadow compartments of social life. These gifts can bring about healing transformation if unlocked and welcomed into communities. Here is an example:

> In Australia for many years the Health Department adopted a policy of institutionalising people with mental health problems. Those classified as sick were simply placed in psychiatric wards of hospitals. This policy was well suited to suburban neighbourhoods. There was a clear definition of who was sick and who was healthy; the 'problem' could be removed and put into institutions; our notions of insanity could be projected on to those who were hidden and we could continue living in our neighbourhoods with an illusion of rationality and well-being. In the process our own sickness became shadow.
>
> Then, due to many pressures (primarily budget), the policy changed. A de-institutionalisation policy was adopted, and people who had been previously locked away were suddenly relocated into hostels in neighbourhoods. There were and still are many ramifications of such a shift in policy. People in the neighbourhoods were scared; people in hostels were still isolated, un-welcomed and medicated.
>
> However, we were fortunate as young community development workers in West End to be part of a process where people in our neighbourhood who defined themselves as 'mentally healthy' started building bridges with those defined as 'mentally sick'. These groups met for dinner on Friday evenings, then for picnics on Tuesdays. A few of us started a self-help mental health group – for all of us – using the methods of GROW, an international self-help movement. What amazed us was how those of us defined as 'well' or 'rational' experienced almost as much inner chaos as did those who were defined as mentally ill. We suddenly all had a safe space to explore what was obvious for some (who had been told for years by psychiatrists), and what had become shadow for the rest of us – our repressed feelings of self-doubt, delusion, paranoia and neurosis.

The policy shift led to a community of people coming face to face with a group who had been removed from consciousness. In the process of encountering one another people were given a safe place to engage with their own shadows. In turn people learned from their officially crazy friends and neighbours to accept and love their own shadow selves. Then, as a community, the neighbourhood became a place that was more appreciative of difference, where all could be more vulnerable in public and freer to express individual and collective eccentricities.

The idea of dancing with the shadow invites practitioners to attend to the shadow with new questions, a fresh perspective, a purposeful interrogation of given rhetoric, alertness to collusion, and a deconstructive orientation that destabilises community analysis as it exists. A dialogical approach to welcoming problems and dancing with the shadow holds the promise that what some people see as bad and unhealthy – problematic youth, racism, intolerance, people with mental health problems – can be welcomed into community as hospitality.

Summing up

The first reflection of this chapter was a call to re-awaken *love* in community work practice. Love as ethics and *eros* was considered as crucial to awakening transformative spaces. Community is then nurtured in the transformational shift towards a soulful other-orientation, a journey from *I* to *we* through dialogue and hospitality. We want to work with colleagues who are alive – the kinds of fools who continually 'fall in love' with life, and who are alert to the potential transformation of the ordinary to the extraordinary that is the daily concern of soulful community work.

The second reflection explored what we call *deepening participation*. To be co-creators of dialogical community, soulful people are needed – people who have been awakened by love. Yet the paradoxical converse of this is that such soulful people are 'made' through participating in the everyday and ordinary things of life, albeit with a particular attentiveness, awareness, animation and imagination. Deep participation invites people into an intimate engagement of their stories and creativity, hospitality towards one another's ideas and perspectives, and the giving of attention and care to building a shared analysis of ways forward.

The third reflection alerted practitioners to the dangers of seeing community primarily as an objectified site or 'place'. Soul seeps away when places become simply functional sites for consumption, property speculation and professionally designed and driven interventions. A re-imagined approach can see community as a process of ongoing place-making that requires people's daily creative endeavours. An approach to dialogical community development awakens people's conscious and purposeful processes of *emplacing*.

The fourth reflection was a call to welcome social problems as gifts that can invoke depth in our community practice and to dance with the shadow that can illuminate social issues with a fresh perspective. Modernist community development techniques try to fix social problems and suppress social shadows. The approach to community development presented in this book concerns itself not so much with 'fixing' a particular flaw, as it does with attending to the details of social life. Community problems and symptoms of shadow are voices calling forward into a dialogue and back to depth – and a deep response begins with developing a new hospitality towards social problems.

We hope that this brief excursion into re-imagining community practice has challenged previously unthought-about 'givens', has destabilised habits of perspective, and has invited the reader into a reconsideration of community development practice. This chapter has laid the foundation for rethinking transformative community processes in the next chapter. We invite you to continue with us in the dialogue.

3 Transformative community processes

Community development is intentionally and hopefully a process of transformation. This chapter considers transformational work through more orthodox community development concepts such as method, analysis, conflict and structures. We explore a dialogical approach that involves a discerning approach to methodology; group and community-owned analysis; careful conflicting; and structuring the work through place-based, community-oriented, democratic people's organisations. These four reflections provide a mud map for how a dialogical approach to community development can transform the social world. They explore the role of a skilled and soulful citizen or worker in supporting 'community' to become a vehicle for social change in which people find their own paths towards development.

The discerning and gentling of method

In the late 1980s we both started getting involved as unpaid community workers in West End, Australia. This meant getting to know our neighbours and getting involved in a variety of community activities and projects with refugee groups, indigenous people, and people with mental illness. It was clear that many interesting and good things were happening. In the midst of all this Peter asked one of his mentors, Dave Andrews (1992, 2007, 2012), 'How do you make sense of all this activity?' In a nutshell his answer was, 'I know it all looks a bit mad, but there is a method within the madness.' This conversation created clarity that disciplined method was crucial within the work, and we have been learning and relearning the skilful means ever since.

A methodical and rhythmic approach: bonding, banding, building and bridging

One of the most useful ways of thinking about the method of community development has been developed by our Queensland colleagues in dialogue with Anthony Kelly (2008). For him, 'method' signifies a way of ordering and structuring the community development process in ways understood as *micro, mezzo, macro* and *meta* (Ingamells *et al.* 2010; Westoby and Owen 2010; Westoby and Morris 2011).

Within our own interpretation of this method the focus of the micro process is *bonding* – nurturing purposeful interpersonal relationships through the kind of dialogue discussed in the preceding chapters. It requires the loving practice of hearing people's stories, articulating with them an understanding of the key issues that they are struggling with, and exploring with them the possibility of sharing their stories with others and trying to do something public about them. This part of the process requires practitioners to be conscious of their own agenda – this may be 'doing a worthwhile project', 'fulfilling a funding obligation', or 'delivering some outcome' – but to hold it lightly, or put it on hold, so the concerns and therefore the potential agenda of the people can be clearly understood.

The bonding process requires a movement towards others and hospitality towards their concerns. Within therapeutic or counselling approaches, this concern would be directed towards finding a therapeutic solution; for example, someone might be concerned about the ever-present noise pollution in their neighbourhood, and a therapeutic solution would be to find new ways of 'coping with the noise' without getting overly angry. A community development approach instead moves the conversation towards an agreement to do something about this concern publicly. It asks questions such as, 'Would you like to do something about it, with others of course?' and 'Are other people suffering the same problem or feeling the same concern?' If there is agreement to explore the issue and possible actions with others, then the micro process can become a platform for a mezzo process.

The mezzo process involves *banding*: working with the people whose stories have been heard and who want to do something, linking them together, and moving what might have previously been felt as a private concern into collective public action. Places are made by complex webs of relationship and some people may already be linked together in different ways – but banding is about coming together around a common purpose for action.

The addition of mezzo to micro processes requires a movement from purposeful relationships, to purposeful and participatory action groups. This mezzo process involves people sitting down together in relationships of mutual trust, agreeing to do something public together as a group, conducting analysis of what are the issues, the issues behind the issues, the players and stakeholders, the possibilities, and the tactics and strategies that might best reach their objectives. This can seem chaotic and disjointed, but the method in the madness is to be purposeful about facilitating a process of weaving relationships and moving towards clarity about a way forward for reflective action.

Returning to the previous example, in a noisy neighbourhood, this process would bring together local residents who share the same concern, forming some purposeful bonds and agreeing that, 'We want to do something about noise in our street or neighbourhood.' The agreement is built upon a mutual trust in one another's ability and desire to journey together. It then requires the group to sit down and consider questions such as, 'What might we envisage a neighbourhood with less noise to look like or feel like?' and 'Who is making the noise?', or 'Who might be our allies in reducing noise?' and 'Who will try and hinder us bringing change?' Strategies will be chosen – for example, campaigning to stop trucks driving down small streets (a campaigning strategy), or agreeing as a group of neighbours not to use electrical tools on Sunday afternoons (a mutual co-operation strategy).

The macro process within the method requires *building* – working with these people who are involved in purposeful and participatory public action, to form and stabilise groups and organisations that can carry the work on in a sustainable way. Sometimes this is referred to as 'structuring the work', which we consider in more depth later in this chapter. Sugata Dasgupta (1968) and Saul Alinsky (1969; von Hoffman, 2010: xiii) argue that it is the democratic nature of these grass-roots people's organisations that is crucial for this kind of work. They must be built and owned by the people and for the people. They are community-based organisations (CBOs) with their 'base', their impetus, their whole rationale grounded in the community.

Returning to the noise pollution example, this process might see the group of active residents form a non-incorporated organisation 'Locals Against Noise Pollution' and build a link with the local neighbourhood centre to work under their auspices for insurance and financial reasons. For the practitioner supporting this work of the people, a particular kind of leadership is required. The preferred approach is to pay gentle attention to both process and structure in a group. Many groups, because they do not pay close enough attention to process, find themselves under threat of fracture as the emergent group leadership just wants to 'get on with it'.

The final process within this understanding of method is described as the meta, which involves *bridging*: linking stable CBOs into alliances, coalitions, co-operative arrangements, networks or federations that enable people to tackle trans-local or even global issues. Wheatley and Frieze (2011) describe this kind of work as 'scaling-across', although people often refer to it as 'scaling-up'. Within the example, the now-formed local group might want to create alliances with groups doing similar work in other localities – in the recognition that it is no good stopping trucks driving through one neighbourhood if it simply means they drive through the adjacent one. A local problem might require a regional solution. In Brisbane in the 1980s, a local residents' group concerned about traffic in their street ended up developing an analysis of traffic planning and roads infrastructure, and became a regional alliance across several suburbs called *Citizens Against Route Twenty*.

A gentle and discerning approach to method

One of the crucial skills in dialogical community development is to be aware of where an individual person or group is situated within the framework discussed above, and to facilitate their engagement with the community development process appropriately. To move too quickly usually leads to an unravelling of the process – either relationships are not strong enough, analysis has not been considered well enough, or groups are not stable. To move too slowly could mean that momentum is lost, or actions and activities become too localised and unable to connect with broader movements tackling national or international forces.

Groups and practitioners need to discern carefully where they are in the process, asking reflective questions such as:

- How strong are relationships between people, groups and organisations?
- How coherent is the community analysis? Does it take into account both obvious and subtle forces and dynamics?
- How stable is the structuring of public action? Is it vulnerable to undercurrents of personality, power or politics?
- Is there movement towards strong organisational forms? Is there sufficient leadership to move this along?

Again drawing on the wisdom of our colleague Anthony Kelly, we refer to this skill as *gentling* (Kelly, forthcoming) – a skill requiring discernment. In the gentling process, a practitioner needs to know when to push people to try something new, to trust the power of the group, to 'walk their talk'. Yet gentling also requires knowing when to back off, letting go of untimely opportunities, giving people a break, hinting at potentials, or holding an idea or initiative lightly. It involves discernment to know that maybe the group is not yet strong enough to tackle a big issue and needs to build strength by tackling a smaller one. Paulo Freire and Myles Horton describe the process as understanding 'the delicate relationship' (Bell *et al.* 1990); and we have previously described it as being in a 'responsive dance'. Sennett (2012: 225) talks about this practice as 'the light touch' required of social solidarity (the community organiser) as opposed to political solidarity work (the labour organiser). He also usefully describes it as practice that 'prefers the nudge to the command' (ibid.: 211).

Our Brisbane colleague Morrie O'Connor introduced a useful idea that we call a 'bonding and banding task'. This is a task that a practitioner might facilitate, not for the outcome of the task itself, but for the value of the process to the group. For example, a newly forming group that has come together to do something about opposing a building development proposal might decide to hold a Christmas party or to have a stall at a school fête. It may not really matter what the task is. The important thing is that the initiative matches the whole group's stage of development and that the group learns more about working together from the experience. Smaller examples might be asking two quieter members of a group to go to the shop together to get some milk for morning tea, giving them a different kind of one-on-one opportunity for a chat; or washing up with someone who you know has something on their mind, to open up a space for them to raise it if they want to.

A dialogical approach to method

The dialogical approach also pushes community workers to be aware of and hospitable to those others not usually invited into the community development process. This approach holds to a tradition of social solidarity with the marginalised, and therefore would start the micro method through entering into dialogue with the invisible or disenfranchised on the edge of a 'community'. However, it does not mean that practitioners cannot also enter into hospitable dialogue with those considered to be at the economic, political or cultural centre of power. The following case study tells a story of community work that takes both the margins and centre seriously:

> Gram Vikas, an NGO based in the Indian state of Orissa, works with whole villages to install cheap but effective water and sanitation systems. Their motivation is research indicating that having piped water to households can have a profound impact on health outcomes and therefore other well-being indicators. Abhijit Banerjee and Ester Duflo (2011: 46) provide an account of how the director of this NGO, Joe Madiath, became committed to this work. It is quite a tale. His crucial realisation was that water and sanitation was 'simultaneously a daily challenge and an opportunity to initiate long-term social change. He explained ... that in Orissa, water and sanitation are social issues' (ibid.).
>
> When the NGO approaches a village to partner with, they insist that they will only commence a two-year process of installing pipes and systems when *everyone* in the village agrees to be connected to the same water mains. Banerjee and Duflo share how '[f]or the high-caste households, this means sharing water with low-caste households, which, for many in Orissa, was unacceptable when first proposed' (ibid: 47). Clearly it takes some time for everyone to agree, but the process of purposeful persuasive dialogue often leads to agreement and action (but not always). If an agreement is struck it is often the first time people of high caste and low caste participate in the same project.

The degree of separation between the centre and the margins is often less than we suppose. The story above illustrates this. It would be easy simply to work among the poor and ignore the wealthy, seeing cultural practices as too stuck for change. However, what we describe as deconstructive movements can also challenge an oversimplified dichotomy of centre–periphery, and purposeful dialogue where everyone can open up new possibilities. While maintaining a social commitment to those on the edge, we advocate respectful engagement with those deemed to be at the centre, as shown within the preceding story. A subtle *geometry of practice* (Westoby and Owen 2010) can build purposeful relationships with those on all points of the spectrum between the periphery and the centre, the bottom and top, the inside and outside.

Furthermore, people at the so-called centre often have at least one relationship with those on the so-called margins – it may be a disabled relative, a son or daughter whose behaviour they find challenging, or a cousin they have visited in jail. Sometimes an encounter can happen in unexpected ways, and if it is not crowded by unforgiving expectations or strident demands (that is, if it provides a hospitable space for the humanity of people in power) it can have unexpected results. Here is another story that exemplifies this:

> It was the height of the World Expo 88 housing crisis in West End. Local residents and community groups had been campaigning for months, raising

public awareness of the issues for local people being evicted from their homes or facing big rent hikes. Gerard and some colleagues had convened the Expo Social Impact Summit, held press conferences, and had stories in national magazines, TV news and local papers – but with no response from the Queensland government. Then the story was picked up by a journalist from the *Catholic Leader*, who was interested in the social justice angle and happened to know the state housing minister through family and church connections. One morning we received a phone call, saying the journalist had convinced the minister to have a look for himself, and they were about to leave – where should she take him?

Gerard gave her a few addresses, and could do nothing else but wait and trust the process. We heard later that he visited a couple of boarding houses, and was moved by what he saw and the people he met telling their own stories, probably much more graphically than the community advocates who had been speaking on their behalf. He was so appalled by the conditions at one place that he wanted it closed down immediately, until the journalist gently asked him where he thought the people would go. Within weeks the state housing department had agreed to fund the state's first housing worker, to be based at the local neighbourhood centre.

The starting place could be dialogue with everyone. Dialogue unlocks the possibility of story, and story unlocks the possibility of genuine exchange of ideas and perspectives, leading to potential change of all parties to the dialogue.

Invitation within method

The dialogical approach to method, informed by ideas and practices of hospitality, also requires some thinking about invitation. Hospitality implies that a community practitioner invites others into the process of community development, and this is how we have described it so far. However, in many ways it is the other way around, with community practitioners being invited into a process by residents or some kind of community organisation. A story from Peter's experience in PNG illustrates the idea of awaiting an invitation:

After three months of work in a remote area our group of ten young Australian volunteers were accompanied by some local guides back to Port Moresby – a four-day walk through difficult terrain staying overnight in villages. An interesting moment occurred each evening as the group of walkers approached a village hoping to find a place to sleep. The group would walk to the edge of the village and then sit and wait. The local guides and porters knew this important protocol. They informed the Australians that it was important to simply sit, let our presence be felt and to wait for an invitation from the village leaders to enter the village. Eventually this would occur, with either elders or their spokespersons approaching the group. The 'leader' of our group would be invited into the village to talk with the leaders and terms would be negotiated for staying the night.

The story illustrates the social practice our colleague Athena Lathouras calls 'lurking with intent'. It is built on indigenous protocol around simply awaiting an invitation through 'sitting on the edge'. While wanting to enter the village there was a decision to place oneself in a space where the possibility of an encounter could take place. There was also a respectful recognition of the inequalities embedded within such social encounters (Sennett 2003) between well-off Australians and local villagers. The intimacy of deep participation, discussed within previous reflections, was preceded by the respectful distance required because of inequality. It is a distance that enables people to see one another, even talk, but also acknowledges the often painful experiences of trying to develop mutual relations across the many economic, social and cultural inequalities of community life. This dialectic tension, emerging between a respectful distance and a close 'lurking' or presenting oneself, leads to the possibility of an invitation: 'Come stay with us'.

In contrast, the following story illustrates that sometimes it is important not to so much lurk, but to intentionally present oneself in what Kelly describes as 'first movement' (Kelly 2008; Westoby and Owen 2010) and then to respond to the response as a way of establishing mutuality as a platform for future collaboration:

> A colleague of ours, Anne Brown, was working for the Australian Centre for Peace and Conflict Studies (ACPACS) and while in Vanuatu decided that as part of the visit she would pay respects to the National Council of Chiefs, as representatives of the customary leadership of the nation. When she visited and paid those respects – presenting herself and her organisation with no 'development' agenda, the chiefs asked about ACPACS. In hearing her response they decided that they would like to learn more from ACPACS. After several conversations they invited her, as an ACPACS representative, to enter into a development partnership with them. From this invitation a long-term relationship developed that was then transformed into a co-operative development partnership that has forged on for many years.
> (Westoby and Brown 2009; Walker 2012)

Within both of these stories there is the careful attention paid to being invited into community development processes. There is no intervention per se, but the creation of an opportunity, an encounter, which can foster what has been previously discussed as co-motion. Clearly dialogical practice within this initial process is not only a process of talking but also a respectful process informed by understanding of cultural protocols and genres and a nuanced discerning of how to negotiate across complex relations infused with issues of power and potential domination.

Mandate within the method

Community practitioners often discuss the importance of building trust within relational work, and the above stories show how invitation is a critical foundation of trust. 'Trusting relationships' can become the mantra that defines the work. From our experience one of the other crucial practices in building and maintaining this trust is 'gaining a mandate'. This refers to the process of a practitioner constantly checking back with people about what 'we' have agreed to do – in terms of analysis, goals, objectives and strategies – and getting active consent to move forward together.

For example, a practitioner might have been talking with someone in a wheelchair about their problems accessing transport options in the neighbourhood. This is the micro process of the method discussed earlier. The practitioner hears their story and could respond, 'Do you know anyone else living around here who is also concerned about this? We could have a coffee together and talk about it.' Or they could say something like, 'I know someone else who has a similar story to you. Would you mind if I shared your story with that person? Maybe we could then get together; what do you think?' In both cases there is a potential movement from the micro to the mezzo process within the method. From the perspective of seeking and maintaining a mandate it is important that permission is sought from that person, or more accurately the decision-making process is moved from oneself – an *I* – to include the person the practitioner has been talking with – a *We*. The mandate to move forward is legitimised within the dialogical relationship. Trust building is strengthened if this process takes place as often as possible. Here is another example:

> Peter was in Vanuatu working with a group of 30 chiefs. The task at hand was to consider the problem of conflict within a particular locality. People were drawing a mud map of the local issues, building an analysis of the causes of conflict. After some 30 minutes of the group discussing conflict, Peter sensed that people were missing some key elements of the analysis. They had got stuck on the issue of a land conflict, obscuring other sources of conflict to do with overpopulation, lack of family planning services and so forth. So Peter chose a moment to interject and sought permission to introduce some new ideas. He didn't just bring new ideas; he first sought a mandate from the group to 'shake the analysis up'.

In the process of negotiating that mandate the group was able to engage dialogically with the new ideas. New strategies were considered, and trust was reinforced between the facilitator and participants. The mezzo method was strengthened through the clarity of the analysis developed by the participatory group. It is this topic of analysis that we now discuss in more depth.

Widening analysis

Many of the previous reflections have engaged implicitly with the issue of analysis. The story at the end of the previous reflection is about analysis: a group of chiefs building an understanding of their situation and a facilitator gaining a mandate to support a group in widening their thinking. Analysis is central to any process of community development, ensuring that people have a way forward, a sense of what to do and an understanding of why they are doing it. It ensures people become aware of the forces that are acting upon and within their places, and requires people to become conscious of the ways that such forces are shaping the way they are living. This is Freire's 'naming of the word and the world' – literacy as a process of being able not just to read and write words, but also to understand the forces impacting and shaping us in the world. Analysis makes conscious or visible these forces – local, regional, national and increasingly global. For example:

> Within Vanuatu some of the key complexities of development are to do with land. Currently there is an intense social struggle related to diverse visions of how land should be owned. Traditionally land has been used to support activities such as subsistence living (gardens, livestock) and ceremony. However, in recent years there are significant pressures at play to change the way local people relate to their land. Customary practices are feeling many pressures.
>
> Within an initiative Peter has been working on with many others, chiefs are trying to make sense of the forces at work around them in relation to land. Locally, population pressures have made it difficult for kin groups to keep allocating enough land to new young families to ensure a sustainable subsistence living. Families are therefore under increased competitive pressure when trying to access good land for food growing. Young people also have new aspirations as a result of global media that expose them to other lifestyle and livelihood options. Sometimes young people do not want to stay on the land. To make it even more complex, land can be claimed by different groups. Some groups that left land decades ago, maybe as a result of colonisation processes, may return and claim a connection to the land.
>
> At the same time there is a push by the national government to develop an income and tax base to pay public servant salaries and provide services, so they promote tourism and other forms of income-generating investment. Such pressure plays itself out in changes to land legislation, allowing families to lease land to foreigners. Internationally, foreign capital aligns with or influences local elites in demanding new forms of land tenure, so they can build large resorts or sell off subdivided plots to aspiring middle-class foreigners.

Drawing from this story of practice it is clear that analysis is complex – it demands that practitioners and local people become aware of all these intertwining forces exerting pressure on their lives.

Within transformative community work the process of analysis goes further than building such understanding. Analysis does not just privilege thinking. It also refers to action: to consideration of tactics and strategies for moving forward. Combined with thoughtful analysis of the situation, there is also a need to develop an analysis of what to do. Referring to the Vanuatu case, tactical and strategic questions could be asked, such as: Do we engage in active non-violent struggle against real estate agents, local elites within the Land Department, and international agents such as the Asian Development Bank and Australian

Government? or, Should we just be pragmatic and learn to get the best deal for our land through leasing and sub-leasing? or, Do we then try to use the money we earn to educate our children and young people in Western forms of living, giving them the chance to find a cash-earning job? It can be difficult to make these distinctions and decisions between alternative analyses.

Practitioners engaged in community processes usually bring well-developed personal and professional skills of what we call *practitioner analysis* – the use of traditional analytical skills (sorting, sifting, questioning and collating) to the understanding of a problem with the goal of devising a solution. Peter's reflection on the complexities of land in Vanuatu is an example of good practitioner analysis. He sat down with a blank sheet of paper and considered the economic, cultural, political and social forces that are at play within Vanuatu, collecting information and sifting and sorting into an analysis of some of the key issues and potential strategies. Practitioner analysis aims to be accurate and astute, and workers need to use all their analytical skills and their acumen in social and political science to understand a situation. However, from the perspective of dialogical community development, while a worker might be conducting this practitioner analysis within himself or herself, they will usually put the analysis 'on hold' or at least 'hold it lightly', to create space for a group to develop their own group analysis.

Building a group analysis

A group analysis is enfolded within a participatory process, actively conducted by people who are affected by particular concerns. It is a group analysis because it will not usually include everyone within a neighbourhood, village, or other kind of place. Usually it will start with a group of people on the 'edge' of a space – women, young people, or some other marginalised group.

Within the process of group analysis the practitioner puts on hold their practitioner analysis, and instead accompanies people in collecting data, sitting with a paper and marker pens, and trying to 'connect the dots'. In this process the people involved build their own understanding of the relationships between issues, problems and actors, in such a way that they discover a way forward. As discussed earlier, a practitioner may intercede and gain a mandate from the people to add to the analysis, or suggest that the group invite an 'expert' to share information that might be critical to building the analysis. The point is that the group analysis aims to be accurate, astute and informed, and to involve the group of people *themselves* in designing actions that are effective and have a high level of ownership and commitment. One relevant practice story that has stuck with Peter for many years is an account by Mackie (2000) of group analysis emergent from women in Senegal:

> Within the story the problem of female genital cutting was seen by many practitioners to be 'cultural' and therefore very hard to change. However, when a local NGO engaged with a community, women were brought together to consider their analysis of the problem and possible solutions. After deliberation they came up with the idea of a 'collective pledge'. It became clear

that people were not so much attached to a cultural practice (the practitioner analysis), but were afraid that their daughters would become unmarriageable if their family was the only one opting out. Faced with the reasonable guarantee that others would also honour a 'collective pledge' it became easier for everyone to act and a snowball effect moved along one village to another. In 1999 the government changed legislation to follow the grassroots movement.

The story illustrates the significance of building a group analysis because not only is this congruent as a community-owned process, but it also disrupts what in this case was an inaccurate practitioner analysis.

Over the years we have also learned that within group analysis it is important to separate the technical tasks. On the one hand, the 'dot-connecting' part of analysis requires that somewhere – maybe on a whiteboard, a piece of butcher's paper, or in the sand – the practitioner gathers the 'data' emerging from people's stories and their perspectives. However, there is a different process that needs to move on from generating data and connecting the dots. This second process involves developing a joint agreement about what to do as a result of examining the data. It is one thing for a participatory group to make sense of what is going on; it is quite another to agree on what to do (tactics, strategies, actions, activities) and how to do it (who, where, when). We refer to the two processes as *data generation* and *agreement generation*. They are both part of the process of analysis, but it is helpful to think of them as distinct processes that are enfolded within one another. Once the group has embarked on both processes then it is moving ahead – it has taken the next step in social change work.

While happy to articulate the simple ideas of generating both the data and agreement processess, we are also aware of many other social methodologies that are very useful for enabling group and community analysis. For example, from his work and research within South Africa, Peter has become close friends with Verne Harris from the Nelson Mandela Foundation (NMF), which hosts dialogue initiatives through their Centre for Memory:

> One of the most intriguing processes is the United Nations Development Programme (UNDP) Community Capacity Enhancement (CCE) methodology. The methodology is based on a six-step implementation cycle, each with a specific objective and small group exercises. The steps initiate and support a process of data generation, group analysis and agreements for social change strategies.
>
> For the past few years, the NMF has applied the CCE methodology to identify communities' concerns both with regard to HIV/AIDS and also to address violence and xenophobia. The main means for achieving this is through community conversations – open community discussions guided by facilitators trained in the CCE methodology. Community conversations provide safe spaces where people can get to know each other, build relationships, express themselves without fear and get to the heart of their concerns. Here, they identify and explore their issues, values and resources. They

72 Transformative community processes

begin to make decisions and take action to find solutions to the challenges they face. They constantly review and reflect on the process they are going through. The process is also shared beyond the community through documentation, arts and the media.

(Nelson Mandela Foundation 2010a, 2010b)

For us the CCE methodology is an exemplary example of a process that enables group analysis. There are of course many others, such as Conversation Cafés, the Art of Hosting and Open Space Technology processes, to name just a few. Each has a series of steps or procedures that are designed to achieve what we have called data and agreement generation.

Another cutting edge method of analysis exemplifying the kind of dialogical practice we are interested in is the 'collective narrative practices' methodology being developed by Australia's Dulwich Centre in partnership with organisations around the world. This approach to building group analysis, like any good micro method, is grounded in people's stories. Yet it uses a set of principles to unearth people's stories in particular ways that enable communities of resistance or sustenance to be created (Denborough 2008). These principles are grounded in practices that enable a practitioner to elicit the 'double stories' of people's hardships and responses – one story of their suffering itself, and another of how they have sustained themselves despite such sufferings. Embedded within the sustaining processes are people's skills and knowledge, which are the starting points for 'development'. Collective narrative practices unearth these stories, skills and knowledge – people's data so to speak – and through methodologies such as Collective Documents, the Tree of Life, the Kite of Life and the Game of Life (ibid.) enable people to build an analysis of ways forward.

Co-creating tools for group analysis

Another important element of group analysis processes, learned from the Dulwich Centre's collective narrative practice experience, is the importance of taking care in co-creating analysis tools that are embedded within local culture. Reiterating ideas discussed in our reflection on deepening participation, David Denborough tells the story of being invited to work with Tamil refugees living in Vancouver and co-creating a methodology:

> The Tamil refugee community in Vancouver were experiencing the stress of inter-generational conflict and some leaders had invited the Dulwich Centre to come and work with them around this community concern. This invitation led to many conversations about what kind of methodology would resonate with people in ways that would lead to easier eliciting of stories and analysis. The Dulwich Centre shared their experience of using the Tree of Life methodology, but local Tamil leaders felt that a tree was not something that really resonated with them.
>
> After some time a kite was suggested. People's eyes lit up – always a good sign of cultural resonance. Tamil people love kites and enough people in the

community could explain in detail how to make kites and the skills needed to fly them. This folk tradition was then used as a metaphor and methodology in which people were invited to draw pictures of a kite and then create and share their stories based on those pictures. People then developed an analysis of what was happening to them within Canada through identifying both 'strong winds' that shape their lives and also ways of 'flying through strong winds'.

(Denborough 2010: 3)

This story illustrates how it is helpful for practitioners not simply to import social methodologies from elsewhere to conduct group analysis, but rather to seek the kind of resonance discussed previously.

Building the other into a dialogical community analysis

In further reflecting on transformative community practice, another question arises: How does an appreciation of 'other' enrich an understanding of these processes of doing group analysis? The question can be usefully explored through an identification of movements that widen our analysis beyond the normative gaze of practitioners and usual suspects. The task of building a dialogical group analysis is to include the 'other' in two distinct ways.

The first widening movement simply is to ensure that 'other' people, who are not usually considered important, are invited into the process of moving from a group to a wider-community analysis. People's conception of community usually includes people more 'like us' – people easier to relate to or easier to access. The 'other' dimension of the movement ensures that the invisible people are considered. They could be:

- the poorest;
- the rural – those on marginal land within rural settings;
- the homeless – therefore unable to respond to a letterbox or door-knock survey;
- out-of-school young people – not at school and therefore requiring practitioners to get on to the streets to find them;
- victims of domestic violence – who often are not able to go to meetings because their partners exercise control over their lives;
- future generations – who have no voice; and
- those 'furthest from the road' – referring to Robert Chambers' admonishment to avoid 'development tourism' (Chambers 1997).

A dialogical group analysis ensures hospitality towards that 'other-community' often considered not so easy to include. The accuracy, authenticity and integrity of the analysis will be profoundly influenced by the degree to which these people can participate.

The second widening movement involves thinking about those usually seen as 'other' in terms of 'enemy' or adversary – people or organisations that are often purposefully excluded. Most community development work is at some point engaged with conflictual kinds of relationships over people's divergent agendas. This is not to deny that solidarity with the marginalised is the primary factor. However, in thinking about the other as enemy or opponents, community workers can diminish the possibility of finding common ground. A dialogical approach, while at times advocating resistance actions against others, does not start with resistance. A dialogical approach at least initially attempts to engage in dialogue with the 'other' who might be construed as enemy – possibly politicians, bureaucrats, corporate leaders, chambers of commerce, or multinationals. Within this commitment to dialogue, it is important to acknowledge the complex deliberative democratic processes that are often required to bring lasting social change. For example:

> During 1988, people in West End were upset with the pre-Expo 88 development. Many were made homeless both by the loss of dwellings, knocked down for development, and by the spiralling pressures of rising rents. In this context, some colleagues organised a large gathering of local residents who came together to watch the movie *The Milagro Beanfield War*, a fictional story about a local struggle against global corporate power.
>
> At the end of the movie people started discussing and debating what they could do in their neighbourhood as a response to the making of homelessness. A coherent analysis was starting to develop. However, it became clear that this analysis was underpinned by a framework where landlords, as 'other', were being perceived as enemies – as 'bad' people. Our friend Dave Andrews eventually stood up and challenged this, advocating that we conduct an action that publicly rewarded landlords who were not putting up the rent and therefore not evicting local people, while also confronting those who were evicting local people for the primary purpose of profit.
>
> Within this emerging dialogical analysis the other – as landlord – was not considered enemy, and strategies or tactics were chosen that reflected this analysis. The chosen strategies included two parallel processes. One process involved a group going on a hunger strike until 50 local landlords could be found who would declare that they were either maintaining the rent as it was or decreasing it in the light of people's economic hardships. These landlords were then presented with bouquets of flowers in a public ceremony. The second process involved groups of people organising to sleep on the street outside the houses of landlords who were evicting local people to cash in on Expo – primarily a symbolic action to confront these landlords with the reality of their actions in creating local homelessness. Such landlords were not sneered at or abused – they were silently and symbolically challenged to confront their own greed.

The story illustrates the importance of rethinking habitual ways of framing the other as enemy, and invites reflection on assumptions about them.

We find it useful to think of these movements as a shift in self-perception of the group, from recognising that it represents a limited perspective *within*

Transformative community processes 75

the community to an acknowledgement that it represents a limited perspective that is *alongside, among* and *in dialogue with* other perspectives in the wider community.

Valuing unresolved tension and contested understanding

Let us go a little deeper into analysing the second widening movement. Taken to its logical extreme, dialogical analysis challenges community workers to include the very people who are identified as the 'problem' within a group analysis, and to build a new analysis *with them* that informs a shared, if not a collaborative, agenda of action. This is the tough bit – what happens when you sit down with opposition or the enemy and attempt to build a shared wider community analysis? It brings to mind a cartoon in which environmentalists advocating 'sustainable development' negotiate with multinationals advocating 'rapacious exploitation' – and end up with 'sustainable exploitation'. It is important to guard against the dangers of being co-opted. Of course any polarising framing (for example, as friend versus enemy or sustainable versus exploitative) is antithetical to dialogue, which is best informed by a diversity of perspectives. Again, here is an Australian-based story:

> For many years Peter and Gerard were part of a collegial community of interest, the South East Queensland Intercultural Cities Forum (SEQICF), which aimed to encourage deep intercultural dialogue and engagement across the region. In 2007 SEQICF designed and facilitated a dialogical process, Out of the Shadows, which aimed to: identify new and emerging intercultural issues in southeast Queensland; document differing perspectives on these emerging issues; and be a catalyst for coordinated responses to prevent inter- and intracultural conflict.
>
> The Out of the Shadows process created a safe space for dialogue, where people from different religious and cultural backgrounds, with a variety of ways of understanding intercultural conflict and different roles and responsibilities, could meet and hear one another's experiences and perspectives. Participants included families, young victims and young perpetrators of violence, cultural elders, community representatives, frontline workers, academics, policy analysts, and government workers in multicultural affairs, the police, social policy, community development and community safety.
>
> There was a process of community engagement in the months before the event, and an invitation to participants explicitly stating 'principles of dialogue' that they accepted as a condition of participating. The main activities through the two-day event were 'fishbowl sessions', a series of facilitated dialogues between eight to ten key informants in the centre of the room, with another 60 or so people watching and listening from rows of seats on either side. These sessions were interspersed with lighter times of musical and dance performances, short films, good food, and plenty of time for informal chat in breaks.

In terms of outcomes, the analysis provided a rich depth of material that informed new directions in policy and practice. Some of these more promising directions emerged precisely from the points of unresolved tension and contested understanding that were highlighted in the dialogue.

In Out of the Shadows and other formalised dialogue processes, it is often necessary to set ground rules or principles of dialogue to frame the nature of the discussion. These may include practices such as speaking and listening from the heart, honouring silence, suspending judgement, listening with perception, looking within one's self, identifying assumptions, and maintaining an attitude of learning and a spirit of enquiry. Facilitators negotiate an agreement with participants to work from these principles. This gives the group a point of reference to guide the process when people depart from the agreement – a frequent occurrence, because people are not used to this way of relating to one another in contested territory.

Furthermore, when engaged in a process such as described within the Out of the Shadows event, dialogical community analysis requires an appreciation of what we call the dynamic of *affirmation* and *scepticism*. Affirmation consists of validating the perspectives expressed. The assumption is that a view expressed is not only valid from the participant's point of view, but that it also expresses something significant about the whole of the matter. Colin Peile's (1994) holographic paradigm, drawing on Bohm's work, suggests that the sharpest focus in an analysis will come from assembling, legitimating and attending to as many views as possible at the same time. In this context scepticism means working from the assumption that any one perspective emerges from a particular point of view, from a particular horizon, and therefore is less likely to express the whole of the truth about a situation, and more likely to express insight, agenda and potential.

A challenge is not just to hear different perspectives and incorporate them into a more holistic understanding, but also to value the dialogue between unresolved tensions and contested analysis. It is often the voices that are considered 'problematic' that open up new possibilities. It is often in the intensity of energised disagreement that people are pushed beyond the recycling of preference, ideology, habit and disappointment.

The challenge for the practitioner-facilitator is to value dissent, hold the tension and keep the dialogue open by maintaining goodwill and an inquisitive 'community of enquiry'. John Forester in *The Deliberative Practitioner* argues that 'much more is at stake in dialogic and argumentative processes ... At stake too are issues of political membership and identity, memory and hope, confidence and competence, appreciation and respect, acknowledgement and the ability to act together' (1999: 115–16). Sennett describes it less obscurely as, 'rather than dropping the [unresolved] issue, people need to stay connected to one another; thorny issues seldom go away' (2012: 241). At times shared insight dawns on a group's life when a creative synthesis opens up a surprising potential at the heart of an apparently implacable contradiction or contention. The moment is often characterised by a pause in the discussion, silence, a deep listening to something said that would usually not have been heard, the realisation of the significance of the suggestion, and the unspoken resolve of the group to take the risk involved and move forward together. At Out of the Shadows one young participant said:

> 'For the Muslims, when we see our indigenous brothers and sisters, and they are still experiencing straight-out racism, both covertly and overtly, it is our community that says, "Well, what chance do we have?"' This insight led to an analysis that the poor treatment of indigenous people sets the standard for ways in which diverse groups feel they are being treated, and to a new resolve to make 'addressing the legacy of colonialism for all Australians' a priority in the ongoing work of the SEQICF.

This emergent analysis linked the experiences of Muslim and indigenous young people in ways previously not considered by the leaders of each of those cultural communities. This linking created new relationships and a sense of solidarity between previously isolated struggles for justice. Clearly such connecting was and is not inevitable. The alternative generative trajectory is that the unresolved tension is simply maintained – instead settling for a kind of respectful civility that maintains the peace.

In conclusion, this reflection has shown how analysis is central to any process of community development, ensuring that people have a way forward, a sense of what to do and why they are doing it. Inevitably there is disagreement and conflict. We now turn to focus on the challenge of dealing with conflict within community practice.

Careful conflicting

In the process of community development work practitioners inevitably meet different groups reflecting differing interests and positions. Given most community workers' commitments and values, conflict is inevitable. This third reflection of the chapter considers ways of working with conflict that reflect a dialogical, soulful and hospitable approach to community development.

The reality of a shit-fight

In 2010 Peter spent some time conducting research on community-based environmental conflicts within Ecuador. One of the interesting stories of practice was that of an organisation called DECOIN (Defensa y Conservacion Ecologica de Intag):

> DECOIN was initially established in 1995 as a grass-roots environmental organisation to find ways to conserve the unique biodiversity in the Intag area of northwestern Ecuador. This area is part of two of the world's most important biotic regions, the Tropical Andes and the Chocó-Darien Western-Ecuadorian Biological Hotspots, including both tropical rain forests and cloud forests.

> Initially focused on conservation and sustainable community practices in the Intag area, where all of the organisation's members live permanently, DECOIN has found itself facing down large-scale mining interests supported by the Ecuadorean state. These interests still threaten to destroy Intag's environment and communities and the example of sustainable development it is creating.

Despite our previous calls to start engaging any conflict with dialogue, we argue that many social conflicts will also require nothing less than what some Australians call a 'shit-fight'. DECOIN has had to engage in such a shit-fight. Initially their hope was for dialogue and co-operation with the mining companies. However, that initial hope had to be superseded by processes of social mobilisation enabling local people to fight for their land, livelihoods and autonomy. In this instance the mining company was backed up by the state in the form of military protection, so social mobilisation also required resistance against the state as well as a private corporation.

We need only to observe the behaviour of some private (Madeley, 2008), and for that matter many public corporations, to conclude that many such corporations are pathological in the sense described by Joel Baken in *The Corporation: The Pathological Pursuit of Profit and Power* (2004). And at the end of the day it is hard to dialogue with pathological people and organisations. Sometimes a dialogical approach will not work. People therefore need to confront, challenge, and hold to account some corporations, while agitating and protesting against their excesses. Many corporations are geared only and ruthlessly towards profit, private speculation, economic growth and increased political power. Some are not intent on making the world or our neighbourhoods better places to live. Here is another story:

> We are closely connected to some colleagues who have been doing community development and social solidarity work within West Papua over the past few years. They have been working with local activists and development practitioners to consider strategic ways forward for non-violent change. Dialogue has been given decades of space; however, there is also the need for mass resistance to the activities and occupation of the Indonesian state. Our own government (Australian), alongside others, is colluding with the Indonesian state in oppressing the West Papuan people by turning a blind eye, overstating the success of quiet diplomacy and enjoying the economic fruits of trade with the West Papuan region. As recently as 2010 there have been serious massacres, video recorded by West Papuan citizens.

Some of the work of our colleagues in West Papua has been documented in previous writings (Rayfield and Morello 2012). Their work highlights not only the problem of corporations, but also the collusion of states – in this case the Indonesian state. Sometimes sitting with our anger towards corporations, states and their collusion for oppressive purposes reminds us of Gandhi's axiom 'It is better to do violence than do nothing.' In a way, we are attracted to violent action as a release of our antagonism. However Gandhi went on to argue that it is better to engage in truth-force (non-violence) than violence, and so the challenge is to reinhabit our better self. The work of DECOIN and our West Papuan solidarity activists provide examples of such inhabitation.

Traditions of conflicting

There are many approaches to dealing with conflict that sit between the two extremes of violence and dialogue. Anthony Kelly and Sandra Sewell (1988) outline several different traditions that can be drawn upon in dealing with conflict: the Maoist, the Alinskian, the Christian, and finally the Gandhian tradition.

Each tradition has a different logic of conflict, with accompanying attitudes and actions that infuse their strategies and tactics. For the Maoist approach power lies 'in the barrel of a gun'. The tactics are those of guerrilla warfare – brief incursions into the territory of the enemy, quick retreat, revival and then renewed attack. Skilful use of violence, surprise, retreat and many other elements are central to the tactics. Our most recent reading of the use of such Maoist approaches has been Indian novelist and activist Arundhati Roy's account in *Broken Republic* (2011) of the struggle of indigenous tribal people of the Orissa state in India.

Within the Alinskian tradition the focus is on a war of 'social surgery' (Alinsky 1969: 133) – a radical confrontation with those in power. While he uses the language of warfare, Saul Alinsky is not advocating violence. In *Reveille for Radicals* he advocates that conflict for the purposes of social goods, such as better housing, economic security, or improved health programmes, needs to be carried out by powerful people's organisations. These organisations must fight in such a way that there will be 'no violence, and yet the battle will be sufficiently dramatic to serve as an outlet for the stirred-up passions of people ... The goal is nothing less than bloodless victory' (ibid.: 140). The tactics include the use of ridicule, threats (often more terrifying than the actual proposal) and constant pressure.

The Christian tradition subscribes to the power of loving one's enemies. It is an approach of 'turning the other cheek'. For many this might sound completely passive, but according to more historically astute interpretations of the biblical scriptures, it is actually an invitation to stand up against attempts to humiliate (Wink 1992: 176). Within this interpretation the Christian approach requires people to stand up to those who attempt to humiliate with a statement that goes something like 'try again; your first blow failed to achieve its intended effect. I deny you the power to humiliate me.' The approach to conflicting is to persuade the enemy through love combined with tenacity and prevailing.

Within the Gandhian approach there is no enemy, or more accurately 'the enemy is within'. There are only opponents to be engaged through the idea of truth-force or *satyagraha*. Within this approach the tactics are again of persuasion, all sorts of orthodox campaigning and civil disobedience, hence the use of the word 'force'. The key to wielding truth-force is not the threat or fear of violence, but the moral power of non-violent action with truth. Some people describe it as a kind of moral jujitsu (Kurlansky 2006: 153).

80 *Transformative community processes*

These briefly described traditions illustrate different social approaches to conflict. Each approach has a different conception of the world and opponents/adversaries/enemies. Such differences in turn govern logics, attitudes and actions that guide practitioners in the inevitable shit-fights that are a part of community development work.

Dialogical conflicting

Moving away from the language of fighting we now consider more carefully the need for dialogue within conflict. While a shit-fight works on the realistic assumption of antagonistic politics (discussed in Chapter 5), the hope is for a more dialogical politic in which people can listen, learn and move towards one another, being hospitable towards the 'other' and therefore becoming community. Here is an example:

> It was 2001 and a Norwegian merchant vessel called the *Tampa* picked up over 400 asylum seekers from a sinking fishing boat near the Australian coastline. The then Australian Prime Minister declared that no asylum seekers from the *Tampa* would set foot on Australian soil, and they were shipped off to the island state of Nauru. The Federal Government used a fear-promoting politic against vulnerable Afghan and Iraqi asylum seekers fleeing war to legitimise this exclusionary and illegal process. As a refugee advocate Peter was outraged and was willing to engage in campaigning – as he in fact did.
>
> However, at that time Peter was also a part-time lecturer. What struck him in the university classes was the unwillingness of many 'progressive' people, who supported asylum-seeker and refugee rights, to create a safe space for discussion with their fellow students. When asking students, 'What do you think of this government's campaign against asylum seekers?' some opened up and shared their fears of 'being swamped by others', and fears of 'people who are different to us coming here'. The progressives in the class immediately jumped on these comments – labelling those 'other' students as racists. Instantly the room was infused by a spirit of deadly debate. People quickly felt that they had to take sides – for or against, progressive or racist, inclusive or exclusive. Peter was somewhat stunned by the rapid process of polarisation and the inability of people to hear each other. He struggled to restore a safe space of dialogue where people were able to remove labels and try to listen to one another, discerning the fears and needs beneath each position.
>
> Peter's response to that experience was also to use a community development approach to find others who shared his concern about people's ignorance around asylum and refugee issues and lack of capacity for dialogue, and to agree together to do something. A group formed, engaged in analysis, discussed tactics and ended up initiating a project called Refugee Learning Circles, which provided learning resources for people to facilitate public conversation around the issues.

Conflict for many is a problem: something scary and divisive. The students in the story above became alienated from one another as a result of the conflict within the classroom. Community workers are no different to most people. Conflict is often feared and purposefully avoided. Practitioners often find themselves trying to back away from conflict. We also know from hard experience that many models of conflicting in our society are not very hopeful; they adopt an adversarial stance looking for winners and losers, and they can quickly lead to violence, scapegoating and humiliation. Conflict often seems to destroy social relations. Because people want to avoid these negative outcomes, they tend to avoid conflict altogether.

However, in our experience conflict is an inevitable part of social relations, and so practitioners need to become adept at the social practice of *careful conflicting* in community development work. Conflict can provide the energy for constructive or generative engagement around differences of opinion and perspective (Lederach 2005). It can be a healthy expression of new-found self-confidence, autonomy or empowerment. Conflict means there is tension between different goals, some legitimate and some illegitimate, and yet within this tension there is often the potential for building new kinds of social relationships.

It is worth saying again that not all conflict leads to the potential to build new kinds of relationships – it depends on a range of factors. For instance, if standing at a bus stop with a man who is drunk and cursing Aboriginal people, then it is hardly the time to bother entering into conflict. There is no relationship and probably no potential relationship with this man, so it would probably be a waste of energy engaging in conflict. It might be better to withdraw. However, if the cursing person is someone known and he is sober, then the opportunity invites a conversation triggered through a question such as, 'Why do you hold such a view?' This creates the possibility of challenging through first hearing the story and then bringing in other perspectives.

In our experience conflict can only be effectively resolved through dialogue when the following principles and practices are applied in combination:

- a commitment to truth;
- a recognition that individuals only have a *relative view of the truth* about anything;
- an acceptance that individuals therefore need to enter into *dialogue with humility*, willing to learn from other people; and
- a particular type of courage, that people are *willing to suffer*: that is, they can let go of their own agendas and perspectives and suffer the process of taking on board someone else's perspective – potentially a very painful step.

This approach to dialogical conflicting invites community workers to bring full attention to such inner dynamics. Questions can be asked such as:

- Do we have a commitment to truth or do we simply want to maintain our own blind spots in order to win the fight?
- Are we conscious that our view of the world is relative or do we think it is absolute?

- Are we entering the process of dialogue with humility that enables us to understand the others' points of view?
- Are we even willing to be persuaded towards their views, or is dialogue our ultimate art of manipulation?
- Finally, are we willing to suffer and let go of ideas, beliefs, perspectives that we have held on to dearly, or do we only expect the other to suffer and let go?

The perspective of dialogical community development requires practitioners to engage in conflict with a primary commitment to nurturing relationships. Techniques of conflict resolution and management are only secondary. People are only really willing to hear someone's story, or to engage with someone else's perspective, if they feel that someone has taken the time to hear *their* story, or to engage with *their* perspective. It is this primary hospitable process of hearing one another's stories that nurtures relationships, and it is within the crucible of such relationships that people have a better chance of accepting or resolving differences.

Finally, a dialogical approach to conflict also recognises that people are sometimes embedded within institutional processes, habitual patterns and ideological positions that undermine their capacity to see afresh, and lock them into polarised interests. For example, the so-called 'left' is attached to a discourse of rights, and the so-called 'right' is attached to a discourse of responsibility. These attachments can undermine the possibility of dialogue to the point where practitioners are obliged to practise deconstruction. Binary ways of thinking such as right–wrong, black–white, conservationists–loggers, economy–environment and rights–responsibilities can maintain conflict in an unhelpful way. As dialogical community workers it is important to destabilise such binaries, support people in the ensuing state of transformative tension, and work with them towards potential synthesis. It is not that the person attached to either side of the binary is the 'enemy', but that they are blinded by their entrenched position and by the patterns and processes where they are embedded.

People are also 'blinded in their seeing'. At the heart of our attitude towards conflict is the acknowledgement of ignorance. Rather than seeking power within the process of conflicting, people should primarily be seeking to overcome ignorance through pursuing an understanding of the currents of their deeper connections with one another.

Structuring not strangling

In the first reflection of this chapter we argued that a crucial part of community work is the macro and meta work of building democratic people's organisations that enables people to sustain and structure their initiatives. This final reflection discusses in more depth the importance of building place-based community-oriented structures within transformative community work, a process that we have called *structuring the work*.

Innovative structures

One of the crucial transitions within transformative community work is the shift from a participatory action group, characterised by informal relationships based on mutual interest – what we call non-formal work, to an organisational structure. Within such a structure a group's relationships become characterised by roles and responsibilities and are defined not primarily in relation to one another but in relation to the group as an entity.

There are many reasons for this kind of transition. Sometimes the number of people involved in a group has grown to the point where they can no longer make decisions by involving all members in a discussion around a table. Once a group has grown to a certain number (usually culturally determined, and also dependent on the co-operative capacities of the people participating) it becomes almost impossible to maintain informal processes, and necessary to set up more democratic ones. Sometimes a group is taking public action or making public statements, and needs a name as an entity in its own right; people may call for more formal, accountable and transparent processes of decision-making; or a group needs to engage with the formal system and structures, usually of the state or other donors, for the purposes of grant acquisition, management, insurance, audits and so forth. Authors such as Henderson and Thomas (2005) have written extensively about what groups should consider when choosing to make this transition.

Within the Australian context the legal options include company, non-profit association, or co-operative structures. We tend to favour the latter two, due to our commitment to democratising both the economy and care (which we discuss further in Chapter 5), whereby economic logics are socialised within the democratic imperative and reciprocity principles of community (Restakis 2010: 96). In our experience the design and choice of organisational form are crucial when groups consider the kind of social or public good they are trying to create. For example, if a group decides to provide a social good for and with people who live with profound disabilities then a co-operative structure would provide an appropriate organisational vehicle. The co-operative structure can lessen the problems of bureaucratisation from becoming dependent on the state and the contradictory logics of applying profit principles to social care. The structure also enables a co-operative to raise capital from funders, members and other stakeholders in ways that non-profit associations are unable to (see ibid.: 107).

In our experience one of the problems for community-based work is that people tend to move too quickly from being an informal or non-formal participatory action group to becoming a formalised legal structure. The leap is made without considering both the risks of making that shift and also the alternative options, such as the one illustrated below:

> We were angry. We had formed the West End Refugee Support Group – a non-formal organisation with roles, rules and procedures, but without the legal trappings (incorporation had been avoided). The group had been welcoming and working with newly arrived refugee families for several years. As the

work expanded it was decided that a legal entity was needed to act as auspice, to take care of some financial grants that were being accessed. However, every time an organisation was approached as a potential legal auspice they wanted 20 per cent of the grant money and also wanted to control at least some of the activities. For example, one organisation approached said 'yes' on the condition that they could decide who should be the project worker.

The members were not happy with these conditions and therefore started thinking about turning the West End Refugee Support Group from a non-formal organisation into a formalised legal structure. This would relieve the need for an auspice. But in considering this risks were identified. The main one being that organic grass-roots energy would become focused on the organisation – setting it up, maintaining it, finding money to pay for insurance and audits and so on. So a few members started to consider what alternative options existed.

Peter and Gerard started talking about setting up a new community-based organisation that could act as a local formal structure, to auspice the work not only of the West End Refugee Support Group, but also a large amount of other organic grass-roots work that was occurring in the neighbourhood. We could see the potential nightmare of every participatory action group structuring their own work through forming their own legally incorporated organisation – a proliferation of organisations all requiring voluntary management committee members, insurance and audit fees. We had seen it happen in other contexts and decided there must be another way.

After some deliberation the need for a minimalist model was identified – a formal incorporated association that would provide the necessary legal and official cover, but would exert minimal control over the organic community-based activities. The idea was that the West End Refugee Support Group and any other local group would be able to utilise this non-controlling auspice for their purposes of interacting with more formal systems.

In May 1994 the Community Initiatives Resource Association (CIRA) was incorporated under the Associations Incorporation Act. The minimalist model was encapsulated in the principles of the Resource Association. It was like a two-dollar shelf company, set up to resource community initiatives. The idea was that any members who wanted to do something had to form their own working group to organise and manage their initiative. The business of the management committee was to manage the organisation as a whole, but not to micro-manage these working groups and projects – it would delegate authority and responsibility to the people doing the work. Through this innovative, minimalist model the Resource Association fulfils the contracting, insurance, accounting, auditing and reporting needs of many local and some non-local groups. It continues to this day and has auspiced well over 100 local initiatives and hundreds of thousands of dollars in cash flow.

(Barringham 2003; Westoby *et al.* 2009)

Those of us involved in the Resource Association have reflected for many years on the beauty of setting up this local structure. We realised that the other options for these grass-roots groups had included becoming either reliant on a larger organisation that would auspice the local work, with all the associated risks mentioned above, or alternatively every action group setting up their own legal structure, which would exhaust people sitting on multiple committees, finding money for insurance and audits and so on. The Resource Association was based upon a different paradigm, where the local structure was to be a shared legal auspice working in a parallel structure with community groups and projects. It only needed one management committee and one annual audit. It enabled many organic grass-roots groups to engage with the formal system of legality and finance (grants, accounts, audits, insurance) without having to worry too much about it. Such groups could focus on what they did best and were set up to do: the work of participatory action. This kind of structuring of the work releases local energy, imagination and action. When reflecting on the work after the first ten years Neil Barringham (2003) coined the phrase 'structuring not strangling', which seemed to describe the approach beautifully.

Small and accountable structures

However, this kind of structuring of the work is becoming increasingly difficult. More and more regulation by state structures, combined with more and more interest in neo-liberal logics of efficiencies and economies of scale, have led to the decimation of small place-based community-oriented structures. Small is no longer beautiful in the eyes of the powerful. Gerard reflects on this shift:

> When I started in the field, in the early 1990s, you could still get funding for small local initiatives. I remember talking with elderly residents who couldn't get to the shops, doctor or hospital. I wrote a funding submission and received $3,000 to organise a church mini-bus driven by unemployed local young people to pick up residents of three local retirement units twice a week. If I put together the same submission today, any funding body I know would want it to be a $50,000 'regional partnership initiative' meeting 'complex needs' across a 'corridor of disadvantage'.

The priorities of the modern state favour the proliferation of large non-profit or for-profit organisations with all the trappings of organisational modernity, such as 'quality assurance' systems, risk-management protocols and workplace health and safety procedures. Such organisations proliferate, soak up resources and space, and demand attention in localities. Yet from the perspective of dialogical community development, they are fundamentally flawed because they have not emerged from people's place-based struggles to build community or tackle community issues – that is, from people's own analysis of their situation. Instead the authority for the work comes from bureaucratic 'needs analysis' and allocations of government money, or alternatively from profitable possibilities. Within such logics, when the money moves the work moves. Such organisations only relate to space; they have not done the work of emplacement, and they remain unaccountable to people who live in the localities they have colonised.

One of the most significant consequences of this kind of shift is that such large organisations are not grounded in the local web of relationships that makes up community life. They find it almost impossible to be *among* this web, and build genuine community with it. After all, they employ professionals who usually do not come from that local place, and who have been trained to maintain their boundaries with local people. Instead they provide services to the 'community' as a territorialised population – an object, not a subject.

The irony of this shift is that the very infrastructure people have been building for years – that creates platforms for meeting, weaving the web of relationships that enables organic support, care and 'community as hospitality' – is de-funded, or simply strangled to death by regulation, compliance and overburdening accountabilities. People become less able to support one another and thereby more dependent on the services provided by such large organisations. Such organisations create a society in which there is plenty of 'grass' but no 'roots' – you can see all the activity, but it is not sustainable.

Structuring beyond the local

This is not to say that structuring the work must only remain oriented towards the local and small. In the resourcing environment described above, dialogical community development must be pragmatically trans-local. It invites the creation of new structures that tackle trans-local issues, and thereby focus on Freire's 'whole' rather than just the 'parts'. It invites building structures that are trans-local but are still grounded within the multiple 'locales' where they are rooted. While the macro-oriented work builds a structure such as the Resource Association, the meta work builds bridging structures that link beyond this local focus but remain grounded within the local.

Chilean economist Manfred Max-Neef (1992) has beautifully told the story of ECU–28, an example of structuring 'beyond the local' within the Andean region of Ecuador:

> The methodology of the project was to mobilise a participatory process of *horizontal communication* between villages that rarely had the opportunity to meet together, and create a shared understanding of their problems through building a regional consciousness.
>
> The project avoided the more orthodox process of peasants from different villages talking to the 'vertical structures' of the state only as individual villages – that is, each village making its own representation about its 'village problems'. Instead, through a series of grass-roots processes supported by the project, village committees were brought together to formulate a regional analysis of their state of affairs – which they could then take to the relevant state authorities *as a whole*.
>
> Through the process of 'provincial encounters' – which consisted of village committees meeting together, learning from one another, building a shared community analysis, they formed a *regional structure* – a Regional Peasants' Congress. Such a Congress was still rooted in the local (people

represented their local villages and reported back to the whole village) yet it created a regional analysis and regional people's power-base.

(ibid.: 25–117)

This story highlights some important processes for building regional structures within a transformative framework, such as:

- building horizontal relationships between people who have similar experiences, but have not been able to share with one another;
- strengthening these horizontal relationships to the point where people can build more formal structures;
- maintaining clear lines of communication and accountability between the local and the newly forming regional structure;
- nurturing participatory leadership where the emergent leaders remain committed to an ethos of ongoing participation rather than accumulation of power;
- recognising that, while larger structures require some kind of role definition, the key ethos should remain relational rather than role-oriented; and
- spending time on building a strong sense of shared values and vision.

It would be possible to look at many other case studies that show how to structure transformative work beyond even the regional and provincial and move into a national and transnational scope. For example, Judy Wicks' work in forming the Business Alliance for Local Living Economies (BALLE) (Wicks 2004), South Africa's Treatment Action Campaign (Green 2008), the La Via Campesina movement (McMichael 2012: 208ff.) and the Shack Dwellers International movement (Patel 2010) are just a few that have intrigued us over the years.

Closer to home, some colleagues have been building a different kind of regional structure on the Sunshine Coast of southeast Queensland. Their work is a response to decisions of some government departments to grant funding only to regionally oriented organisations. The consequence was that many years of local community effort invested in building local neighbourhood centres came under threat. Large organisations, often with no local base, were applying for and winning state funding opportunities. They had the capacity to employ consultants to prepare impressive applications – and then ironically started to network with the local neighbourhood centres to build local contacts, understanding and credibility. The local neighbourhood centres in the region decided to fight back:

> In 2007 four local structures: the Caloundra Neighbourhood Centre, the Hinterland Community Development Association, the Maroochy Neighbourhood Centre and Nambour Community Centre, decided to get together and start a process of forming a regional structure that would be able to compete within the regionally oriented funding market, yet be structured in such a way as to remain grounded within the local work of the

neighbourhood centres. The Sunshine Coast Community Co-op was formed. It acts not as a 'super-structure' that swallows up each local organisation, but as an enabling structure that respects each of the organisations. Each organisation is developing capacity to engage with the issues, both in its own areas and also across the region.

(Buckley 2007: 2)

The story of this organisation illustrates some innovative ways to structure the work so that local issues can be engaged with at a regional level, but still remain small enough for local people to participate. The structures remain as people's infrastructure – built from the bottom up, drawing on horizontal relationships (between neighbourhood centres and associations) and yet able to interact with the vertical formal system (usually donors or/and government). Such a model provides an alternative pathway to the conventional practice of large NGOs simply dropping in with a ready-made 'blueprint' approach to provision of services.

Structures as people's structures, not service-oriented agents

The approach of the large non- or for-profit organisations critiqued above is to legitimise their work and 'dropping in' on localities by demonstrating a need for provision of their services. They often become experts at creating need, and then argue to communities and governments (often the donors) that they are the experts at addressing that need – ironically through their services (McKnight 1995), which are provided to the detriment of community-based responses to local challenges. The following story considers a case study of how to re-imagine the emergence of people's structures as opposed to service-oriented structures:

During the 1990s many refugees within Brisbane became tired of the 'service' provided by the torture and trauma clinic based at a local hospital. The focus of that service was clinical work, with strong assumptions about refugee trauma and the need for medically oriented treatment. By the mid-1990s several leaders among Cambodian and El Salvadorian refugee groups decided they had had enough of this clinically and medically oriented service, and initiated a collective process of building their own structure. Over the next couple of years these leaders engaged in the micro and mezzo levels of community work: building relationships with diverse groups, forming an action group, and conducting some community-based research. Finally after much deliberation they formed an incorporated association, called the Queensland Programme of Assistance to Survivors of Torture and Trauma (QPASTT), to work with refugee individuals, groups and communities within a framework that incorporated clinical, group and community work alongside human rights advocacy.

This case study involves refugees moving from being the passive objects of a hospital service system to structuring their own work in mobilising action and eventually community organising. Not surprisingly, the resulting organisation does not pathologise refugees. It is not service-oriented – services are created, but alongside other community and social action. QPASTT, governed by refugees, compatriot professionals and other volunteers, continues to be a vehicle for refugees to find space to heal, for refugee groups to advocate human rights and for the creation of 'community' between refugees and non-refugees. The governance of the organisation is firmly grounded within the 'co-created community' between refugees and non-refugees. It is a people's structure, and offers a lens on alternatives to service-structures.

In conclusion, this reflection has shown how at particular times within developmental work community processes might need to be sustained through structuring. We have paid particular attention to the complexity of this structuring work, focusing on the potential slippage away from local accountability and also towards service-orientation rather than solidarity. Practitioners are instead invited to experiment in developing and nurturing innovative people-centred structures.

Summing up

These four reflections have provided an overview of the ways in which a dialogical approach to community development can transform our social world. We have shared our understanding of the role of a skilled and soulful worker in supporting 'community' to become a vehicle for social change in which people find their own paths towards development.

The first reflection introduced what we call *method*. Method refers to a systematic way of doing dialogical community development work. We explored the methodical and rhythmic work within what can be called the micro, mezzo, macro and meta processes of a community development process. The push and pull of a gentling approach and gaining mandate was also outlined. The implications of a commitment to solidarity and hospitality in methodical dialogical practice were also explored.

The second reflection examined the complex work of *analysis*. Within community development work analysis includes the process of thinking and action. A process of widening analysis starts with practitioner analysis, but holds it lightly; then moves on to a group analysis (people doing analysis together); then widens the process involving various others moving towards a more inclusive community analysis; and finally pushes dialogue with others to the point of holding unresolved tensions and contested understanding.

The third reflection explores how practitioners might *carefully conflict* within their practice. Conflict is not only inevitable; it is often desirable. Escalating conflict, where necessary, might be important for transformative work. While bringing suppressed conflict to the surface might sometimes be necessary, it is important to at least try a dialogical approach to start with, and then move on to utilise various other traditions of conflicting. In saying this we have acknowledged that the dialogical approach has limits – it might not always work.

90 Transformative community processes

The final reflection considered the complex business of *structuring* transformational work. The beauty of innovative local structures is that they do not strangle local energy and enthusiasm. We then pursue the need to build structures that are beyond the local, while remaining firmly embedded within the local. People's structures, emerging from their aspirations and impulses, are posited as an alternative to service-oriented structures delivered *at* people.

4 Analytical interlude
What weakens dialogue within community development

This analytical interlude examines three of what we consider to be the most significant issues that weaken the possibility of dialogue within contemporary community development practice. At first glance the reader might question why we do not explicitly address some of the obvious challenges – such as people's lack of propensity to listen, people's inclination to get into polarising debate and people's tendencies to monologue. Or we could simply discuss the challenges of putting into practice the ideas discussed in Chapter 1 – such as the difficulties of reaching for the other and understanding, the challenges of community as dialogue, or the lack of people's ability to 'see the whole'. However, our sense is that such topics have already been well discussed elsewhere.

This interlude instead attempts to bring attention to three overlooked, subtler and, in our opinion, core dialogical challenges of our times. These challenges have also been framed negatively as 'what weakens dialogue within community development', attempting to name what can be summarised as cultural, political and material forces. Each of the three reflections also offers positive practical ways forward to address the discussed challenges.

We have put this analytical interlude at the centre of the book because in our experience holding an analysis is central to integrating theory and practice. Practitioners, while building on a positive vision of the world, also build a way forward from an analysis of what is wrong. The three trends identified are ideological positions, therapeutic culture and growing inequalities, each of which is discussed in turn.

Ideological positions: captive to fundamentalisms, exclusivity and prescription

Ideology plays a significant role in people's understanding of life and their intention in the social world. As Michael Freeden says, 'ideologies map the political and social worlds for us' (2003: 2–3) and for many they are 'a way of imposing some pattern on the world – some structure or organisation' (ibid.). In an appreciative understanding of the term it makes sense that we are all ideologues. People need some kind of map, pattern, structure and organisation for thinking and acting.

Viewing ideology appreciatively it can be seen to energise people, give a sense of security, and provide what appears to be a clear analysis, each of which is now considered. One of the virtues of ideology is that it provides people and groups with an agreed and uniform way of viewing the world, a common language, which in turn makes it easier to generate a certain amount of energy. People are often mobilised and energised through commitment to a clear way of viewing the world, combined with an agreed and uniform rationale for action. Ideologies can also provide a sense of security. In a world that is becoming more and more complex and confusing – with so many political and religious options, so much information, and so many calls to loyalty – adopting a particular ideology sometimes enables people to relax. Someone has finally found a truth (although they might see it as *the* only truth and *the* way) and it makes people feel safe and secure. Furthermore, ideology can provide useful lenses through which people analyse a given situation. For example, a Marxist political ideology provides a powerful analytical tool to see the relationships between capital and labour in a certain situation. If someone subscribes to Marxist ideology they will have a sharp awareness of labour exploitation. In the same way, if someone subscribes to a particular feminist ideology they will have a sharp insight into gender relations. Ideologies can then sharpen analyses of the world and can bring insightful perspectives to an issue.

However, while starting this reflection with an appreciative understanding of the value of ideology, we have also come to see two ways in which it usually undermines dialogue. This undermining occurs first when people are unaware of the ways their worldview is underpinned by ideology, and second when they become attached to their ideological positions. These dynamics restrict their contribution to dialogue and their capacity to create a 'free and friendly space' (Nouwen 1975: 15) that invites others into dialogue.

Ideology is filled with shadow. Subtle shifts of understanding and intention can swing insight and action in the direction of liberation and emancipation on one hand, or in the direction of repression and totalitarianism on the other. For example, one of the shadow dangers of ideology is that the energy, sense of security and sharp analysis described above might become captive to fundamentalism (Hollis 2001) and people become ideologues. Religious fundamentalisms arise from all traditions, for example the Christian 'moral majority' in the USA, Hindu fundamentalists as a political force in India, and Islamic fundamentalism growing in many parts of the world. Materialism, hedonism and narcissism flourish as contemporary forms of cultural fundamentalism (Hollis 2005: 164). Political expressions of fundamentalist ideology appear in the form of hegemonic neo-liberalism or narrow interpretations of Marxist, feminist and Green philosophies. Embedded within these fundamentalist-oriented understandings of ideology are strong bounded-set positions usually underpinned by very strong dualisms such as right–wrong, orthodox–unorthodox, or natural–unnatural. Such fundamentalist ideology can give people a passion, safety and commitment that can evoke amazing energy, but at a potential cost to community as dialogue and hospitality. We are not suggesting that fundamentalisms do not make sense under certain conditions, such as when people or groups have experienced ongoing humiliation or disenfranchisement. We are simply arguing that when people slide towards fundamentalist ideologies then dialogue becomes almost impossible. We are reminded of Yeats' classic 1920 poem *The Second Coming*, written at the time of the looming Irish civil war:

> Things fall apart; the centre cannot hold;
> Mere anarchy is loosed upon the world,
> The blood-dimmed tide is loosed, and everywhere
> The ceremony of innocence is drowned;
> The best lack all conviction, while the worst
> Are full of passionate intensity.
> (2000: 158)

Damage occurs when there is a shift: from using multiple ideologies to understand a complex world, enabling people with conviction to take action infused with uncertainty; to people taking polarised ideological positions and adopting fundamentalist stances, fuelling passionate certain action. When this shift occurs, people who have lost the capacity for reflexivity become divisive and anti-dialogical, undermining the possibility of community. Often real challenges to dialogue occur when non-reflexive ideologues refuse to recognise that their view of the world is ideological, drawing on language such as 'common sense' or 'natural'. Others are then perceived to be attached to 'unnatural' ideas, and are easily dismissed.

As would be clear to the reader by now, our understanding of community is not built on the basis of uniformity, exclusivity or exclusion; instead its foundations are intersubjectivity, a pluralistic social participation and agonistic politics (Mouffe 2005). Such agonistic politics implies that there will often be ongoing differences that are in some way irreconcilable, yet where there is still the possibility of respectful engagement within that difference. In such spaces people work to maintain a conversation despite the tension of disagreement.

A dialogical approach to community development invites practitioners to develop the skills of attention, observation and engagement *with* people who have differing perspectives. Bringing people with differing perspectives into a dialogical process introduces many more pairs of eyes, which enables, and in some cases forces, community workers to look more carefully at what is happening. It can enable discernment of a narrative thread that emerges from the dialectic between content and relationship. There is more chance of 'understanding' with many perspectives offered – one goal of dialogue. A soulful orientation adds to a dialogical approach in that it prefers to approach a problem or issue with a sense of mystery. What is happening in a given situation is a mystery that can only be unravelled through constant attention. Non-reflective ideologues become arrogant – people are too sure, too soon, of what is happening.

An approach informed by a dialogical commitment also expands conceptual frameworks to engage with actual experiences. Soulful people still advocate ideals with conviction. They of course subscribe to some kind of ideology, in the sense of a map, pattern, structure and organisation to help understand the world;

but they do not do it arrogantly or exclusively. They do it reflectively and reflexively. Their primary focus is on the *lived* present rather than an *ideal* present or future and this orients them constantly towards curiosity and dialogue. Such people still inspire energy but they do it creatively, imaginatively and experimentally. They remain open to being challenged, dialogued with, and confronted. An appreciation of mystery and the hope for expanded conceptual frameworks implies that people actually see more attentively than people who are blind to or attached to their ideological positions could ever wish to do. It requires that community workers adopt a teachable attitude enabling them to learn about many perspectives, themes and windows of analyses that can unravel complex relationships and dynamics within social spaces.

Therapeutic culture: managing anger and anxiety, coping with distress and undermining social agency

The second theme, and from our perspective a most pervasive and yet almost invisible trend, is an ever increasing anxiety and anger among people and the corresponding colonising process of *therapeutic culture*. Frank Furedi (2004, 2005), a British sociologist, argues that Western societies now live within a therapeutic culture that medicalises human distress, which in turn leads to a reliance on technical and professional interventions to reduce that distress.

Furedi echoes the earlier ideas of North American depth psychologists James Hillman and Michael Ventura as articulated in their adventurous book *We've Had a Hundred Years of Psycho-therapy and the World's Getting Worse* (1993). Hillman and Ventura cite examples such as clients sitting with a therapist explaining how they are angry about the increasing levels of noise pollution surrounding their houses. Clients will say something to the therapist like, 'It's driving me crazy'. For the likes of Hillman, Ventura and Furedi, therapeutic culture orients the therapist and client to collude with each other in developing psychosocial strategies to *cope* with such anger rather than engage in socially and politically oriented processes that transform the causes of distress. The therapist's answer will therefore be something like, 'How are you going to cope with the noise?' or, 'How will you deal with the anger and frustration you are feeling towards those making the noise?' People take the path of least resistance enabling them to 'feel better', of course until the next issue arises that stirs up the latent anger.

Most people find themselves doing this all the time – they cope through turning their own music up louder when tired of the constant noise in the neighbourhood. Hillman and Ventura argue that such a coping strategy might not be very helpful in the long run. It certainly lacks a dialogical and transformative commitment to engaging with the 'why' and 'who' of causing the noise pollution, which in turn undermines collective engagement with such an issue.

The relevance to community development work is obvious. Within the trend towards therapeutic culture, an individual's distress or suffering is usually medicalised. People are labelled as traumatised, angry, anxious, not-coping, or fragile, and are diagnosed with all sorts of problems such as post-traumatic stress disorder (PTSD) and attention deficit hyperactivity disorder (ADHD). In a parallel process, social groups experiencing distress and suffering are labelled as at risk, vulnerable, needy and problematic. Whole populations of the marginalised – such as young people, the aged, refugees, Aboriginal and Torres Strait Islanders and war-torn populations (Pupavac 2004) – are labelled as not-coping. The problem is located *within* their social body, legitimising instrumental and technological kinds of interventions.

One of the biggest problems with this model of human vulnerability and powerlessness, transmitted through therapeutic culture, is that it coincides with a far wider tendency to dismiss the potential for people to exercise control over their own lives. There is a decline of belief (including self-belief) in people's individual and collective agency to make change happen. People instead become good at their 'complaining muscles' so to speak, rather than their 'dialogical muscles' – reinforcing their sense of vulnerability and powerlessness.

Another indicator of such diminished social agency is the tendency for people to turn for help to professionals, particularly therapists and counsellors, and even professional community workers, instead of to friends and other community members. Community, created through the conviviality of friendship and association, has historically provided the social space for people to be together in grieving, mourning, and recovering from the distress of a range of losses, or alternatively challenging the causes of distress. Therapeutic culture cuts across this soulful expression of community and moves towards forms of professionalisation and medicalisation of care. This in turn undermines the use of humanising and transformative dialogical muscles that enable people to work together to challenge the causes of social suffering. A dynamic is then set up that could be understood as a positive feedback cycle, whereby the atomisation of society and dissolution of organic community feeds into therapeutic culture, which in turn undermines the social agency that 'traditionally' contributes to community.

Our sense is that there is the need for an alternative way of thinking and acting. Instead of supporting the trend towards professionalised and medicalised care, community practitioners can offer a way of re-socialising concerns through nudging people towards, or inviting people into, dialogical processes. People together can rediscover and relearn how to create community for the purposes of both supporting one another through life's inevitable distress and also taking collective action when necessary.

Growing inequalities: disrespect and accompanying humiliation

A significant distress of many marginalised people is their awareness of being 'on the wrong end' of material inequalities. Richard Sennett's work (2003, 2012) has helped us make sense of these material forces, which, from our perspective, also profoundly weaken the possibilities of dialogue. His particular contribution is an analysis of growing inequalities and how they in turn both undermine people's 'capacities to co-operate' and produce a 'cynical society' whose 'denizens are ill-disposed to cooperate' (Sennett 2012: 134). He also stretches our analysis of what weakens dialogue in his reflections on how difficult respect is when inequalities grow.

At the core of Sennett's thesis is the notion that contemporary forms of capitalism are leaning towards a 'zero-sum competition' with 'winner takes-all extremes' (ibid.). He argues that social cohesion is inherently weak within such capitalist systems (ibid.), and is even more stressed under the conditions of contemporary turbo-capitalism.

This reduced social cohesion, produced through increased inequalities, undermines the possibilities of dialogical exchanges. Sennett argues that dialogical exchanges are made possible by an emphasis on the qualities of social relationships, particularly the 'power of duty and honour' within those relationships (ibid.: 136). However, modern capitalism has produced: (1) a form of consumerism that has resulted in children becoming more dependent on the things they own rather than one another, thereby undermining the possibilities of strong social relationships; (2) capitalist logics, which diffused into workplaces also undermine honour and responsibility; and, (3) contemporary culture, which produces the unco-operative self. This all adds up to a social dynamic that reduces co-operative capacities and weakens dialogue.

Furthermore, Sennett argues that the complex social dynamics centred around how respect and dependency interrelate also challenge dialogic relations (2003). His analysis of how many marginalised people within unequal societies end up in relationships of dependency – upon welfare, or low-paid alienating work, or aid initiatives – is very useful. A community worker engaging with marginalised people, often in conditions of dependency, can encounter a deep resistance to opening up to dialogue. There could be a lingering resentment, a building anger and/or a simmering indignity.

Harvard University conflict-resolution specialist Donna Hicks offers insight into the humiliation of indignity (Hicks 2011) – understood as something different to disrespect. Thirty-three years of conflict-resolution work led her to understand that, 'emotional riptides wreaked havoc on the people and [any] dialogue process' (ibid.: xiii). She concluded that 'the force behind their reactions was the result of primal insults to dignity' (ibid.). Dialogue is undermined or weakened when people who are treated badly, suffering indignity, find it hard to let go of their positions, perspectives and pain. Slovenian philosopher and cultural critic Slavoj Zizek pushes this kind of analysis further, arguing that within wealthy societies we now live with the 'institutionalisation of envy' (2011: xiii), ensuring and amplifying such resentment, anger and indignity. These feelings, all produced by welfare or aid dependency, clearly do not create a good emotional platform for dialogue. Reaching 'for the other' or for 'mutual understanding' is counter-intuitive when humiliation poises people for a fight.

Seeking connections across gulfs of difference is challenging. Inequalities produce many challenges – albeit individually mediated and made sense of – that can undermine people's self-respect, their self-love, and their capacity to reach out. With greater inequality and the corresponding increased chance of experiences of humiliation, there is often less self-respect. There is also an accompanying inclination towards dispositions (Bourdieu 1984) that imply 'Go away

– you are different!' People bunker down with 'people like themselves' thereby reproducing social distance and inequalities. These dynamics produce what seminal authors Richard Wilkinson and Kate Pickett call social pain (2009: 212), an idea echoing Pierre Bourdieu's notion of 'social distress' (1999) and Wendy Brown's concept of 'social injury' (1995). People experiencing painful material inequality manifest their suffering in many destructive ways – from mental health issues and obesity, through to crime and imprisonment.

Of course a dialogical perspective on community development sees potential within the social pain produced by such inequalities. If not silenced or managed by therapeutic interventions (as per the previous reflection), people's experience of social pain can lead them, sometimes 'nudged along' by community workers, into dialogic conversations with others. These conversations create possibilities whereby a mutual understanding of common experiences can then lead to social solidarity and collective action. Potentially then, while inequality reduces social cohesion *across society*, it can lead to social solidarity *among* those suffering. The felt private pain, through dialogue with others, can be understood as social pain and re-imagined as a public issue animating collective action (Daveson 2000).

Summing up

Three trends that weaken dialogue within community development have been discussed, providing a rich analysis of challenges facing community workers who are committed to dialogical approaches to community development. A soulful orientation, a social and ecological practice and deconstructive movements require engagement with these trends that can inform careful, considered ways of working with others.

The reflection on *ideological positions* sheds light on cultural and historical patterns of thinking that undermine dialogue. In identifying ideological positions as a crucial challenge for dialogical community development we suggested that many people, in their search for security, an easy and simplistic analysis of society, and a sense of 'community', find it very hard to open up to dialogue. Non-reflexive ideology tends to emerge or be constructed from closed-set, bounded systems of beliefs with clear 'ins' and 'outs'. We offered an alternative way of thinking with an appreciative attitude towards reflexive ideology, expanded conceptual frameworks, and a delight in mystery.

Drawing on Frank Furedi's work, our discussion about *therapeutic culture* argued that people and professionals increasingly collude with one another to find solutions to social problems via technically oriented therapeutic interventions. Within therapeutic culture, rather than addressing the causes of social distress – often related to moral, social and political processes – people focus on individually *coping* with the distress and/or complaining about it. In contrast we argue the need for people to reclaim their dialogical muscles, developing social solidarity with one another and mobilising for action.

Our reflection on *growing inequalities* focused on Richard Sennett's research on co-operation, respect and inequalities, alongside Donna Hicks' scholarly

98 *Analytical interlude: weakening dialogue*

work on dignity. Kate Pickett and Richard Wilkinson's cutting edge research on inequalities and their social consequences were also considered. Clearly increasing social inequalities are producing material conditions that weaken social cohesion and undermine platforms for dialogue. However, our understanding also explores how the resultant social suffering can be a catalyst for dialogue among those who suffer, thereby being a crucible of social change.

Finally, we are not proposing that community development practitioners go into spaces and places and name these trends in public ways; these trends are, after all, part of the analysis that practitioners first have to understand and internalise themselves. Many people would not be able to make sense of this practitioner analysis. The sterile ways of thinking, being and doing that result from these trends have seeped deep into people's conscious and unconscious ways of living. Community workers can only hope to enter into dialogue with people gradually, bringing a fresh and subtle perspective informed by such an analysis. Within a space of dialogue arises the possibility of new ideas, of 'in-between' ways of thinking, being and doing – and new kinds of community.

5 Caring for different spheres of community life

In Chapters 2 and 3 we explored broadly how a dialogical approach to community development can deepen our understanding of living and working in communities. Chapter 4 explored our practitioner analysis of what weakens dialogue within community development. We now examine the different spheres of community life that practitioners need to care for, named as the ordinary, economic, political, cultural and ecological spheres. In many ways these spheres of life are intertwined; however, they have been pulled apart for the purposes of understanding how a dialogical framework of practice is diffused within each one. This everyday practice of community development has been named as *caring*.

Caring is a crucial disposition within dialogical community development. Care can be contrasted with the notion of *cure*. Cure implies the end of trouble: if someone is cured, they do not have to worry about what was bothering them any longer. In contrast, care carries a sense of ongoing attention and curiosity. If an understanding of community development is informed by a paradigm of cure, then the focus will often be on instrumental interventions and technique. The primary concern becomes: What techniques will be used to solve or remove the problem? Such an approach undermines the tenets of the dialogical approach explored in the previous chapters. However, if an approach to community development is to be informed by a paradigm of caring, then 'problems' will be approached in the kind of way discussed in Chapter 2. Problems invite caring and curiosity. A dialogical approach promotes reaching for a deeper understanding of shadow, story, discourse and dynamics at work in social contexts.

The practice of community development would change remarkably if practitioners thought of it as ongoing care rather than the quest for a cure. More time would be taken to watch and listen, trying to discern the patterns that make sense of the deeper mysteries of daily community life. Problems within such spaces offer a chance for reflection that would otherwise be precluded by the swift routines of life. The approach to community development outlined here acknowledges, despite its implied paradox, that a muscled, strong-willed pursuit of change can, at best, actually stand in the way of substantive transformation and, at worst, cause more problems.

Caring for the ordinary

Despite the movement towards a more sophisticated view of community development, it is important to remember that much of the caring aspect of community building is done through being aware of and involved in the ordinary. Ordinary activities might include sharing a cup of tea or coffee, standing in line at a social security, welfare or NGO office in support of someone needing help, taking a stroll through the local park with someone who wishes to simply chat, or taking the afternoon off to cook up a meal with some friends. These everyday events work as a kind of social glue that connects ordinary people with one another, building community around the everyday concerns of life.

Sometimes as authors we watch the way community development workers live (ourselves included) and get the sense that community workers' lives are the antithesis of what is dreamed of. People do not walk their talk. The lives lived – charging around from meeting to meeting, project to project, heads full of analyses of global geo-politics and national trends – squeeze out any time or space for the ordinary life of community. As an antidote to this, instead we dream of a conviviality of community life in which people have time for one another, in which beauty and art are welcomed, in which the rhythms of work blend with the pleasures of recreation and friendship – in which the ordinary is considered significant.

As practitioners with specialised skills and knowledge, community workers should have developed an acute self-awareness and sense of personal power; but none of this should detract from the ordinary activities of caring in community. If practitioners do not have time for family, friends and play, then they are potentially undoing community while trying to nurture it. There is no space in this frenetic busyness for community as dialogue or community as hospitality.

Doing ordinary things with extraordinary love

In the whirlpool of activity that is modern life, we are reminded of some pertinent words of wisdom from Mother Theresa. For her, at the heart of living is the requirement to do 'ordinary things with extraordinary love' (Devananda 1986: 65). The extraordinary activist efforts of Gandhi, in South Africa and then in India, were balanced by the ordinary simplicity of significant parts of his daily life. It could have been easy for Mahatma Gandhi to forget the daily routines required of living in an ashram – working on the land, spinning yarn, preparing food, and teaching and playing with the children. However, he lived and modelled his dream at home.

As community workers run around manically trying to build community, trying to make a better world, it would appear to be increasingly important to ask questions such as, What is this world, this community that is being dreamed of? The answer usually alludes to a nurturing, wholesome web of relationships full of wonderful ordinary living. For us (as authors we acknowledge that we might be saying more here about our own vision of the good life, shaped by our class, age, gender and race, than anything else) it is about people walking in parks, drinking coffee, sharing a beer or glass of wine and chatting while picking up the kids after school. It is a soccer game, cricket or tennis match among friends on a Saturday afternoon, or a weekend camping trip out into the countryside. It involves open homes, talking at the kitchen table while cooking dinner, a cup of tea at the fence, nursing mums' groups, playgroups or birthday parties creating happy, messy chaos in lounge rooms and backyards. This is community with depth – or our version of it! Others will have their own versions. But community workers all around the world would be wise to pause and ask themselves if they have time to participate in such activities, or in their earnest commitment to building community are they too busy to be a part of it?

Beware of idealism

A major obstacle preventing community development workers from enjoying and participating in the ordinary is a sense of idealism. As discussed in the Analytical Interlude, idealism and conviction in themselves are wonderful; they inspire hope, energy and action. But they also have a shadow side, often appearing as rejection of the ordinary, and neglect of the mundane. Idealism can inspire a grandiose vision of change, which can actually become an obstacle to participating in the simplicity of ordinary community life. Here is an example:

> In our classic inner-city neighbourhood of West End, the politics of the left is expressed through factionalism – the International Socialists versus the Democratic Socialists versus the Socialist Alliance, not to mention anarchist factions beyond count! The result is that some of the most passionate and committed people in our community find it difficult to work together, let alone be inclusive of 'ordinary' garden variety neighbours who are 'compromised' by their bourgeoisie values and mortgage.
>
> Gerard recalls how it all came to a head one night during World Expo 88, when the community mobilised in support of a squat in some flats that had been cleared for redevelopment. About 30 of us sat against the walls of an empty lounge room, discussing the events of the day – police presence, outstanding warrants, media attention, electricity workers cutting off the power, how the squatters were travelling emotionally, and how they would feed themselves that night. At that moment the squat was on the front line of the community resistance to Expo, and many diverse people were there to offer support.
>
> We were discussing tactics and ethics, a debate between experienced campaigners and tough survivors of the global peace movement. The debate became tense as people disagreed and tried to persuade the group to come round to their viewpoint. The discussion got louder and angrier, and polarised around the opposing ideals of a well-known Christian pacifist and a non-violent Dutch environment activist recently returned from action in the rainforests of Borneo. Neither had the awareness to know that they were dominating the room and alienating people. Neither would back down, but we were all a bit surprised when suddenly they both flew across the room, at one another's throats in a classic cat-fight! Neither was much of a fighter,

so no one got hurt. But what was sad was that the ordinary people who had come along to offer support – some venturing into social activism for the first time – were completely alienated, and many did not return.

Community practitioners all need to develop an awareness of the ways that idealism distracts from caring for the ordinary.

Caring for the economy

Ordinary life is in many ways associated with the household. Interestingly the word 'economy' originates from the Greek word *oikonomia*, meaning the organisation of the house and a prudent and ethical use of its resources (Booth 1993). Informed by this etymological understanding, our perspective is oriented towards the idea that caring for the economic sphere requires a renewed focus on the micro level of what can be understood as locality-, home- or community-oriented economics (McKibben 2007; Princen 2010) and also the articulations between this micro and macro level as per Max-Neef's (1991) human-scale economics.

However, for many decades of the twentieth century, the economic debate has been dominated by macro-level binary modes of thinking, focused on the either–or choice of adopting a capitalist economy based on free-market principles, or developing a bureaucratic socialist economy. Neither of these dominant approaches has proved itself to those who care for the economy in the service of a people-centred, life-enhancing approach to development.

Current hegemonic forms of growth-oriented, free-market capitalism operate almost by definition on the basis of what is expedient, and are therefore open to question on ethical grounds. Anything so obsessed with selective advantage and profit cannot be trusted to provide either moral guidance or long-term stability. The cataclysmic economic events since 2008 have added to the argument against this model of development with capitalism facing ongoing crises (Harvey 2011). Authors such as David Korten (1995, 2000), Raj Patel (2009) and Vandana Shiva (2005) have provided a pertinent analysis of the dangers of global capitalism – or what Shiva calls the 'death economy'. On the basis that people do not want a death economy, and that the post-2008 economic meltdown has undermined people's commitment to 'turbo-charged capitalism', we along with many others are searching for new perspectives on caring for the kind of economy that will enhance people's lives.

Fostering a community economy

For community practitioners searching for new perspectives and guided by orientations such as solidarity, economic development implies the development of a 'community economy' sometimes understood in terms of a moral economy (Owen 2009), a living ecological economy (Shiva 2005), a Buddhist economy (Schumacher 1974) and a social or solidarity economy (Amin 2009). Such an approach is underpinned by a moral imperative for everyone to have enough, with particular reference to the marginalised and future generations.

A people-centred economy honours people's freedom to engage in economic transactions – an acknowledgement of the importance of the market – but also attempts to overcome the widespread failure of market mechanisms to promote social justice or ecological sustainability.

Such an economy can also be understood within a 'diverse economies framework' (Gibson-Graham 2006), recognising that there are multiple economies operating at any one time within a geographical space. The visible capitalist economy can be displaced from its hegemonic status and viewed as one kind of economic structure alongside other non-capitalist ones. Most people participate in economic exchanges that are non-capitalist (for example, sharing tools between neighbours) alongside capitalist, and fostering a community economy can be enhanced through focusing on the former exchanges. Here is an example of the limits of a market-oriented economy that provides insight into the possibilities of seeing and fostering a more people-oriented one:

> The inner Brisbane neighbourhood of West End is a place where people love to live. It's close to the university, the river, the central business area – the amenities are fabulous. However, in recent years the rents have risen exponentially as processes of gentrification have taken hold. In this context we have watched two parallel rental housing economies at work.
>
> The market economy is the more visible one. The rental contract is often mediated through the real estate industry that has a vested interest in high rents: the more the rent, the more the agencies' fees. The more vacancies the agencies create the more re-letting fees they earn. Often local 'free' newspapers are linked to real estate industry interests, who are their biggest advertisers, and they publish constant hype about the market rental rates that could be charged. If you are a landowner in the area and read these papers you would regularly lick your lips with the taste of potential profits. On the whole this market housing economy pushes lower-income households out of the area. It is an economy of social exclusion based on the contradictory logic and mythology of the market. The logic is that the household who can pay one dollar more than any competitor gets the vacancy, while the mythology is that this is somehow a fair way to allocate shelter.
>
> On the other hand we know plenty of tenants living in the area who are known by their local landlords. The 'contract' between these landlords and tenants is mediated through a relationship that has some other kind of meaning and connection, and therefore has some scope for dialogue. Within this relational economy the rents are significantly lower than those being charged in the market. The relational economy is guided by an ethic other than profit, and enables a whole diversity of people on lower incomes to continue living in the area – it is a more inclusive economy.
>
> Of course, individual real estate agents also bring varying levels of compassion and types of relationality to their industry, and we have heard beautiful stories of agents, usually the Greeks who have strong historical roots and social ties to the area, defying the market in ways that preserve their community.

Such a case study illustrates the powerful potential of building relational and human-scale moral economies. Not everyone need be driven by the profit motive that is usually the focus of a narrow market orientation. In the relational economy both the relationships between landlords and tenants, and a commitment to maintaining some lower-cost rental options for people in the neighbourhood, take priority over maximising profit. This relational, living and human-scale local economy balances economic objectives with social and ecological objectives.

Building economic institutions with social objectives

Another element of this vision for community economic development is that earnings, spending, savings and investments remain primarily in localities, generating work and jobs for local people and furthering other local social and ecological outcomes. This kind of local economy focuses on building structures such as savings and loans co-operatives, local micro-credit groups, community credit unions, local industries and social enterprises.

The 'how to' for building such social economic institutions has been articulated within various community economic development frameworks. While not wanting to outline them in any depth it is worth noting that some of the frameworks drawn upon within our practice have included:

- Michael Shuman's (2007) 'local economic development' framework;
- Alison Mathie and Gordon Cunningham's (2008) 'assets-based community development' approach; and
- the British Department for International Development (DFID)'s 'sustainable livelihoods' framework (Pawar 2010: 73).

They each provide different analyses of what the problem is, what the possibilities are and the methodology for bringing change towards community-centred economies.

One vehicle for such change, a favourite of ours seeing as we are both members of one, are co-operatives. Co-operatives are one way of building local relational economies, because they ensure both member and/or worker control of the organisation, and link business imperatives into the kind of broader ethic of co-operation and community-oriented values. Furthermore, they are experiments in democratising economies, subjecting the logics of business (usually to survive and make profit) to member control. These democratic and other values are outlined within the seven principles of the International Co-operative Alliance – inspirational for those re-imagining economies. As attested to in the 2012 United Nations International Year of Cooperatives, co-operatives need not be perceived as at the margins of the economic sphere of society, but can be vibrant economic, ecological and social contributors. A 2007 United Nations report argues that, 'through their self-help enterprises and their commitment to members and their communities, [co-operatives] generate an estimated 100 million jobs worldwide' (United Nations General Assembly 2007: 4). Furthermore, John Restakis, in his book *Humanizing the Economy:*

Co-operatives in the Age of Capital, argues that co-ops account for over 800 million members in 85 countries around the world (2010: 3). We have both been members of several co-operatives and here is one story:

> We currently work part-time for Community Praxis Co-op Ltd – a not-for-profit workers' co-operative established in 1998 that provides training and consultancy services to non-government organisations, community-based organisations, and government. All members of the co-operative sit on the Board of Management and have a key say in the direction of the co-operative. Three per cent of all income goes into an 'ethical dividend' that we give away to foster other co-operatives and respond to community needs. The ratio of pay is four to one (4:1), a relational commitment limiting greed and exploitation by ensuring that the highest-paid worker (usually someone with a doctorate or a consultancy) never earns more than four times the hourly rate of the lowest-paid worker (usually an administrative worker or a student in the role of project assistant).

Within our city are many other community co-operatives. During the past 13 years Reverse Garbage has built a recycling business, employing local people who source and sell industrial and other discards, and supplying materials to household projects and artists who create recycled art works. Nundah Community Enterprises Co-op is another social enterprise that employs people with learning difficulties and health issues. This co-op runs a successful café, catering business, egg-retailing venture and property maintenance business. Such co-operatives are an integral part of the vision of rebuilding local economies by establishing and growing businesses that have social objectives.

We are also fond of two stories from other parts of the world that illustrate how community development practitioners can be involved in building economic institutions that focus on a relational moral economy: Mohammad Yunus' work of the Grameen Bank (1999) and Judy Wicks' work of the White Dog Café in Philadelphia and the accompanying Business Alliance for Local Living Economies (2004; Wicks and Klause 1998).

There are huge challenges to building new legal structures that enable community-oriented people to invest in such local relational economies. Questions arise such as, How do we ensure our pension or superannuation funds are channelled into legal structures that could invest in local work with social objectives? or, How do we move away from an over-reliance on government or philanthropy to build such economies? A number of colleagues are involved in experiments of building such structures. Here is a story of one of them:

> Over many years some Brisbane colleagues have built Foresters Community Finance into a viable organisation with a legal and ethical structure to invest funds into work that will provide social housing, arrange premises for community organisations, and cultivate other kinds of asset bases for neighbourhoods. Foresters Community Finance specialises in supporting community development through investment and business, rather than just relying

on government funding and philanthropy. Their ethical investment fund is only one of many mechanisms that offer options to rebuild local living economies. They argue that we need to rethink our returns on investment and include ecological, social and community returns in our calculations.

Such structures are sometimes seen as representing a new 'fourth sector' – neither government, private or non-profit. The fourth sector is made up of hybrid structures, experimenting with business models but driven by social and ecological objectives.

In considering the importance of reviving local economies we want to be careful in our argument. We are not just for reviving local associationism. As becomes clear in the rest of this reflection (if not already) we are also conscious that most businesses are non-local and are focused on extracting money from communities. Caring for economics requires, then, the dual strategy of reviving locally owned and locally oriented economic and social actors, while also challenging the way current economic logics extract from communities. As per our Chapter 3 reflections, we argue that this work will require macro and meta processes enabling alliances and federations of socially oriented economic actors to challenge extractive processes.

Challenging greed

Building on the last comment, caring for the economy does not simply mean that local relational economies are nurtured; it also implies challenging some of the 'givens' of the current manifestation of the market economy. Deconstructive thinking helps to destabilise the orthodoxies of many economic fundamentalisms. For example, it is important to advocate a transformation in the way wages are allocated, destabilising the rationalisations used to legitimate greed. The obscene disparity of income levels between high- and low-income earners is an abomination to anyone committed to an ethical, relational or community-oriented economy. One *Guardian* article highlighted how within some corporations the 'ratio between bosses' rewards and employees' pay has risen to 98:1 ... meaning that the work of a chief executive is valued almost 100 times more highly than that of their employees' (Finch 2007: 41).

Many commentators believe it is this growing inequality and undermining of economic egalitarianism that will thwart much of social progress. Studies indicate that it is people's sense of relative poverty that undermines their health and good will, and often provides the impetus and motivation to participate in anti-social activity and crime (Wilkinson 2005; Wilkinson and Pickett 2009). In opposition to this kind of trend an ethos could be re-cultivated that is committed to a decent living wage, rather than just a minimum wage, and shames those who receive disproportionately high wages. This is not talk of a 'politic of envy' (a disparaging slogan being used with regularity against those who mention the word class), but a politic based on ethical imperatives and a reconsideration of the moral economy. There is an opportunity to reclaim a commitment to social justice that implies genuine movement towards an equal society. Praxis oriented towards the politics of enough and substantive equality, rather than simple equity or equality of opportunity, is crucial – ensuring all people are guaranteed enough to live happily. This is an imperative grounded in the passion of personal experience for Peter:

> I have spent many of my days talking with people who are desperately trying to survive – young and old. I have spent time living in a shanty town of Manila; I have eaten meals with the poor of Phnom Penh and New Delhi; I have sat with families and stumbled with my bad Zulu in the townships of South Africa; I have sat with young people in Vanuatu dreaming of a future despite having to support extended families of 20 people. These people live on the crumbs of the rich.
>
> Then I see a job advert linked to a company in the 'development industry' (often funded by public money through AusAID) and learn of consultants earning the equivalent in one hour of three months' income of the poor. These companies and consultants are adept at rationalisations: 'Such high wages must be developed to keep people from moving to the private sector', or 'These people work so hard that it is deserved.'

Such rationalisations are simply ways of legitimising rampant greed (albeit often fuelled by fear) – greed that is destroying an economy that would otherwise have the capacity to genuinely care for the poor. Clive Hamilton's diagnosis of 'affluenza' (2005) accurately describes the ailment that blinds so many to the possibilities of global social justice.

Examining economic orthodoxy for signs of madness

Along with such rationalisations there is much economic orthodoxy that needs to be challenged. We are reminded of the satirical question: Who believes that you can grow something infinitely within a finite system? The answer is 'mad people and economists'.

Current economic orthodoxies legitimise trading activities such as shipping apples from the UK to South Africa to be waxed and then back again to the UK for consumption. From a short-term economic perspective it appears sound: the activity generates trade and the employment of people in South Africa. However, from every other kind of perspective it is madness. Ecologically it is a disaster – think of the fuel consumption and refrigeration costs. Politically it undermines South Africa's food security and sovereignty – its people could be growing apples for their own consumption. But such practice is assumed to be legitimate in the name of an orthodox economic principle such as comparative advantage. Our sense is that some of the greatest social and political struggles will be faced in restructuring the international trade system away from the kind of activity represented by the apples being shipped back and forth; instead towards rewarding businesses that produce and sell as locally as possible, and that only work with other bioregions and nations when necessary.

Our approach to community economic development clearly requires a certain level of economic literacy. To unravel rationalisations and unmask orthodoxies such as those mentioned in the previous discussions requires an awareness that is willing to cut through all the mystification of technocratic economic elitists, whether of government treasuries, chambers of commerce or the World Trade Organization. It is important that people are able to deconstruct and destabilise the current economic discourses that legitimise speculative and shareholder-oriented economies in the name of the ever present spectral need for growth. It would be wise to trust our intuition and yet complement it with a hard-headed analysis. Economics cannot be separated from politics. The terms 'scientific' and 'pure' economics are merely technocratic disguises for an imperfect, politically charged exercise. Economics is a socially and politically constructed lens that can support either a struggle for fairness, equality and justice, or the legitimation of greed and 'free enterprise'.

Facing our economic selves honestly

At the same time as growing awareness awakens people to the myths and orthodoxies of current political economy, it also challenges each of us to be honest with ourselves. A dialogical approach to caring for the economy points out that many of the problems encountered in current economic discourses are in fact the product of our own collective and individual shadow problems. Many of us, deep down, are committed to the status quo to the extent that we are unable to imagine an alternative household, relational or human-scale economy. It is too easy to blame the banks when many people readily accumulate huge debts to finance an affluent lifestyle.

For example, the growing crescendo of voices highlighting interconnections between the economy and environmental sustainability challenges us collectively and personally. Books such as George Monbiot's *Heat* (2007) confront each of us more than ever about the impact of our personal decisions on the environment and the economy. For Peter, choosing to fly for holidays and also choosing a job that requires many flights – for example, to Vanuatu as part of a development partnership – has a profound impact on the environment and therefore on the lives of the poor who are most vulnerable to the impacts of human-made global warming. This impact provokes an honest look at the connections between our choices and their consequences.

In Australia there is a bumper sticker evoking the Gandhian mantra, 'Live simply that others may simply live.' It strikes to the heart of the matter and calls people to recognise the interconnectedness shared as economic, social and ecological beings. Underdevelopment is directly connected to overdevelopment. Many decades of development experience have illuminated that global development will not take place simply through a transfer of technology and/or utilisation of more resources. 'Development' is a matter of sustainable, just and equitable utilisation and distribution of the resources at hand, and reduction of overconsumption patterns that overutilise limited resources. It would seem wise to insist that ethical commitments and ecological realities should inform economic strategy.

Re-imagining wealth as 'life-projects'

Raff Carmen, in quoting Ivan Illich, unveils a central problem of modernist economics: the *paradox of scarcity*. This idea expresses the 'truth' that, once people choose the option of modernist economics, there will never seem to be enough:

> Economics always implies scarcity. What is not scarce cannot be subjected to economic control. This is true of goods and services, as it is of work. The assumption of scarcity has penetrated all modern institutions. Education is built on the assumption that desirable knowledge is scarce. Medicine assumes the same about health, transportation about time ... Being immersed in it, we have become blind to the paradox that scarcity increases in a society with the rise of GNP. This kind of scarcity which we take for granted was – and largely still is – unknown outside commodity-intensive societies.
> (Carmen 1996: 59)

Working in Vanuatu has made the truth of Carmen's analysis very clear to Peter. The Paramount Chief of Vanuatu and some of his colleagues expressed it in these words:

> When we first visited your country [Australia] we were amazed at the wealth. Then we realised that if we aspired to this, changing from our underdeveloped economy to yours, we were destined to always be poor. We would only be aware of our scarcity of resources and riches. We would lose our self-respect and confidence. So we turned our back on that model and started rethinking our customary economy in which we have traditionally traded in shells, mats and other goods made and collected. We are very wealthy when our reference becomes these goods. So we are rebuilding our economy on this basis.

On one of these work trips, a colleague of Peter's handed the chiefs the book *Ancient Futures: Learning from Ladakh* (Norberg-Hodge 2009). It is a book about how some of the Ladakhi people of the Western Himalayas resisted 'development' and are returning to a human-scale, intimate, gentler, natural economy. The chiefs were astounded, and became totally absorbed with the story. For the Vanuatu chiefs, here was the story of a group of indigenous people far away geographically struggling with the very same thing they were.

Since then Peter has been working with the chiefs to rebuild an equivalent 'life-project' (Blaser *et al.* 2004; Westoby 2010) in which the aim is to develop a vision and strategy for their collective lives that is infused with their own definitions, goals for life and deliberation about how to connect needs and satisfiers (Max-Neef 1991) in ways that build such a life. It requires resistance to the respect-destroying version of life depicted by aspects of modernity. Rebuilding a life-project embraces the diverse economies framework (Gibson-Graham 2006), recognising that people can choose to participate in various economic practices, both capitalist and non-capitalist. This vision and strategy also engages with conventional development in numerous ways, including variations of assimilation, accommodation and resistance. This work with the chiefs of Vanuatu has given Peter cause to stop and reflect:

> It was in the context of such a conversation that I became more conscious of a lack of my own life-project. In the light of human-induced global warming I am becoming increasingly aware of my own vulnerability. Awareness grows that my work is so linked to a global cash economy and my personal food security is so deeply connected to the industrial food economy that I lack any self-reliance. Clearly one cannot go back to a pre-industrial age of self-sufficiency, nor am I particularly nostalgic about such an epoch; one is constantly reminded of how hard such a pre-industrial life is for many in rural Vanuatu. Yet I am gradually becoming conscious of participating in a completely unsustainable livelihood pattern. It becomes clearer that I live without a life-project that infuses me with a vision of how to live sustainably. I've become captive to the impulses of modern consumerism and addicted to an increasing amount of 'satisfiers'.

Peter's work with the chiefs also highlights the significance of a dialogical approach in that both chiefs and Peter were learning from the partnership. Development was not about a transfer of information, resources and technology from Australia to Vanuatu, but about a dialogical process of exchange in which both parties to the dialogue were opened up to new possibilities. The new possibilities opening up for Peter involved honest acknowledgement of something lacking in his development vision.

Such awareness is an imperative enabling community workers to give legitimacy to a new economic development vision. It starts with everyone – not everyone else! From that starting point it is possible to participate in a broad voluntary movement of community-oriented citizens willing to live simply while collectively modelling an alternative household and human-scale relational economy. In a parallel process, such a movement can also challenge state and transnational governance bodies to develop polices and initiatives that enable local, national and global economic and environmental justice. The movement consists of people able to acknowledge their own greed, selfishness and fear, and also able to live simply and ethically, enabling a global economic and ecological balance that cuts through both the underdevelopment that is killing others and the overdevelopment that is killing us.

Caring for politics

Rebuilding community-oriented places will require not only caring for the ordinary and the economic, but also vigorous processes of politicking. Dialogue and economic restructuring does not take place in a vacuum devoid of political processes. Politicking, while not being necessarily about party politics (which is not to say that people committed to community work should not be thoroughly involved in party politics) is most certainly about engaging with issues to do with power, democracy, participation and citizenship. This reflection on caring for politics considers the importance of democratic political processes within our dialogical approach to community work.

The project of democratising

One technical skill of community as dialogue is that of engaging with people's stories and accompanying them in the transformation of their own narratives. Dialogue requires more than just listening to people's narratives – it requires a transformation of narrative. Our Australian colleagues Anthony Kelly and Ingrid Burkett, drawing on the insights of Paulo Freire, set out how this transformation can be achieved through shifting narratives 'from nouns and adjectives to verbs' (2008: 39). For example, they write about how it is more useful to think of poverty as 'poverty-making', accurately implying that there are actors involved in a complex array of activities that lead to people's experiences of being poor – and that it is not just a 'given state of affairs' (ibid.) that people cannot do anything about. The understanding of poverty changes 'from a *state* to a *process*' (ibid.).

Democracy is a classic example of a term requiring this kind of grammatical transformation. Reframing the noun democracy as the verb *democratising* potentially highlights the social dynamics at work within any political process – usually either for or against the process of democratising. Democracy as noun is often talked about in binary terms of democratic–undemocratic, in which Australia or the USA and countries 'like us' are described as being democratic and 'other' countries as undemocratic. In contrast, the Derridean deconstructive movement destabilises this simplistic binary and invites the rethinking of democracy as a 'project of democratisation' requiring constant renewal.

Thinking and illuminating the contest over democracy can be transformed simply by 'getting some verbs into it'. If people are lacking the freedoms to engage around their concerns, there is a problem. If some people are protecting entrenched powerful interests or some key people are purposefully blocking engagement, then there is a risk that the project of democratisation will reach a state in which it has stalled. On the other hand, if people are actively engaging around their concerns or are challenging elites, then the project of democratising is a process that has some life in it, and all actors are determining its future.

One of the tasks as community development practitioners is to care for politics, because one of the crucial imperatives is the project of democratising all social, cultural, economic and political contexts. Democratisation is central to making the political sphere of participation meaningful whether that sphere is state, civil or customary. Democratisation is one of the cornerstones of an approach to community development in which people have a right to voice, can act publicly and are able to influence decision-making processes. Dialogue and deliberation thrive in a space where the project of democratising is vibrant and well. Many significant development outcomes – those that genuinely reflect the way people want to live – are dependent on people's democratic ability to participate in the process of deciding how they should live.

While arguing for a universal 'project of democratisation', we recognise that the *forms* of democracy emerging from that project will be shaped differently within different social, cultural, historical and economic geographies. What democracy looks like within Australia will be different from that emerging in Vanuatu or South Africa. Democratisation is however worth fighting for within any context: it is a universal desire and an instrumental imperative.

Supporting the public agora

So what does it mean to make the project of democratisation central to community practice? One of the classic essays on democracy was written by nineteenth-century French liberal Alexis de Tocqueville (1835), in which he used the concept of the *agora*. Originally the marketplace and meeting place of the city-states of classical Greece, the agora is understood by de Tocqueville as 'the assembly' where people's concerns are discussed collectively and publicly. Polish sociologist Zygmunt Bauman (1998: 86–7) likens the contemporary idea of civil society to the concept of the agora, seeing it as an interface between the public and private spheres of social life. Historically there has been an evolutionary process whereby the agora has, officially at least, been opened up to everyone. Originally in ancient Greece it was for 'citizens', defined as a particular group of men. In modern parliamentary democracy it has opened up to include almost everyone through universal suffrage. For Geoghegan and Powell in many ways the process of present-day community development 'may be conceptualised as the late modern agora – as the site of political, or at least politicised, assembly of citizens' (2009: 15).

From our perspective as community workers, democratisation involves supporting people on the margins to learn about the political system and how they can use it to take what they might have perceived as their private concerns into these public assemblies for discussion and dialogue. After all, feminists and others have taught us all that 'the personal is political, the private is often public'. In supporting people on the margins to access their right to practise democracy, community workers often take on a coaching role, or what we earlier called an accompanying role, walking *with* people and sharing with them what has been learned about influencing decision-making. In community groups this might mean, for example, standing with people who are being scapegoated or ostracised to stand up to bullies, find their allies, and work with others towards group processes that are inclusive and respectful. Here are some other examples:

> Our colleague Dave Andrews has found that, in Australian church contexts, the most marginalised people are those whose poor personal hygiene means they smell bad. Dave has supported many poor, smelly Christians to attend the service, talk to the Rector, get to know the church wardens, and cope with the formalities of participating in Parish Council!
>
> In a government context, we have found that politicians love their constituents, and so-called ordinary people can be very influential. For example, at a meeting with the Housing Minister, Gerard was one of several

well-informed, politically astute, professional housing advocates who found themselves sidelined as the Minister listened deeply to the everyday experience of the tenants in the delegation. These tenants were nervous but their personal stories and heartfelt analysis were highly influential. In another instance, a young person who bounced up to the Mayor at a youth festival and said 'we need a youth space in our suburb' was heard – and professionals were able to act on the 13 consultants' reports that had argued the same case over the previous seven years!

In supporting such people on the margins to voice their concerns, practitioners enter into a two-way process of nurturing democracy: democratising the people, and at the same time caring for and democratising the system – preserving the health of institutions ordering life by asking and supporting them to accommodate and respond to the full diversity of their constituency.

A dialogical approach to community development also orients practitioners to nurture multiple agoras as sites for people in dialogue and decision-making. The more human-scale agoras there are, the more the project of democratisation is working. Fiona Caniglia, a local colleague of ours, has worked with others to put two democratising grass-roots institutions into the fabric of politics in Brisbane: 'Politics in the Pub' invites politicians to meet their constituents on the ground of the constituents; and the CAN Awards are an annual recognition of the value of grass-roots contributions to the civic life of the city. There are many other examples from around the world. For example, the Sri Lankan citizen-led online journalism site Groundviews 'uses a range of genres and media to highlight alternative perspectives on governance, human rights, the arts and literature, peace building and other issues' (Groundviews 2012). Such citizen-led use of information and communication technologies, mobile devices and social media is creating new platforms for social change and democratisation in many places (Thomas and Bromley 2010).

Translating the private into the public

For community development workers another element of caring for the sphere of politics is the work of *translation* – ensuring people are able to take their private concerns into public assemblies. The process is one of people working *together* as an act not only of individual but also of collective citizenship. This is complex work. Sociologists and political scientists conceptualise the difficulties in terms that they call the 'agency-structure dilemma' (Giddens 1984; Bleiker 2000). Some argue that, while people can exercise agency (for our purposes as community workers, this means that people can act collectively in ways relevant to their concerns), the structures of society are all-powerful in denying or limiting the effectiveness of that agency. Many argue that structures related to class, gender, race, economic and political interests are so powerfully entrenched that it is naive to believe that people at the grass-roots can act to bring about change. But we are buoyed by the memory of occasions when people on the margins have realised that they are not isolated and powerless, and have taken their concerns into the public agora, sometimes finding unexpected support. We saw a beautiful example in Brisbane in 1988:

> A group of property owners and speculators calling themselves the West End Progress Association had been actively talking up the gentrification of the area and supporting property development. They began to move into the public arena, and started to get community and media support. They became bolder and more vocal and began making statements on behalf of the community.
>
> At this point, the local indigenous community started talking about the establishment of an indigenous cultural centre in Musgrave Park, a long-time meeting place for traditional and urban aborigines, including a group who lived on the streets and slept in the park, many drinking heavily. The Progress Association called a public meeting to oppose the initiative and propose to 'clean up' the park, seeking a public mandate for their campaign.
>
> On the evening of the meeting, hundreds of people gathered in the auditorium at the local high school – one of the biggest local gatherings we have ever seen. The Progress Association executive was beaming from behind its tables on the stage, and opened the meeting with invited speakers against the cultural centre. People began asking questions from the floor, and it started to become clear that a lot of people had not been convinced by the case put by the speakers, and that in fact there were many in the room who liked the idea of a new cultural centre and were keen to support the aspirations of the indigenous community.
>
> Eventually, it was Jim Bellas who exposed the sectional interests and the hidden agenda of greed at the heart of the meeting by asking one of the key speakers, 'Aren't you the guy who owns several properties in the area, who opposed public housing in your street, because it would lower your property values?' There was an outcry that confirmed the dominant mood of the meeting, and a buzz grew as people realised they were far from alone in their views. It was a magical moment when people realised the potential of collective citizenship: this was a public meeting, and the will of the people was looking for a way to be expressed. The few people who were still opposed to the cultural centre started to get up and leave and the Progress Association guys on the stage moved to close the meeting.
>
> Then Paddy Jerome, an old Aboriginal Anglican minister who saw the people of Musgrave Park as his flock, spoke from the back of the room: 'Mr Chairman. Before you close the meeting, I believe there is one more item of business.' The auditorium hushed as he made his way down the side of the packed hall, and slowly climbed the stairs on to the stage. He stood at the lectern, and spoke very clearly and with great care: 'I move that this public meeting SUPPORTS the establishment of an indigenous cultural centre at Musgrave Park.' There was a huge cheer – a near-unanimous endorsement of Paddy's courage in providing a touchstone that articulated the will of the people, and a sense of justice being done by the people themselves, in the face of those in power who had tried to manipulate the event to their own ends.

While stories like this keep community workers believing in the power of public expression of private concern in a democracy, it is important to develop a realistic approach to the complexities of caring for the political sphere. Care can be taken to avoid, on the one hand, believing that people can always (or even usually) make an easy translation of their private concerns into the public agora, and, on the other hand, giving up caring about such democratising processes. History has provided many cases of social transformation resulting from marginalised people's participation in decision-making processes as social and political agents. A realistic approach requires a deep care of the political process, and an even deeper – and tougher – commitment to keep trying to accompany people in translating their concerns while being conscious of the deep structural barriers to social change. Here is another story:

> For several years Peter has been following the work of the national Local Governance and Community Development Programme (LGCDP) in Nepal. This programme works with social mobilisers at village level to support change processes. Evaluations have shown that such mobilisers need to become citizen mobilisers, adept at supporting households, groups and communities to not only develop 'transactional' projects (economic and service-oriented), but also to develop 'transformational' processes that support people to have a voice (what we call translation), and actively participate in decision-making processes of local government and service-delivery agents (Jha *et al.* 2009). Furthermore, a crucial learning from this programme is that not only do the marginalised need support in gaining such voice, but capabilities need to be developed within government and service-delivery agents to be responsive and accountable to that voice. Overall, initiatives commonly known as 'social accountability' are necessary to support demand-oriented transformation of public bodies.

Community development workers, while involved in the praxis of supporting group processes of translation (in the above story also understood as transformational work), also need to be committed to the broader project of democratisation. This project requires a public sphere large enough, an agora creative enough, to engender the engagement of diverse groups – even those totally disagreed with. Within a thriving politic, diverse groups of people are all attempting to translate their concerns into the broader assembly. This is imagined as the role of the contemporary state: to be a public institution maintaining a thriving politic of debate and discussion. And while recognising the significance of the state we also imagine thriving debate and discussion within other political spheres ordering life, whether they are civic, customary or subaltern. Skilled community workers will nurture this broader diverse political project, while simultaneously supporting those on the margins, who usually have limited capacity for translation, to engage fully in democratising their contexts.

Constructive or destructive politicking

Drawing on the work of Belgian political scientist Chantal Mouffe (2005), it is useful to consider two possible constructive processes and one possible destructive process at work within such a pluralistic agora. Of the constructive, the first is that of public dialogue and the second is *agonistic* engagement. Within the first process, people move the dialogue on the basis that people and parties can listen to one another, understand one another, move towards one another, and develop some public agreement that encompasses the diversity of views. We do well when we foster the philosophy of Socrates, the ancient champion of dialogue who maintained that the purpose of dialogue is to discover and do what is right, and therefore valued the experience of being corrected or becoming convinced by others more than the experience of convincing them to adopt his views.

In contrast, agonistic engagement implies ongoing differences that are in some way irreconcilable, and yet there is still respectful engagement within that difference. People work to maintain some conversation despite the tension of disagreement. In agonistic politics there is often an adversarial but still respectful social relationship. It acknowledges both the legitimacy of the other's position and the legitimacy of contested ground in democracy. Both of these dialogical and agonistic approaches can be understood as pro-social and are informed by an orientation of hospitality in the sense that attention is given to the other as human, and therefore as worthy of respect.

However, sometimes dialogical or agonistic engagement deteriorates into a somewhat destructive *antagonistic* relationship in which the other is no longer seen as a legitimate opponent or adversary, but an enemy who is considered illegitimate. There is little space for respect; political relationships and activities are devoid of social foundations. They may have lost their soul; and they are probably moving towards violence. The implications of this should be clear: nurture a body politic that maintains respect at its centre. Within the agora, community workers can hope for dialogue towards consensus, they can at least work for agonistic engagement and they can work against antagonistic dynamics.

There is another chapter in the story of the Musgrave Park cultural centre public meeting that illustrates some of the potential and limitations of dialogue or agonistic politics:

> In the weeks following the public meeting, a group of those who had connected at the meeting banded together to attend the next few meetings of the Progress Association, and attempted to continue the dialogue over the preferred future of our neighbourhood. At the first meeting the Progress Association executive sat at the front of a room facing rows of chairs. It was not long before one of the local rat-bags called on the group sitting in rows to move their chairs into a circle, and the executive to join them. Unfortunately, the Progress Association were not open to other views, were not willing to give up their power, and reacted as though this was a hostile takeover – they stopped attending their own meetings. The opportunity for dialogue was lost. The organisation faded quickly from public view. We assume they

continued to pursue their own sectional interests together, but they did not seek a public mandate again.

Reflection on this story, one of antagonistic politics, invites consideration of the need for openness from all parties in the process of agonistic engagement, the difficulty of holding sectional self-interest in dialogue, and the messiness that people bring, with their complex personalities, agendas and egos, as they engage in public processes.

The struggle over community as a paradigmatic site

A final reflection on caring for the political sphere re-engages with the thinking of Jacques Derrida (2001). Derrida understood community not only as hospitality, but also as a discourse that has become what he calls a *paradigmatic site*. In this sense paradigms are linked sets of ideas, concepts or processes that provide an explanation and justification for a particular view of reality. Derrida argues that, once a particular view of reality becomes dominant, then social and political processes regulate and discipline people into certain ways of ethical being, thinking and behaving that are consistent with such a view. Derrida's insight is that community, as a paradigmatic site, is becoming an important locus of struggle in the regulating and disciplining processes of ordering how people live. Community development practitioners are a part of this struggle – contesting the meaning of community when the term is used in ways that are antithetical to hospitality and solidarity.

For example, in countries such as the UK and Australia, community is now being constructed as a place only for 'civil people'. People are constantly told they must act and behave in particular kinds of social ways, and are conversely called anti-social if they do not. Peter was recently walking the streets of Dublin in Ireland and was struck by the number of signs informing citizens that they 'were under CCTV surveillance due to anti-social behaviour'. 'Anti-social' is perceived to be anti-community – which, from the perspective articulated within this book, resonates with sanitised conceptions of community as some kind of place without problems. Until 2010 in the UK there were anti-social behaviour orders, or ASBOs, which were politically sanctioned punishments against those considered uncivil. There appears to be the re-establishment of a moralistic order echoing pre-1960s' notions of deserving and undeserving, based on simplistic binaries such as deviance and normality.

In a parallel process in Australia, community is now a discursive site not only for civil people but for 'responsible workers'. Within this discursive frame people are deemed to be pro-community if they are responsible workers and taxpayers first. Citizenship, with its accompanying rights, becomes a secondary concern. For example, the Australian government-sponsored *Welfare to Work* programmes reorient people's self-perception in the light of this discursive pressure. If someone is not first and foremost a responsible worker – that is, if they are unemployed – then they are not fulfilling a social contract called 'mutual obligation'. To break that social contract incurs loss of income security and transformation into a *non-citizen* of community life. Fuelled by this kind of thinking, community becomes closely associated with its etymological roots that have previously been described as munitions. Within this approach, people invoking community are in fact meaning such things as: 'Get out' and 'You are not welcome here', or adding, 'If you live here we have the right to engage in surveillance over your life' and 'You are to become like us.' It is the world of the gated community. It is hardly community as hospitality and dialogue.

Within such a context one of the challenges for community development workers is to then care for the political sphere through entering this discursive struggle over community with a different understanding and therefore a destabilising agenda. The agenda argued for in this book is that of community as an open site of dialogue and hospitality to the other – others who are different, strangers, young, non-consumers, non-producers, instrumentally non-useful, old, disabled, deviant, refugee, asylum seekers and so on. Such people will often fall out of the bounded sets of so-called, self-defined 'civil people', 'workers' and 'responsible people'. Derrida's invitation is instead for 'communities of hospitality', 'community as hospitality' and, fundamentally, 'community as ethics' (Caputo 1997a: 124).

Caring for the cultural

Alluding to such hospitality, dialogue and ethics we now turn to a concern about caring for the cultural sphere, first focusing on the issue of diversity. We argue that, in the same way that genetic diversity enables a biosphere to survive change, so cultural diversity enables rapidly changing communities to not only survive but thrive (Capra 1994: 10). In the light of this, a core assumption of our development practice is that cultural diversity enables people to deal creatively and imaginatively with challenging issues. A communal monoculture may lead to a lack of imagination and therefore a lack of transformative options. Within this assertion are not only instrumental hopes – that diversity enhances a community's capacity and transformative options – but also aesthetical hopes – diverse cultures and many of their accompanying social practices make life more interesting and exciting!

In *Ecology and Community*, Fritjof Capra outlines the dynamics and conditions of an alternative kind of generative community characterised by diversity, but complemented by a vibrant network:

> Diversity means many links, many different approaches to the same problem. So a diverse community is a resilient community. A diverse community is one that can adapt to changing situations, and therefore diversity is another very important principle of ecology ... But it's not always a great advantage, and this is what we can learn from ecosystems. Diversity is a strategic advantage for a community if, and only if, there is a vibrant network of relationships, if there is a free flow of information through all the links of the network. Then diversity is a tremendous strategic advantage. However, if there is fragmentation, if there are subgroups in the network or individuals

who are not really part of the network, then diversity can generate prejudice, it can generate friction, and as we know well from our inner cities, it can generate violence.

(1994: 10)

This is why it is imperative to develop an approach to community development that has an appreciation of both the fragility and the importance of cultural diversity, acknowledging the accompanying complexities. Here is one of Peter's experiences:

> The work of building diverse community that celebrates and loves difference is fragile. I have spent the past several years involved with diverse refugee groups in my home town of Brisbane. This involvement has made me aware of huge human diversity, the complexities of human relationships, and the challenges of community cohesion and coexistence within many of our contemporary social geographies. For example, my work over years with Sudanese refugees has immersed me in the complexities of coexistence:
>
> - between ethnic groups or tribes from within Sudan – many of whom have been fighting against one another for years;
> - between religious groups – Arab northern and western versus Christian southern and eastern Sudanese who have been at war for decades;
> - conflicts of generation and gender;
> - between Sudanese and other recently arrived groups, such as those from the former Yugoslavia or from nations of the Pacific;
> - between Sudanese and Australia's indigenous peoples;
> - between Sudanese and many Anglo-Australians, such as the older woman from a white working-class suburb who rang the police, because there was a group of young black men in the park near her home:
>
> 'Are they threatening you?'
> 'No.'
> 'Are they misbehaving?'
> 'No.'
> 'What are they doing?'
> 'They are kicking a ball around.'

Each of these challenges to cohesion and coexistence is also immersed within broader national and international discourses – that are currently 'anti-Arab', hostile to Muslims, and fearful of 'others' (Hage 1998, 2003).

Clearly working within this kind of complexity is a significant challenge for community development workers in the context of increasing migration and the resulting demographic diversity. Accompanying this is a growing fear of the other as strangers, portrayed as dangerous, destabilising and threatening. It follows then that this aspect of community development is crucial in an age where some people can say, 'genocide is an act of community-building' (Szeman 2000). Many intercultural conflicts and wars are legitimised in the name of 'community' – the kind of community not oriented towards hospitality but instead towards 'wall-building' (Brown 2010). With such thoughts in mind, it makes sense for practitioners to address the question: How do we nurture diversity in the fragile web of social relationships that are at the heart of hospitable and dialogical community?

Being hospitable to the enemy within: an ethic of plurality

It appears that many of us live and work in times and places where, more than ever, people need to face and love their differences. As alluded to in the previous paragraph, societies around the world are threatened with potential chaos and political disintegration. With the fear generated by such potential there is a tendency to project the enemy on to the other – whether it be Muslims, gays, whites, blacks, conservatives, liberals, greens or socialists – and such a tendency could easily lead society in a downward spiral of endless exclusion and expanding violence. Our response to this tendency is to argue that it is imperative that people cultivate an ecological attitude that affirms cultural diversity *and* organic connections. The way to achieve this is to understand and practise hospitality in a way that people have rarely had to practise it before.

Learning about hospitality requires facing this enemy within ourselves, and becoming hospitable to that enemy – an enemy that demonises others. This is a challenge: a dialogical approach to community practice means first a dialogue with ourselves, understanding the shadow parts within – acknowledging that deep inside many of us there are racist, sexist, bigoted, class-conscious selves.

A dialogical approach that reawakens love is not afraid of such selves. Cultivating a love for these selves enables individuals to look them in the eye and transcend them. It is possible to be friends with the enemy within and find less need to look for the enemy 'out there'. In doing this people are free to utilise what culture and intelligence has taught – to 'be ethical' with the full knowledge of who we are. People can develop what William Connolly (1999) calls an ethic of cultivation, cultivating a deep plurality within ourselves, and then also in our neighbourhoods and our nations.

Fostering centripetal dynamics of connection

There are also many centrifugal social dynamics at work, pushing people apart, creating distance and disconnection. They fragment and disintegrate the possibility of community as dialogue and hospitality. Many interest groups actively work against a socio-cultural configuration that affirms diversity and connectivity. They do not want to see people coming together to hear one another's stories. They see community as an opportunity to build walls (Brown 2010).

Obviously we see one of the roles of community development workers as recognising, naming and opposing such distancing and disconnecting centrifugal dynamics, and instead nurturing centripetal dynamics that bring people together to listen to one another, learn from one another, and creatively find solutions for living together. The challenge is to create platforms that enable such listening and learning to take place. Here is another story:

In 2010 Peter was visiting the UK, conducting research around intercultural youth conflict and violence. During that research trip one highlight was visiting the community organisation Peacemaker, located in Oldham on the outskirts of Manchester. The organisation had been set up in 1997 by a group of young British Asians, 'deeply concerned by the depressing slide into segregation which they were witnessing around them' (Peacemaker 2012).

As a response Peacemaker set out to reverse this 'slide' by cultivating opportunities for young people from different communities and ethnicities to meet one another. Initiated by young people themselves, Peacemaker drew on networks and contacts to foster deep plurality in the neighbourhoods of Oldham. They have played a key role in fostering active engagement of young people, nurturing community cohesion and identifying strategic initiatives. They work with young people directly – both in and out of schools – and with adults and community groups, creating spaces where people can first come to terms with their prejudices and, second, take this learning and apply it within their own communities.

(Peacemaker 2004, 2006)

This story is representative of so many grass-roots organisations working hard to reverse centrifugal trends and to instead foster centripetal community dynamics. When platforms for dialogue have been laid in which people of difference have come together, then places that thrive are more possible – they are ecologically sound and balanced, full of vitality, and capable of transformation.

Earth care

Having considered the need to care for the ordinary, the economy, politics and the cultural, we now turn to what many, including ourselves, consider to be one of the most challenging imperatives of our day: care for the earth. The Earth Policy Institute has calculated that globally an investment of approximately $110 billion per year is needed to restore health to the planet (Brown 2012). A few years ago this scale of investment may have seemed impossible, but as was seen in early 2009 during the global financial crisis, governments around the world were able to pump much more than this into rescue packages for a failing global economy. Many, including the Australia Institute, saw the irony. They argued that:

> The most interesting thing about the worldwide approach to bailing out the financial system is how pragmatic policy-makers have been. No one, from the US Treasury Secretary to [then Australian Prime Minister] Kevin Rudd, will put their hand on their heart and say they understand the full nature and extent of the problem.
>
> Nor will they look the voters in the eye and declare that, after spending trillions of dollars to bail out banks, they are certain that the problem will be solved. On the contrary – when it comes to the world of finance, we all have to accept just how complex the systems are. We can't really expect certainty, and we can't really guarantee success. Rather, we all just have to comfort

ourselves with the thought that it would be irresponsible to sit back and do nothing. It is, it seems, self-evident that we should at least try.

But not, apparently, when it comes to climate change. Even though most of our bankers can't explain the risks associated with the derivatives they have purchased over the years, our climate scientists are expected to be able to predict the weather to a high degree of accuracy in 70 years' time. Even though economists can't predict the rate of GDP growth, inflation or the exchange rate next month, those determined to do nothing about climate change demand certainty about what the price of emissions permits will be in 20 years' time.

In the last month, trillions of dollars have been found [to bail out banks]. New regulations have been introduced. And countries have all committed to work collectively in the pursuit of a common goal. Unfortunately, none of this effort has been aimed at reducing greenhouse gas emissions; it has been aimed at something far more important – sustaining the banking system as we know it.

(Australia Institute 2008)

This Australia Institute commentary illuminates the ideological 'smoke and mirrors' game represented by vested interests wanting the current economic trajectory and logics to remain in place, while choosing to block ecological investments. Today's powerful interest groups appear to prefer focusing on climate adaptation – both technical and political – rather than investing in ecological mitigation (Parenti 2011). An alternative ecological investment, focused more on mitigation, as advocated by the Earth Policy Institute, would enable work on projects such as reforestation, stabilising water tables, protecting biological diversity, restoring fisheries, restoring rangelands and protecting topsoil on croplands, while trying ultimately to decarbonise the economy. Such an investment is deeply connected to also caring for the economy, politics and the cultural as outlined previously.

In many ways 'earth care' represents the convergent needs of caring for all of the spheres discussed within this chapter together. To focus only on one represents an analytical failure to see how a crisis of one sphere amplifies another 'expressing itself through another' (ibid.: 7). Current economic models are destroying the earth, and now the earth needs restoration. More human-scale, people-centred and relational economics are required. The current political stasis has resisted effective translation of many ecological concerns into the public agora. Governments around the world, in collusion with corporations and many citizens, have ignored the plight of the whole life-support system – they/we are in denial (Homer-Dixon 2006; Parenti 2011).

The dark spectre that sits behind this possible collapse of the earth is of course human-induced global warming, watered down in name by governments and other stakeholders as 'climate change' – giving the impression that human activity is not a key cause. Here the interface between a truly global issue and local places is profound. In the Pacific there is the rapidly approaching need of 'environmental refugees' from places such as Kiribati, with their President travelling to New

Zealand in 2008 looking for a new home for his nation. In Asia, consider Aceh and its vulnerability when the 2004 Boxing Day tsunami struck, and large areas of Bangladesh that are under threat of disappearing should ocean levels continue to rise. In Africa, Ethiopia is experiencing more famine as weather patterns make sustainable agriculture more difficult. In Australia increasing ferocity of drought and fire make life tenuous in both cities and the bush. As political geographer Christian Parenti argues within *Tropic of Chaos: Climate Change and the New Geography of Violence* (2011), across vast geographical tracts, mainly between the Tropics of Cancer and Capricorn, where climate change is more felt, there is an emergent catastrophic convergence of crises (ibid.: 7). Earth care is the arena in which the biggest challenge is to act locally *and* globally, avoiding the binary of either–or.

Working locally and globally

People working together as communities can act both locally and globally. As noted previously, the word 'economy' is closely connected to the notion of household, which is also the starting place of earth care. Household action is the initial base for taking responsibility. George Monbiot's book *Heat* (2007) has already been mentioned as one example of a treatise on how to make significant changes at the household level. The permaculture movement has shown how people can grow food within households and local neighbourhoods, and how appropriate technologies can be utilised to enhance local food production. Earth care does not imply a Luddite anti-technological stance.

However, the household is not the only level of involvement in earth care. The contribution of community development is in mobilising people collectively to participate in these issues at every level of the public agora. People with a vision for earth care can be involved in local councils, regional organisations, national initiatives and of course global alliances. To put it bluntly, there is the need to scale up and across household-like action in a massive way to make the kind of ecological impact required to restore any semblance of health to the planet.

Alternative institutions

In participating in this multiple-level agora it is also important to be clear about strategy. We draw on North American eco-philosopher Joanna Macy (1983) who, along with Molly Young Brown (Macy and Brown 1998), provides a useful framework for conceptualising strategic options, signposting three key ways forward. The first strategy involves 'analysis of structural causes and creating of alternative institutions' (ibid.:19). This strategy requires understanding the dynamics of the current military-industrial growth system. Macy and Brown pose questions such as, 'What are the tacit agreements that create obscene wealth for a few, while progressively impoverishing the rest of humanity?' and 'What interlocking causes indenture us to an insatiable economy that uses our larger body, Earth, as supply house and sewer?' (ibid.). Many other questions could be asked and myriad social movements are at the forefront of asking them – and in doing that are challenging powerful interests.

124   *Caring for community life*

However, as community practitioners we are challenged to not only tackle the causes of the problems, but also create new institutions that reflect the 'dreams' of new ways of consuming, growing, producing, commuting, working and travelling. At a local level the dream is created and modelled through community initiatives such as re-localisation work, transition town initiatives, community gardens, city farms, community-supported agriculture (CSA), permaculture demonstration sites, bicycle and car co-operatives, local energy production, new public transport systems, and bikeways. The work then needs to be structured through macro and meta processes (see Chapter 3) of organisation into coalitions, federations and networks of groups and organisations that have the capacity to scale-up or -across such work on a much broader level. Here is a story of scaling-across:

> The Northey Street City Farm in Brisbane continues to be a source of inspiration in modelling an alternative mode of production. Local people come together and work in the gardens, learning about sustainable urban agriculture. The farm brings refugee groups together to grow their own kinds of food. It fosters awareness and celebration of earth cycles with annual harvest and equinox festivals. It supplies organic plants, food and seeds through the markets and nursery. However, it has also become a hub for diffusing ideas and building a network of community gardens across the city.

The building of such a network is an example of a scaling-across process, enabling local work to connect to broader social processes of change.

Changing hearts and minds

Macy and Brown's second strategy calls for a 'change to hearts and minds' (1998: 21). This requires careful and honest dialogue with ourselves and with other people around the concern of earth care. Dialogue should be gentle so as to draw people in, enabling them to overcome fear, apathy, selfishness and ignorance. For Macy and Brown, such dialogue is aimed at shifting 'perceptions of reality, both cognitively and spiritually' (ibid.).

Initiatives such as the *Roots of Change* study circles developed by the International Society for Ecology and Society show how people-in-places can structure up strategies for changing hearts and minds. Conversation groups, coffee circles, reading groups and Politics in the Pub are all processes that can be engaged in the gentle but critical work of changing people's hearts and minds. In South Africa our friends Allan Kaplan and Sue Davidoff, with other colleagues, have established the Proteus Initiatives and Towerland retreat centre. Their work focuses on creating a learning environment that fosters ecological ways of living through reconnecting with nature. Schumacher College within the UK is another of our favourite sustainability-oriented educational organisations endeavouring to change the hearts and minds of many people.

One of the challenges is to embark on these difficult conversations with people who do not currently share the same concern. The planet seems to be at an ecological tipping point. People's consciousness about the issues and urgency is shifting in such a way that what Macy (1983) calls 'The Great Turning' *might* be occurring. However, plenty of people are still not convinced of the ecological challenge, or if convinced, are simply unable to act purposefully to bring about change in their lives or neighbourhoods. Rather than engage such people through disseminating more information, community workers could make a critical contribution by opening up new conversations infused with the practice of dialogue, creating spaces and platforms for ordinary people to reveal their fears, come to terms with their doubts, and gradually to embrace alternatives. Within these conversations, practitioners need to be equipped with stories of alternatives – models of how people can live new lives in their local neighbourhoods – and stories of how people have bonded and banded together to challenge corporate and governmental power that is blocking such change.

Holding actions

Macy and Brown's third strategy is that of 'holding actions' in which some people mobilise around the issue of protecting environmental sites that others are still trying to utilise in unsustainable ways (1998: 17). This strategy requires still more radical action, which will probably mean confrontation. Although within this book we have advocated dialogue as the primary means of engagement, we have also recognised the importance of agonistic politics, often embodied in more visible and dramatic public actions:

> Within his visits to South Africa over several years Peter has been keeping tabs on the community mobilisation processes against the plans of Royal Dutch Shell and SASOL (the South African owned nationalised oil company) to conduct gas extraction, or hydro-*fracking* in the Karoo Desert. Many people are deeply concerned about the impacts of this technologically and chemically laden process on the quality of ground and surface water. Over the past few years there has been a mass mobilisation process led by farmers and other groups arguing that not enough is yet known about the impacts of these technologies and chemicals on the water tables. These mobilisations represent 'holding actions' indicating, in this case, that people who live close to and off the land want to protect the water and land for more sustainable purposes.

Certainly as we follow the increasing expansion of mining and logging interests around the world, from Panama and India, through to Ecuador and Mongolia, there seems to also be a groundswell of resistance. Many people, particularly indigenous groups, want to hold on to their land and their older more sustainable practices of livelihood and resist the extractive practices of modernity.

For some commentators (Guardiola-Rivera 2010) some of the most significant challenges of the twenty-first century are between an indigenous and an industrial worldview. The latter is focused on expropriation, expansion and growth; the former on interconnectedness, sustainability and wholeness. Indigenous nations around the world, each with its own particular worldview, are engaged in deep struggles to maintain their living cultures (ibid.) as opposed to being assimilated into consumer cultures. Many are also fighting literally for survival against the monolith of corporate turbo-capitalism (Roy 2011). Our practice is one that values and supports such living culture, attempting to create space for indigenous peoples to maintain languages, initiate intergenerational projects that keep culture alive and to foster ongoing memory.

In conclusion it might also be useful to remember that, for many people around the world, earth care does not just represent issues of conservation – instead it is about survival. Many people in the world live off the bountiful supply of the 'global commons', but this commons is increasingly being fenced in by the colonising actions of corporations in collusion with governments. For example, national parks are formed that marginalise tribal people from their livelihoods; corporations as well as illegal groups overfish areas that destroy the fishing commons for local villages; and forests are logged as export crops, destroying local commons food sources and water tables.

At the core of a commitment to earth care in community practice is then a commitment to the local and global commons (Poteete *et al.* 2010). Modernity and capitalism enclose all spaces within a profiteering economic grasp. The practice of guarding some local and global spaces from this encroachment is becoming ever more critical (Patel 2009; Harvey 2011).

Summing up

Words such as *critical* and *imperative* have echoed through Chapter 5. These words have not been chosen lightly. They are infused with passion, belief and hope. They have been chosen to highlight the importance of community development impacting on these key spheres of community life.

The first reflection explored caring for the *ordinary life* of community: valuing the mundane, the commonplace, and the everyday events that are the social glue connecting ordinary people with one another. As workers, we probably need to be less busy and less idealistic, and attend to the challenge to do ordinary things with extraordinary love.

The second reflection considered the impact of growth-oriented, free-market capitalism on communities, and explored the building of alternative, local, human-scale, *relational economies* with social and ecological objectives. At the same time as these economies are revitalised, people need to be challenging the state and transnational governance bodies to develop policies that enable local, national and global economic justice. A movement is needed of people who acknowledge their own greed, selfishness and fear, and yet choose to live simply and ethically. This would promote a global economic and ecological balance that cuts through both the underdevelopment that is killing others and the overdevelopment that is killing us.

The third reflection considered the importance of democratic *political processes* within community work. People begin the process by transforming their understanding of the world so that it enables agency, moving from private concern to public action. This is the beginning of a wider project of democratising all our social, cultural, economic and political contexts. We reflected on the need to support the public agora through different 'people's assemblies', and the work of *translation* – ensuring that people connected in community are able to collectively take their private concerns into the public assembly. In this context, we care for politics by nurturing both dialogue towards agreement, and dialogue in the tension of disagreement; and by defending democracy through resistance to antagonistic and exclusionary politics.

The fourth reflection looked at caring for the *cultural sphere* of community life, by nurturing diversity in the fragile web of social relationships that are at the heart of community. We argued for an approach to community development oriented towards an appreciation of both the fragility and the importance of a diverse community ecology. The practice of being hospitable to the enemy within requires cultivating an ethic of plurality and fostering centripetal dynamics of connection that bring people together.

The fifth reflection considered the urgent and imperative need to *care for the earth*. Governments around the world, in collusion with corporations and many people, have ignored the plight of our whole life-support system on planet earth. They are either in denial or focused on political adaptation attempting to protect their interests. However, people working together as communities can act both locally and globally. To put it bluntly, action on a massive scale is necessary to make the kind of ecological impact required to restore any semblance of health to the planet and avoid a catastrophic convergence of crises.

Recently Peter heard someone say, 'What's economics got to do with community development?' We imagine different people asking the same question in relation to any of the spheres of community life discussed above: 'What's politics got to do with community development?' and so forth. We hope you are now convinced of their relevance.

6 Dialogue and training for transformation

Chapter 3 considered how a dialogical approach is diffused into transformative community work processes. This chapter goes further to explore transformational training as a way of engaging people in community development work. In many ways the chapter makes more transparent our indebtedness to the 'social learning' tradition of community development (Campfens 1997) that informs a dialogical framework of practice. As stated in the Introduction to this book, dialogue locates the work within an orientation of learning. So while much community development is about organising, mobilising, building and so forth, we see these as emerging from the process of people learning *together* about their world.

In naming this chapter, we have drawn on the title of Hope and Timmel's (1984) classic handbook *Training for Transformation*, again located clearly and explicitly within the Freirean approach to dialogue within community development. However, we use the term 'training' carefully and offer the following caveat. Brookfield and Holst (2010) note that training is often used within discourses of vocational and workplace training. The focus of such training is on instruction and the underpinning philosophy is usually a neo-liberal political economy whereby training needs are driven by employer needs. They argue, in a way that is similar to our Australian and South African experiences, that the 'term training has suffered a downgrading to the point that ... many adult educators in North America [and elsewhere] ... avoid using the word' (ibid.: 66). In contrast, a different reading of the training landscape provides examples of training being used within more radical traditions – often focused on democratic and participatory processes. For example, Brookfield and Holst discuss, among others: the Highlander Folk School with its focus on leadership training and training for citizenship; the Citizenship Schools of the 1960s and their training of teachers; the Sandinista National Literacy Crusade in Nicaragua, focused on training local people and local leaders; and Brazil's Landless Workers Movement, with its training of people in co-operatives.

In distilling the practices of such a radical training tradition they identified the following key themes:

- training as the mastery of action (practice) and the mastery of principle (theory) conceived dialectically;

- a central element is affective and relational – building the skills, understanding, and confidence of people;
- a significant amount of training takes place in the actual activities of social movements: it is training in action;
- training is a mutual relationship where both the trainer and the trainee are trained;
- training is participatory and democratic in methodology;
- training is not neutral: it is oriented to serving the needs of specific sectors of society; it attempts to advance social change activism towards a more participatory and democratic society; it is, therefore, as much a political act as it is a pedagogical act.

(ibid.: 85)

With this kind of genealogy of training as a foundation we feel more than comfortable talking about *training* for transformation.

In this chapter Martin Buber's term of 'possibilitator' (Yalom 1980: 409) has also been appropriated to describe the kind of change agents that are to be supported through such transformational training. Part of our strategy for building a just world is to nurture a network of people understood as possibilitators, who are skilled as catalysts for transformative work. Through our work experience we have realised that what is crucial to effective community development is not lots of money; neither is it buildings and infrastructure – clinics, schools, roads or water. Instead what is crucial is the quality, creativity and analysis of people who dream of a better world for their shanty-towns, neighbourhoods or villages and want to take some form of public, collective and transformational action.

Our use of 'possibilitators' is also informed, or more accurately inspired, by Derrida's deconstructionist hope that the possibility of things is 'sustained by their impossibility' (Caputo 1997a: 32). For example, for Derrida, law that represents justice is something impossible to attain – once people believe they have arrived at law that represents justice, the dialogue about what law and justice mean and how they relate together becomes ossified. Injustice then triumphs. Drawing on such a perspective then alludes to the impossibility of much of what is yearned for within a progressive and ethical project of community development. It is the ongoing dialogue that is crucial – it is history unfolding. However, in highlighting such a proposition about impossibility, Derrida also proposes that the impossible remains possible – as a gift, a hope, a telos. For us, change agents as possibilitators signify the impossible dream of emancipation and yet the ongoing commitment to working that dream out in dialogue and practice.

Furthermore, drawing on the Italian revolutionary Antonio Gramsci, such possibilitators are imagined to be the 'organic intellectuals' of community life (Mayo 1999; Ledwith 2005). They are people who dare to think and act differently in the face of the hegemony that determines how much of current social life is perceived and lived. Many readers would possibly be more comfortable with the idea of 'transformative leaders'. While happy to also use such a term,

130 Dialogue and training for transformation

we prefer 'organic intellectuals' and 'possibilitators' for the extent to which they signify slightly different intensions; that is, bringing second-order change that transforms people's capacities not only to survive the current system but also to change the actual system itself.

We propose that community development workers have an important role in providing a transformational training space, enabling possibilitators and organic intellectuals to develop their dreaming and also their skills and strategies. These change agents can model a new attitude, a new caring and a new vision. They are people who can bring a fresh energy and who can facilitate the awakening of awareness, imagination and powerful action. They are people who can create a fresh dialogue and hold it open with integrity, hospitality, depth, respect and solidarity. In our experience some of the most exciting work has happened when a cadre of such possibilitators has come together with the intention of defending a locality, transforming a sociality, or prosecuting a cause. There is great camaraderie in the shared work. There is great resource in the soulful stories and hard-earned life experiences of any group of diverse and committed people.

For some people, the notion of change agent reflects a modernist and ultimately colonial approach to development. They question why any kind of expert or outside knowledge is needed to bring change and development. For many people, the idea of an education or training role implies that someone 'knows better'. As trainers we are very appreciative of this critique and recognise the potential dangers of change agents in many cases – that of easily slipping into colonial or neo-colonial thinking and practices, or disembedding work from local sociocultural roots, as discussed in Chapter 2. However, as Miles Horton and Paulo Freire argue within the book *We Make the Road by Walking: Conversations on Education and Social Change* (Bell *et al.* 1990), it is important to develop an approach to education and training that both respects people and honours their knowledge – avoiding colonial approaches to practice – and yet can 'move' people into new understandings of their world. One of our training mantras, one learned but adapted from Freire's work, is 'always start with the people, but don't stay there' (ibid.: 66). Social change does require new ways of thinking and acting, and often therefore some kind of movement.

This chapter presents some simple signposts to rethinking community development work in training such possibilitators and organic intellectuals. These signposts include: education as a spacious soulful imagining; texts and stories as resources for sparking re-imagination; methods and models for transformative training; the significance of inspiration and empowerment, not information; and finally, the logic of wishing, willing and action.

In our approach to facilitating learning we use processes both of training (focused on learning and practising skills) and education (a broader process focused on building understanding). It is helpful to make the distinction between the two. We can make it clear by way of an example. Imagine your child, favourite nephew, father, maiden aunt or partner is going to sex education. Now imagine they are going to sex training. You can easily imagine the difference. With the former you would be fine; with the latter you may be hesitant, to say the least!

Space to re-imagine

One way of understanding the broader context for training change agents is as a failure of the imagination of modernity. A failure of imagination implies that most people can no longer imagine a community or society based on anything other than *what is*. The media have dominated people's dreams; formal education systems have dominated people's minds; people's heads are so busy with the information superhighway that they have lost the capacity to imagine a world that might be different. There is little space to dream; little space to articulate alternative models of living; little space to re-imagine community – altogether too little space to create a society in which people care for the earth, economy and *polis* in a new way. There appear to be no other possibilities.

The worlds taken for granted are an imaginative construct

It would be clear to the reader by now that it is an assumption of our approach to community work theory and practice that the worlds taken for granted in the economic, political, cultural, ecological and social spheres are an imaginative construct. As constructs, these worlds can be imagined differently from other perspectives. It follows then that such imaginative constructs can be challenged, and counter-givens entertained. Recognition of these processes of challenging and entertaining is central to the goal of rethinking training within a dialogical approach to community development. We suggest that people can gain new imaginative literacy with the nurturing of an appropriate kind of transformational training space. Such spaces are explored below.

It should also be noted that the goal is not to create a new hegemony in terms of what *should be*, but to create a transformational training space that enables participants and possibilitators-in-dialogue with others to imagine new possibilities for our world.

Creating space for imaginative literacy

The story below illustrates a problem that many people have, being so preoccupied within the parameters defined by the current 'given', that there is very little space to begin imagining a new world:

> A young, highly intelligent, and most accomplished young student wished to have an audience with the Grand Master. The young student sat down and the Master asked if he wished to have a drink of tea. The student said yes, and the Master started to pour. He poured the tea until the glass was full, and then continued to pour until the glass was overflowing, and still kept on pouring. The student jumped up, startled by the tea flooding over the table top and down onto his legs, 'Master, the cup is full to overflowing!' The Master continued to pour, the tea spilling out onto the table and floor. 'As you are,' the Master replied.
>
> (Patkar 2006: 34)

132 *Dialogue and training for transformation*

To nurture imaginative literacy, space and silence are needed; or to work with the metaphor, it is crucial to stop pouring tea into a full glass and find another glass. In Peter's life there is a recurring dream reminding him of this lack of space:

> In the dream I am usually trying to do something or go somewhere. I am racing for a plane or a taxi and I am trying to fill my bag or pack. I always have problems filling my bag – some items fall out or refuse to remain attached. I often miss the plane or taxi. In my dream I am then presented with an alternative; usually it is someone, a friend or relative, who is sitting silently or walking up into the mountain to meditate.

For Peter the dream has become a story, an image that presents options for living. One way is *doing* – the way of the activist; the other is that of *being* – retreat, silence, attention and conversation with others that can spark imagination. Neither option in isolation is the correct way; there is the need for both. Such a middle path cultivates *both* engagement with the world and time taken out, alone or with others to re-imagine a new world.

Creating spaces that support imaginative literacy

The training work of re-imagining can be nurtured almost anywhere. We have sat with groups of people in caravan parks in the suburbs, in garages beneath community organisation offices, and under huge trees in Vanuatu and Papua New Guinea. These are people's spaces. We are not advocating a training approach that creates spaces disconnected from people's realities, or removed from their everyday world. It is best if possibilitators are not removed from their lived settings, so that the process of regaining imaginative literacy is connected to their daily endeavours.

Emotionally, the spaces need to be safe. A safe space does not mean that boundaries are not pushed, or that 'givens' are not destabilised. Training for transformation can well be painful. Nevertheless the training setting must be a space in which people do not feel that they will be coerced or attacked. George Lakey (2010) refers to such a safe space as 'the container', arguing that:

> there are boundaries to learn, people need to risk: to revise their conceptual framework, try a new skill, unlearn an old prejudice and admit there's something they don't know. To risk, people need safety. To be safe, they need a group and/or a teacher that supports them.
>
> (ibid.: 14)

Geometrically, the spaces are usually circles, disrupting tendencies for domination and therefore opening space for dialogue. As University of Washington researcher Tracy Thompson puts it:

> in a *well-functioning* Circle, members experience a strong sense of belonging, a compelling commitment to shared goals, a high level of accountability to

themselves and the group, a robust climate of joint problem solving and learning among peers, an intense feeling of involvement, and high trust relationships.

(2011: 42)

Note the emphasis on 'well-functioning', recognising that while circles have the capacity to disrupt more hierarchical geometries (for example, triangles) there is no inevitability. Circle-work requires skilled practice guided by clear methodologies – as discussed in our third reflection of this chapter.

Intellectually, the space is alive with the dynamism of dialogue where ideas can be tested, assumptions deconstructed, alternatives considered, critical feedback exchanged and proposals interrogated – but with a commitment to respectful dialogue rather than divisive debate. In our experience, debate often only leads people into defending known territory and old ways of imagining. Dialogue instead can facilitate deep listening, the letting go of non-essentials, and the appreciative consideration of new ideas. This is the kind of space in which possibilitators imagine new ways of transforming their worlds. One story of dialogue and learning that has inspired us comes from the New Zealand Social Entrepreneur Fellowship:

> This Fellowship has been gathering for several years within New Zealand and has focused on creating a learning community for social innovators as action-learners. They have based some of their learning practices on Peter Senge's work, arguing that 'a learning community happens best in an environment that encourages dialogue, feedback, contemplation and empowerment' (Hutchinson 2012: 66). The core of their learning practice is enabled through regular retreats whereby social entrepreneurs come together and share their stories, peer mentor one another, and elicit feedback.
>
> Importantly these retreats have been framed as dialogues, heavily influenced by David Bohm's work (ibid.: 68) and the idea of 'the "U" of a social innovation dialogue' (ibid: 72), which they understand as an allegory for a conversational journey. This social innovation dialogue 'U' process involves moving through three phases: (1) Sensing – enabled through check-in circles, strategic questioning, suspending; (2) Presencing – enabled through 'letting go' and 'letting come' (new inspiration/ideas); and (3) Realising – enabled through discerning what is emerging, 'crystallising insights', 'prototyping new activities'.

(ibid.: 71)

Creating circles that foster this kind of emotional and intellectual space are conducive for imaginative literacy. They unlock new possibilities for people enabling them to get unstuck and step on to new ground.

Stories for sparking re-imagination

While space is crucial for transformational training, *stories* are also vital resources for training in re-imagination. They potentially provide the models, images and pictures that enable people to imagine a different kind of world. Two kinds of stories are explored in this reflection – authors and books as *written* stories, and people, groups and organisations as *lived* stories. In many ways, drawing on our understanding of Freire's practice of dialogue, these stories represent the codes that can be used to trigger conversations within community-based training settings.

Paulo Freire talks about literacy as learning to read both the word and the world. Within this tradition of literacy, learning is not simply about acquiring the function of reading text – a function of learning the word; it is also about the process of becoming conscious that illiteracy is a key symptom of powerlessness. Illiterate people become aware that their lack of knowing the word is intimately connected to their marginal place in the world. Within this Freirean tradition of literacy, the 'reading' of stories described below can be conceptualised as acquiring literacy in our imaginative lives.

Written stories that ignite imagination

As young community development workers in the 1980s we were sustained by our reading of religious stories that inspired the imagining of an alternative world. There is something soothing for the soul when reminded that everyone dies and no one can take their wealth and riches with them. There is also something enriching when challenged to live by the ethic of the 'golden rule', common to most spiritual traditions: 'Do unto others as you would have them do unto you.' The ancient religious texts also ignite possibilities that seem beyond contemporary realities. They inspire a hope and evoke a memory that within the stories of history the apparently impossible can come true. Such ancient history flows into more contemporary histories – who would have ever dreamed that the repressive regime in the Philippines under President-Dictator Marcos could have been removed so quickly, or that the Berlin Wall would suddenly be dismantled?

Offering such stories are important within training processes; it is often the power of story that unlocks imagination. Note that when talking of texts and stories we are not referring to textbooks. Textbooks are often too dry and technical to inspire imagination; they tend to, at worst, simply prescribe ideological positioning and, at best, offer sets of abstract propositions and principles. In contrast to textbooks, the texts we use for sparking re-imagination are full of story, narrative and real people. In these texts, story connects with people's reality. Readers can locate themselves within a story and identify with characters and events – this is the source of their power.

For those wishing to sustain a lively imagination that also inspires the building of a community-oriented world, it is useful to collect stories that inspire efforts and re-imagination. People are constantly being fed stories through newspapers and television, and many of these stories tell of a world that people do not wish to keep replicating. Instead, transformational trainers can provide soulful, alternative stories that engage people's imaginative faculties. As authors we turn to storytellers and poets who write with depth, integrity, passion and insight: people such as Tim Winton, Michael Leunig, Epeli Hau'Ofa, Margaret Atwood, Ben

Okri, Frank Moorhouse, Jeannette Winterston, Allen Ginsberg, Pablo Neruda, Leonard Cohen and Salman Rushdie. We also enjoy introducing our trainees to thoughtful *essayists* who reflect in critical and imaginative ways on contemporary society, such as Clive Hamilton, Amanda Lohrey, Peter Singer, George Monbiot and Alain de Botton.

Other important stories for those involved in community work are the stories and writings of *author-activists* who articulate different dimensions of practice wisdom, and fuel the various global traditions of community development. Again, they are not ideologically oriented textbooks, but instead are writings that reflect on experience and are informed by certain values, perspectives, praxis and imagination. They are essential as education tools because they invite learners of community development to consider differently imagined worlds. Examples of such author-activists that have greatly influenced our lives and community development practice traditions have been, among others, Mahatma Gandhi, Jayaprakash Narayan, Fritz Schumacher, Dom Helder Camara, Frantz Fanon, Jacques Ellul, Paulo Freire, Martin Buber, Manfred Max-Neef, Miles Horton, Sheila Rowbotham, Aung San Suu Kyi, Satish Kumar, Joanna Macy, Saul Alinsky, Parker Palmer, bel hooks, Henri Nouwen, Jean Vanier, Steve Biko, Desmond Tutu and Nelson Mandela. These author-activists have stood the crucial test of practical action. Their actions were inspired by new ways of imagining how their communities could be. They often challenge the 'given' world of the powerful – whether colonial powers, nuclear interests, dictatorships, patriarchal leaders, domesticating educators or warmongers. Their written stories initiate people into their struggle to live and build alternatives to the 'given'.

Living stories that inspire imagination

The second types of story that we use in training for transformation are the living stories of people, groups and organisations (after all, not everyone likes to read). Many people can be transformed through meeting and experiencing people, groups and organisations that *model* alternative values, commitments and worlds. This implies the importance of documenting the lives of such individuals and the case studies of groups and organisations – they tell stories that it would be great for people to hear.

The reading of lived stories as text is primarily about people gaining some power over their own imaginations, and thereby over the range of possible presents and potential futures. The goal is not imitation of others' imagined and lived worlds, but a gaining of power to make choices about how to imagine and live present and future lives. This process of gaining imaginative literacy destabilises previous solidified imaginary tapestries.

As authors and practitioners we gain inspiration and fresh imagination from people of all walks of life. Many of the refugees we have worked with in Brisbane have challenged us and called us to imagine a world of peace, solidarity and hospitality. We have been deeply touched by their exposure to the harsh realities of brutality and irrationality, and their resilience in the face of alienation and exile, as Gerard relates:

My son Ciaron knows the story that his first visitor in the world, the first of our friends to appear in the maternity ward of the local hospital after his birth, was a refugee from Peru who was a member of the Sendero Luminoso – the Shining Path guerrilla movement. Ciaron has no memories of being nursed by this guy as he opened up more and more about his experiences of torture, violence and imprisonment in a world far from our comfortable inner-urban home. He moved out of his flat and out of our lives before Ciaron could walk. But when I have recalled his story around the table over the years my voice has carried an echo of his passionate belief that any price was worth paying for the struggle against oppression. His story is embedded in Ciaron's identity, his way of imagining the world.

Furthermore, so is the story that he was named not after, but at a time that we were getting to know, Ciaron O'Reilly – a West End local who has become an international peace activist imprisoned for disarming bombers at American airforce bases in the USA and Ireland. Now these stories inspire Ciaron as a young physicist to take an expansive view of his place in the world, and of the possibilities that could unfold over a lifetime.

The stories of our refugee colleagues are gifts that constantly destabilise the 'given' world. They remind us of the interconnections between a supposedly peaceful Australia and a world at war. The traces of chaos and the tentacles of globalising forces deconstruct our imagined safe, moral, relaxed and comfortable, fortress Australia. Through their stories, we are challenged to re-imagine Australia as a country that not only extends hospitality to the refugee, but also engages ethically and peacefully with the causes of refugee movements.

Along with refugees, many of the young people we have worked with in Australia, South Africa, Papua New Guinea, the Philippines and Vanuatu invoke hope within us. Many of their lives are incredibly difficult. Their futures are precarious. For many of them the rural life is impoverishing and no longer the vehicle for their growing aspirations. They flock to the cities – to peri-urban or inner-urban shanty towns. We find ourselves despairing for their future. Yet they seem to have hope, and through their hope they inspire hope in us. They make music, create small enterprises, enjoy football or basketball, and care for one another; they work hard for meagre incomes, pay for education, and create groups that get involved in their slums or neighbourhoods, holding clean-up days, health days and fun days. Sometimes they get involved in the criminal economy, or turn to the ever growing security industry for employment; sometimes this is their only hope. The point is that they continue to imagine a world that has a place for them despite the difficult 'given reality'.

It is also helpful for a cadre of possibilitators to share their stories with one another in ways that inspire and sustain their work together. There is great resource in the soulful stories and hard-earned life experiences of any group of diverse and committed people. Often our task as transformational trainers is to watch the group process and pick the right moment to create space for learning experiences, to tell our own stories in ways that reflect on the work, and to draw others into sharing their stories and the insight they offer.

Groups and organisations that keep the dream alive

Many groups in our own neighbourhoods also inspire us to keep on dreaming and living a hopeful life. These include groups of activists; reading and learning circles; collectives building alternative economic realities such as local economic trading schemes (LETS), the Justice Products Shop, community-supported agriculture (CSA) schemes and savings and loans circles; and groups focusing on solidarity and service, refugee support groups and indigenous reconciliation groups. These are just a few local groups among many that model a living story invoking alternative presents and futures.

Organisations also provide an essential tool in empowering change agents to imagine and work for a new world. They do this by modelling new patterns of thinking, acting and structuring work into the socio-political fabric of civil society. Part of our role as trainers is to link people with such organisations in a way that will enable them to sustain their imagination and their work as possibilitators. As trainers for transformation it is important to look out for, participate in and nurture organisations that provide a culture, a tradition, a spirit and a structure that is alternative to the assumed 'given'. They can be organisations focusing on anything from local to global development. They may be corporations, co-operatives, associations or networks, but they have one thing in common – they inspire people to imagine and work for a community-oriented world.

In Australia there are many organisations that inspire hope and renewed imagination. Here are just a few of our favourites:

- Jabiru Community, Youth and Children Services – standing up for families, young people and children within particular neighbourhoods;
- Food Connect – supporting alternative food sources to big agribusiness and monopoly food stores;
- New Farm and Sandgate Neighbourhood Centres – modelling alternative local planning processes;
- the Community Living Programme – working with young people, people with disabilities and many others;
- the Queensland Programme of Assistance to Survivors of Torture and Trauma (QPASTT) – working with refugees and asylum seekers within our city;
- the Dulwich Centre – working to support collective healing and change processes within indigenous communities; and
- the Change Agency – working to support activists and social mobilisers in campaign strategies and tactics.

Around the world we continue to be inspired by organisations such as the Highlander Research and Education Centre in the USA, the Community Development Resource Association (CDRA) in South Africa, the Centre for Development Alternatives (CEPAUR) in Chile, Schumacher College in the UK, and the Self-Employed Women's Association (SEWA) of India.

In our experience these kinds of organisations are the nodes and hubs within a web of organisational relationships that continue to energise possibilitators when there is despair. Their example keeps the dream alive and models the structuring of change.

Methods and models for transformative training

While space and stories are crucial for transformational training, in our experience it is helpful for facilitators not only to have been inhabited by the faculties of dialogue and also skilled at dialogue generally, but also to be conscious of the various models and methods available to guide their dialogical practice. Different models have different steps, as well as different ways of integrating elements of experience, new knowledge/theory and application of knowledge. We approach this reflection through first discussing the models generally drawn upon within our work, namely the experiential, elicitive, spiral and participatory learning and action models; and, second, explaining our particular approach to transformational training called 'deconstructive conversation'.

The models named above are certainly not a definitive list, but simply reflect those utilised within our practice. Although these can each be captured diagrammatically (Westoby and Shevellar 2012) we caution over-reliance on such depictions. They simply provide a guide on how to structure dialogue within a training setting in ways that provide the greatest possibility of transformation.

The experiential model

The experiential learning model is the first and most simple one we have drawn on. This model is drawn from the work of David Kolb (1984). It involves first inviting participants into remembering a concrete experience of their own or creating an experience within the training setting, through a role play, or introducing a case study (such as one of the stories mentioned above). This first step is then followed by observation and reflection upon those experiences. Crucial dialogical skills are here required mainly in the form of ordered questions – How did the experience (from the previous step) feel? What happened? And so forth. Generalisations, or the forming of abstract concepts, based upon those previous reflections then follow. Finally the application of those generalisations to new situations is extrapolated. In practice the model is a spiral rather than a circle in that the four components of the cycle keep repeating, creating new and deeper experiences, reflections, generalisations and applications.

> In a training exercise we have used all around the world one of our first processes invites people to sit in small circles and share memories of a positive or healthy experience of community they have had in their life. From these stories dialogue is then opened up about what people meant by community when telling the story of their memory, and what characteristics made it an experience of community. From all these reflections generalisations are made about the diverse ways people think about and experience community.

This story of using experiential training highlights the significance of not giving a lecture about the meaning of community, or not introducing a reading about different definitions of community, but instead offering a space and a process for people to reflect on their own experiences of community and then as a group making sense of the diverse experiences arising.

The elicitive model

In many cross-cultural settings the elicitive model is useful to guide the dialogue process (Lederach 1995). First, the elicitive model begins with concrete experiences through a series of discovery-oriented activities. Such activities are designed to act as catalysts for participants to discover what they do, and how they do it. Second, participants name and categorise the processes they use. Third, participants engage in what Mennonite peace researcher John Paul Lederach refers to as 'contextualised evaluation' (ibid.: 60). In other words, once participants have a heightened awareness of what occurs in their situation they can examine it more objectively and consider the strengths and weaknesses of the approaches utilised. Fourth, participants re-create and adapt their approaches, based on their evaluation. Finally, through either simulations or real-life experiences, participants try out their adapted models through practical application.

One of the crucial differences between this and other models is that the elicitive model explicitly privileges culture (ibid.: 7), hence the use of it within cross-cultural contexts. It is an approach grounded in the view that culture and indigenous (or endogenous) knowledge is the 'seedbed' that gives rise to processes and models that better meet local needs. Over many years of practice we have learned that elicitive training is an approach that achieves both respect for people's knowledge and movement of these people into new social territory, a requirement of most community development practice. In this transformational training approach, the content is elicited from the context and experiences of the participants, and the journey forward is a mutual dialogical journey of educator–trainer and participants in co-discovery (ibid.: 65).

The key principles for this kind of elicitive training are: people in their setting are a key resource, not passive recipients; indigenous or local knowledge is a pipeline to discovery, meaning and appropriate action; participation of local people in the process is central; building from available resources encourages self-sufficiency and sustainability; and empowerment involves a process that fosters awareness of self-in-context and validates discovery, naming and creation through reflection and action (ibid.). Here is a story of elicitive training:

> As part of a five-day workshop in Vanuatu Peter and some fellow trainers invited the chiefs and other community leaders to create, in small groups, two role plays – one based on their experience of a successful reconciliation ceremony and another based on their experience of an unsuccessful one. These role plays acted as discovery triggers. After the role plays (which led to much hilarity, always helpful for transformational training) dialogue was initiated around the steps utilised in both stories – a process that made

explicit what had initially been experienced as implicit. From this process the chiefs and leaders could 'see' their own models and engage in a process of evaluation – they could start to articulate what made some of the reconciliation ceremonies successful and others unsuccessful. From this they created a new model that they named 'sustainable reconciliation ceremonies'.

The story provides an example of how elicitive training, building on people's own knowledge and stories, can also be used to transform people's understanding, making culture clearer and enabling people also to exercise evaluative and adaptive capacities. In such a context any attempt to have directly challenged the chiefs to rethink their reconciliation ceremonies would have been resoundingly rejected as colonial interference. But a respectful training process infused with dialogue, and that starts with people's own experiences and knowledge, can trigger change.

The spiral model

Our third approach draws on the spiral model, which initially utilises the experiential learning cycle by inviting participants to reflect upon their experiences. Like the elicitive model, it seeks categorisations and pattern formation. However, differentiating the third step within the spiral model is the inclusion or insertion of new theory and information. Such theory or information is used to disrupt previous ways of thinking.

In the preceding story this could have meant inserting a story of how chiefs from another country have developed a more sustainable model of reconciliation ceremony. The Vanuatu chiefs then not only have their own experiences and evaluative capacities to draw on, but also the new knowledge arising from the story provided. The fourth step in the spiral model is to connect with this new knowledge, practise any necessary skills, and to strategise and plan for action. Finally, the fifth step calls for applying strategies in action.

The participatory learning and action model

Another approach to training – one well known across the world – is the participatory learning and action (PLA) model. This approach is articulated well by Pretty *et al.* (1995) and also Kumar (2002), drawing on Robert Chambers' (1997) work. These authors all observe that, while participatory processes are well known and employed regularly by facilitators, they tend to be relegated to a set of tools and techniques rather than understood in a broader framework for dialogue and social action. For this reason, we depart from the usual way of thinking about PLA techniques and instead locate them within a broader spiral dynamic. We understand participatory techniques (such as the use of community maps, charts, socio-lines, photography, art, theatre and so forth) as potent means of triggering dialogue. In this way, they are dialogical tools upon which a powerful collective analysis can be built. This analysis through reflection is not the endpoint, but the means by which action is designed, and agreement to act gained. Once action is taken, new opportunities for data collection emerge.

Dialogue and training for transformation 141

One of our colleagues, Nicholas Haines, has spent the past few years working in Cambodia with a focus on training farmers. In 'Creativity and technique: a participatory approach to farmer education in Cambodia' (2012) Nicholas shares his story of wrestling with how to conduct community-based education and training processes that are dialogical and learner centred when many of the pressures work in other directions (for example, donor centred, or performing to a culturally assigned social hierarchy).

He accounts for needing to shift the practice from 'shallow discussion to deep creativity' (ibid.: 140) and from 'testing recall to honouring stories' (ibid.: 141). However, he also discusses the importance of the PLA approach whereby it, 'challenges [him] to bridge the gap between espoused values and values in practice ... provid[ing] a conceptual way of structuring the learning process' (ibid.: 144). Furthermore, it guides his Khmer colleagues through providing them with a framework for 'challenging anti-participatory attitudes and behaviours' (ibid.), offering instead a practical alternative, which can be construed as dialogical.

Each model discussed above provides a systematic, disciplined way of working with people's stories and experience, of integrating new ideas and/or theory and moving towards action. However, this notion of using models also needs to be understood carefully and implemented flexibly. Our experience as trainers makes clear that, while it is very useful to enter a training space with a clear model to frame the process, it is critical to be able to either let go of, or at least hold lightly, any model once it becomes a barrier to learning. Holding on and letting go capture the craft of being able to relinquish the steps embedded within each model and be present to what might be happening in a learning space. Dialogue is the primary orientation – the models can simply play a role in supporting dialogue. If they are no longer doing that, then practitioners can easily deviate or abandon such ideals and focus instead on the goal at hand.

While having written appreciatively about these models, the limitations should also be acknowledged. Models are reductionist and can never capture the complexities of the work. They are abstractions and give the illusion of neutrality. Embedded in this discussion is an assumption about the capacity among facilitators for analysis and, among participants, a capacity for reflection.

Having briefly discussed the models most often drawn upon in our practice we now also explain in more detail our particular approach to transformative training – named as deconstructive conversation.

Deconstructive conversation

We came to an understanding of the importance of deconstructive conversation in training through our own explorations of our inner worlds, and find it useful to frame our approach in terms of a particular way of understanding the therapeutic task. For example, when people start in therapy they often subscribe to a way of viewing themselves – understood at least by the therapist as a relatively stuck perception of who they are. This view of self essentially becomes *the story* of how someone imagines themselves to be and how they describe themselves to others. This story could be called someone's *mythos*. It is not a story or myth based on facts, but only on perception – a memory of a life, filtered through all sorts of lenses. In response to this the therapeutic task is to 'broaden' the myth, or 'open up the presented story' (Gibney 2003: 120), to fill it out, creating what psychologists such as James Hillman (1983) have called a *healing fiction*. Within this process the therapeutic task is to awaken imagination in such a way that people do not limit self-perception to the realm of old stories, often stories imposed by damaged parts of the self or inherited from others. This can lead to tension. However, if people can hold an ongoing dialogue with the emergent stories – the other parts of self – then a more creative, dynamic and whole person can emerge.

This understanding of the therapeutic task is in some ways similar to the deconstructive task of trainers within our approach. However, it is not so much about engaging with the contradictions of the psyche, but about engaging with the contradictions of the social worlds. The task is to initiate a deconstructive conversation that destabilises the given *mythos* that participants have assigned to their reading of the social, cultural, ecological, economic and political worlds. This deconstructive process requires both a destructive process, as people let go of the 'given *mythos*', and a reconstructive process as people open up the presented stories and re-imagine alternative worlds. The container for such deconstruction and reconstruction is the process of dialogue, less technically named here as conversation. Four stages within this potentially transformative process of deconstructive conversation can be identified and described:

Acknowledging different possibilities

Each person comes to a training space with an imagined social, economic, cultural, ecological and political world – a story, a myth of how they see the world – usually how they see it *should* be. These stories in no way reflect the complex reality of what is or could be. They reflect an individual's *one* reality. The story has of course been informed through parental and educational socialisation, through the lens provided by gender, race and class locations, as well as by media and political propaganda. Hence, within any training space hosting several people there are many stories, many *mythos*.

Stage one of the transformational learning process invites participants to recognise this – through an encounter with the other, to recognise that as an individual 'I do not really know the truth', and that 'my given reality is just one reality'. It requires what Arjen Wals and Fanny Heymann (2004:134ff.) call 'frame awareness'. The shift begins when participants are invited to become aware of *difference* – often through simply listening to others.

We often facilitate a simple training exercise in which the whole group listens deeply to one another's stories of their personal journeys. In some contexts, we then follow this with the task of stepping out into the neighbourhood, beginning a conversation with a stranger who is very different from them, and listening deeply to their stories of their experience of the place. This awareness is a critical process in 'destroying' the narrowly imagined world, the 'de-' part of the deconstructive conversation.

Imagining new possibilities

In the light of this awareness of difference and the deconstruction of a narrowly imagined world, stories of an alternative world can then be explored. These stories might be the kind of written and lived stories discussed earlier in this chapter, or they might simply come from the participants as they listen deeply to one another's diverse experiences of the world. They do not provide any 'true' story. They simply broaden the *mythos*, unravel the old stories, present options for 'reframing' (Wals and Heymann 2004:135) and increase the possibilities of embracing new stories. We often use an educative process of reflecting on the work at hand through considering insightful writing, visiting innovative organisations, or interviewing gifted practitioners. This process introduces the cadre of possibilitators to many ways of seeing the world – or seeing many worlds. In Freirean terms, they regain or at least refresh their imaginative literacy.

Creating space for dilemma and struggle: which possibility?

The third transformational training stage requires the nurturing of a space for internal struggle in which a dialogue around these stories, perspectives and multiple imagined worlds can occur. Old stories are evaluated alongside new ones; some myths are broadened; others are narrowed. There are many tensions and dilemmas, and it is important to encourage one another to engage with these stories with honesty and courage. In moments like these, support for choices can be found in the stories of people such as Oscar Romero, a story learned from many of our friends from El Salvador, living in Australia as refugees.

> Many before us have struggled to make the choice to engage with the marginalised in a struggle for genuine community and justice. Oscar Romero's classic moment of internal struggle in the desert of El Salvador is an example. In the desert he knew that he had a choice: either to back off from the soul demands of solidarity and struggle, accepting the world as given by the Salvadorian government and US allies; or to dig deep and find the courage to push on, imagine the world as different, advocate another truth in opposition to the government and stand alongside the poor in a struggle for justice.

Usually the stories are less heroic than Oscar Romero's. Often the stories that invite dilemma or struggle are simply those of other participants in the dialogical training space sharing their experience of life as a refugee, or being unemployed. People's perspectives – which may have been deeply influenced by the media's versions of refugees or the unemployed – are disrupted by this new story. People then have a choice – whether to engage openly with this other story, for example acknowledging the profound pain of exile, or the depressing assault of unemployment, or not.

It is hard to manufacture these kinds of 'conflict spaces' in a training room. They usually occur in the crucible of engagement. It is not a romantic or abstract task. It usually requires the 'mainstream' colliding with the 'margins' – a process identified by Movement for a New Society founder George Lakey (2010: 32ff.). Within most training spaces the people attending represent stories that are more closely aligned to either the mainstream or the margins. It is often when these stories – reflecting different mainstream or marginal experiences of life – collide, that a more real, raw, 'gutsy' and substantial dialogue can occur.

Transformation or regression: new possibilities

Finally there is a stage of either transformation or regression. When confronted with different versions of the world and the accompanying invitation to act that those versions provide, some people give up the struggle and remain content with the given reading of the world that they brought to the training. Others embark on the transformative journey to engage with the ever critical work of social solidarity through a reframed reading of the social, cultural, economic, ecological and political world. They become committed to the process of ongoing action-reflection that reshapes the way they frame their understanding of the world.

This is an iterative process. As soon as people stabilise a certain *mythos* of the world that is decided to be somewhat 'real' – that is, the frame through which the world and its experiences are viewed – then from the perspective of deconstruction, they have become somewhat stuck – dialogue is arrested. In stabilising a frame people can become unaware and unattentive – they remove difference and the possibility of dialogue. It is important therefore to maintain an ongoing deconstructive conversation that destabilises any entrenched or habitual *mythos* and ensures the ongoing development of imaginative literacy. In doing this people enter the territory of uncertainty and ambivalence in which they become 'unsure' – and yet we would argue this is paradoxically the place from which people can develop a deep commitment to the struggle for a socially just world.

Warning: seek a mandate before deconstructing!

A final cautionary note, echoing our discussion about 'mandate' within Chapter 3: implicit within this approach to transformational training is also the need to have gained a mandate to *do* training. This simply means talking with people honestly, openly and lovingly; being clear about the process of deconstructive conversation; acknowledging that it might shake them up a bit; offering support; and then gaining their explicit assent before proceeding. It ensures that people freely enter into the process of dialogue with full awareness and consent. Gerard will never forget the woman he met at a Ministerial Advisory Committee who was the chair of a state-wide housing advocacy group. He asked how she got into this line of work.

I was an ordinary single mum living in a run-down house in an inner Brisbane suburb. This bloke just came around one day, and knocked on the door, and we started talking about the way the neighbourhood was changing. Pretty soon there were other people coming over, and the kitchen table was full of documents and plans. Then I was going to more bloody meetings and got elected chair and ended up spending most of my days at it. But I honestly didn't know what I was getting myself into at the start. I didn't even know I was being bloody 'community developed'! I certainly didn't ask to be.

Her reply provides a warning: be careful, ask permission, and gain a mandate to engage in this kind of deconstructive conversation.

Inspiration and empowerment, not information

Permission is one thing, inspiration another – the former easier to muster, the latter sometimes difficult to nurture. Inspiration as a word implies taking something in, hence the 'inspire', which quite literally means 'breathing in'. In the previous reflections, it was the stories of people, communities or organisations that can be 'taken in' as inspiration leading to greater confidence, hope and animation. From our perspective inspiration becomes a training metaphor for taking new ideas and new stories with their accompanying new energy deep into the self so as to be a resource during the hard times. A crucial part of the transformational training process is that people 'take something in' that leads to transformation of self, which is a key catalytic process for community transformation. Possibilitators need plenty of this inspiration, and it is the community worker's job within training settings to ensure people have 'breathed in' enough stories to face the challenges of transformational work. In our experience this requires training processes of empowerment rather than just information transmission.

Clearly, as important as information can be, in itself it is neither empowerment, nor does it necessarily lead to inspiration. However, information has become the main exchange in a world described as 'the information society'. Within many training spaces and processes it is assumed that information provides power. In our experience this is a fallacy. Here is a story from Peter's work in South Africa (Westoby and Sokhela 2012) that aptly demonstrates the point:

For four years Peter was working in South Africa with an initiative called the Better Life Options Programme (BLP). This initiative was aimed at supporting adolescent girls around issues of sexuality, reproductive health and reproductive rights. A part of the initiative was education and training, through adult-initiated and also peer-oriented processes. In the early days of the programme we tended to mimic similar initiatives that focused on providing information to young girls: ensuring they 'knew' about HIV, sexually transmitted diseases, their bodies and so forth.

However, after some time and through a deeper listening to young girls' experiences, we realised the issues were more about power and poverty than about information. Young girls were getting pregnant because some teachers would only exchange good grades for sex; or young men in the community would demand sex as the ritualised part of a boyfriend/girlfriend relationship; or young men would refuse to use a condom; or police ignored reports of rape. We learned that any useful and transformational training strategy could not be limited to an exchange of information. In this case the training needed to focus on empowerment strategies appropriate to the girls' diverse experiences: assertiveness skills (able to negotiate a 'No'), accessing female condoms, advocacy towards local police, peer support groups of girls, and economic activity to lift them out of poverty (for example, selling condoms to their friends worked for them and for us).

In this story, while the explicit focus became gaining skills of assertiveness, accessing female condoms and so forth, the implicit exchange was about empowerment. The young girls needed to both *feel* inspired enough and also to have acquired the *confidence, relationships, skills* and *resources* related to empowerment to partake in social change relevant to their real, lived experiences. They needed to believe that change could happen and that they could make it happen. This is a function of their experience of the training process more than the training content.

Empowerment and capacity building

Transformational training then invites not only processes of storytelling, dialogue and reflective action (as per the previous reflections), but also processes that do nurture confidence, relationships, skills and resources (or at least linkages to people who have resources). Research from recent 'capacity development' literature, particularly the work of Jan Ubels and his colleagues (2010: 174–7) and Robert Chambers' evaluative work on 'scaling-up' participatory practice (2005: 119ff.), provides various ways forward to ensure transformative trainers continue to focus on this kind of empowerment and inspiration as opposed to information transmission.

For example, good practice invites participants in training to discover inspiring stories through initiating local-level action research and action learning processes. These stories can then be disseminated through existing networks, particularly through horizontal learning peer-oriented processes, whereby people in one locality could visit people doing something inspiring in another locality. Doing this enables people to gain confidence – seeing it done elsewhere; and build networks – meeting the people who have done it elsewhere; and acquire skills – learning from those people.

Ubels *et al.* (2010) and Chambers (2005) also build on a long lineage of research and reflection going back to Reg Batten's (1962) seminal work on training within community development work. His writings argued that it is important for community development initiatives taking training seriously to accompany local change agents, or possibilitators, in understanding their local situation and working contextually. It is not a case of 'we provide training' and then 'send people out'. Transformational capacity building needs to be a process of supporting local possibilitators *in situ*, helping them to learn how to navigate the complexities of their daily activity. We have also found it very useful to accompany such capacity-development and training with the development of a set of sayings and stories (Chambers 2005) that reflect the transformational heart of the community work. Examples of such facilitator sayings are 'hand over the pen', 'hold your agenda lightly', and 'start with the people, but don't stay with the people'.

Embodied learning experiences, empowerment and potent trainers

Transformational training processes in which participants learn through embodied experiences are also a powerful way of ensuring training remains as empowerment rather than being information-oriented. Returning to the above South African story:

> Several years ago, Peter was running a workshop for the BLP with the long-term, peer educators at a national conference in Cape Town. The topic of that national conference was on boys' responsibilities within reproductive health issues. During day one of the conference, several workshop activities focused on the key topic and by the end of the day all the peer educators appeared to have digested the 'content'. They could all verbally affirm with confidence that boys and young men should take more responsibility within sexual relationships around condom use and so forth. During the evening, as Peter reflected on the day and planned the next, he decided to try to 'test' the 'affirmations' and figured the best way would be to use an applied theatre approach adapted from forum theatre techniques (Boal 1979, Schutzman and Cohen-Cruz 1994: 2).
>
> He pulled aside a couple of the young people and quickly devised a script in which the two of them, now as actor and actress, would create a scene in which a young man proceeded to seduce a young woman at home after a night out on the town. Within the acted scene the boy would offer the girl alcohol, which she accepted after a small amount of protest, and then they would fall into the flow of seduction, with her agreeing to have sex and, eventually, even agreeing to have sex without a condom, because first no one had a condom with them and, second, he insisted that he 'loved her'.
>
> The next day the scene was acted in front of all the other peer educators with much laughter and delight. As per the applied theatre methodology Peter then asked the two actors to restart the scene from the beginning and also invited spectators – more accurately named 'spect-actors' within forum theatre methodology (Schutzman and Cohen-Cruz 1994: 1) – to call 'Stop!' at any time and come out and replace one of the actors. They could then continue to act out the scene as they saw fit and both 'spect-actors' would see if a different outcome could be achieved.
>
> During the next 20 minutes or so, the scene was replayed about half a dozen times, usually still leading to the similar outcome of the young man sleeping with the young woman, although usually with a condom. However,

what astounded Peter was that all replacements within the forum theatre process *replaced the girl*. In addition, this replaying usually attempted to negotiate a better outcome through *modifying her behaviour* (such as not accepting a drink in the first place), or being more assertive about her sexuality ('I will not sleep with you'), or being more resourceful ('I have a condom with me'). It should be said that, with respect to the latter, usually having a condom with her was seen to be either 'sluttish' by the boy, turning him off from wanting sex with her (in the theatre scene that is), or irrelevant (that is, 'I do not use condoms').

After winding up the first stage of the applied theatre – six replacements of the girl – Peter referred back to the previous day's sessions about male responsibility within sexual relations and protection. Questions such as, 'What have you seen today?' and 'In what way does what you have seen relate to yesterday's workshop?' were asked. It was suggested that maybe the group should consider what relation those sessions might have to the applied theatre experience. No one seemed to 'connect the dots' and it was at this moment that Peter's previous sense of being 'astounded' was reinforced with an intellectual curiosity about the now [failed] training process initiated during day one.

Peter then asked the two initial actors to replay the scene and this time himself called 'Stop!' and replaced the boy. Moreover, this time Peter had a condom with him, and both actors agreed that if they were to have sex the male would want to use the condom. Again, 'spect-actors' were asked, 'What do you see?'

The peer educators were now themselves astounded not only at how 'easy' it was to change the outcome of the story (with both actors being happy and even being able to enjoy an alcoholic drink or two), but also at their own inability to have 'connected the dots' between the previous days' discussions about male responsibility and the actual attitudinal and behavioural change required. All that was needed was for someone to replace the male and take responsibility!

Peter's educational curiosity remained. Reflecting on this 'aha!' moment in attempted transformational training became a key motivator to consider first the importance of applied theatre and other forms of embodied learning (Pettit 2010) within transformative training and, second, the central role of the trainer as a facilitator of dialogue – recognising that no technique in itself will necessarily trigger transformation.

Reflecting on this experience focuses on the failure (for transformational purposes) of both orthodox training practices, and even an embodied training experience as technique – it still required the attentive dialogical intervention of the practitioner-trainer. However, if the practitioner had not utilised the applied theatre process then the learning would have remained as non-empowering information that failed to transform heart, mind and behaviour.

This is further illustrated in a more detailed reflection on a story of Peter's practice in Vanuatu told earlier within this chapter:

A fellow trainer and I were sitting at morning tea on the third day of a five-day *storian* [storytelling dialogue] with 30 ni-Vanuatu chiefs and other community leaders. As facilitators we were thinking about how to trigger reflective thinking and planning around using customary peace-making processes to address a number of identified conflicts. For us the key to effective community-based training, understood as a process of action learning, was designing the right questions. After some thought we came up with the following questions, which were posed to the group: 'What are the steps you have used in non-sustainable peace-building ceremonies (that is, ones that have not worked, or lasted)? and 'What are the steps you have used in sustainable peace-building ceremonies (where the peace has lasted)?' We asked small groups of six participants to consider the questions and come up with role plays that told the stories of unsustainable and sustainable peace-building ceremonies.

The large group divided into small groups and there was immediately a buzz and energy as people discussed, shared stories and then started constructing role plays of the stories they wanted to share with the large group. Eventually it was time to act the stories and for an hour or so there was much laughter, but also there seemed to be a growing awareness that 'we are learning something important here'. After all the stories were role-played a plenary session unpacked the differences within the unsustainable and sustainable peace-building ceremonies. Some key wisdom was discovered by the group and a 'new' model was identified, and written up as a set of key steps for implementing sustainable peace-building ceremonies within community life. People then moved into a session to talk about how to move forward, addressing some real-life conflicts within their communities using the new wisdom.

The story above is an example of drawing on both an elicitive approach (Lederach 1995), working with the existing resources within a culture and community, and also the experiential learning cycle (Kolb 1984), ensuring that the learning is experiential (as per the role plays), can be generalised (as per the 'new model') and leads to practical application. However, what made the training experience powerful for the participants and trainers alike was the buzzing that occurred when invited into creating role plays. Again embodied learning practices unlocked energy and new ways of engaging with the community challenge at hand.

One of our comrades within Community Praxis Co-op, Dr Polly Walker, lives in the USA. She, along with several other colleagues, has been a central figure in inspiring us as practitioners to draw on performance, theatre and other forms of embodied experiences in training. She constantly invites us to take new risks. She has worked with colleagues to compile a wonderful collection of stories entitled *Acting Together: Performance and the Creative Transformation of Conflict* (Cohen *et al.* 2012), which tells stories both of resistance and reconciliation and also of building just and inclusive communities from such diverse places as Former Yugoslavia, Uganda, Palestine, Peru, Cambodia and many more.

Resisting the seduction of content-focused technologies

Finally, we briefly consider a pertinent critical issue relevant for re-imagining transformational training – the overuse of content-focused technologies (such as computer-based slide presentations), which contributes to the domestication of training. Such trends move in the completely opposite direction to what we have been advocating – such as the use of embodied learning experiences, performance and theatre-oriented practices and appropriate capacity building. The seductive power of technology is that it ensures that lots of information can be provided to students and learners with ease and little reflexivity. It is a seduction that often destroys or at least mutes the role of dialogue within learning spaces. Peter again reflects on a more recent experience in Vanuatu, illustrating the significance of Marshall McLuhan's (1964) maxim that 'the medium is the message':

> Within my work in Vanuatu I often work in outer islands where the learning spaces are under trees, in traditional huts and on grassy knolls. There is rarely electricity. I love going to these places with a roll of butcher's paper and big felt-tip pens, ready to sit in circles with the people. However, I am stunned by the number of times other development professionals ask if they can see the computer presentations or posters that I am using within the training. In reply, I ask them whether they think such use of computer technologies could possibly be experienced as empowering and inspiring to people who do not have the ongoing use of such technologies. I remind them that with the use of such technologies it would be easy to go and share lots of information; it would be easy to provide a 'shock and awe' display of wealth and technology; but it would be very difficult to enter into a dialogue about the concerns and resources related to their experiences of their places.

Peter's analysis implies that such a content-centred approach would not inspire possibilities of a new world; it could only create either a sense of deficit in terms of what people do not have in the villages, and/or yearnings to leave the villages and head to the city or Australia. What really inspires people are stories – stories of how other communities are tackling the same kinds of challenges they are experiencing. In this sense the learning space facilitates empowerment, not through the depositing of information and the utilisation of content-oriented technologies, but through the exchange of inspirational stories. Such inspiration and empowerment enable people to move through the challenging sequence of wishing, willing and acting, which is the focus of the final reflection.

The logic of wishing, willing and acting

David Yalom (1980: 286–350) has theorised the psychological links between the concepts of wishing, willing and acting. This discussion connects these concepts for the purposes of transformational training. Awareness about the possibility of a new world, a new kind of community, is not enough. Awareness does not bring social change, even though it is a good starting place. Yalom has illuminated the steps between awareness and action in ways that we have found useful as facilitators of transformational training. Within our approach to deconstructive conversation, then, there is the process of moving towards awareness of new stories, of how the world can be viewed and responded to; but there is also a process of gentling people towards action.

Within this framework the first step in moving towards action involves reclaiming the ability to *wish*. It is not so much that people have an inability to wish, but rather they distrust or suppress their wishes. Deep down, many people desire a different kind of community, a different kind of relationship with their neighbours, a different kind of economic order. However many people also seem content with the world as it is, so it can become easy simply to distrust our desires.

At the heart of our proposition is the idea that, if people do not want something, or do not trust their wanting, then they will go nowhere – or, put more colloquially, they will simply 'go with the flow'. Gerard remembers the axiom that expressed this for him: 'Even a dead dog can swim with the current.' Therefore, as per our previous reflections, at the initial stage of transformational training it is important to engage with people's stories in ways that reawaken imagination – particularly in enabling people to express their desire or wish for a new kind of world, challenging the 'given', or re-trusting their dreams and heartfelt desires. North American Jungian psychologist James Hollis puts it beautifully:

> As Schopenhauer argued in the last century, will is the life force seeking its own expression ... Will is expressed through the body, through desire, through dream, and through the evanescent visions we may have throughout our life, the vision of the larger life.
> (2001: 49)

Unlocking willingness that is captive to despair

The second step to consider is that reclaiming an ability to wish usually requires a process of reclaiming feeling. While Yalom considers the reclaiming of feeling as a therapist, we have found it helpful to incorporate Joanna Macy's observation (1983) that *despair* is at the heart of losing the imaginative capacity to wish for a better world, and the task of engaging with despair is central to reclaiming that capacity for many people.

For Macy, despair is both a result and cause of separation, disempowerment and supposed apathy. However, becoming conscious of despair is also a key to regaining power, change and possibility. Repression and denial lead to self-damaging patterns of psychic numbing. Part of the transformational training agenda is therefore to unlock this despair, for which Macy provides five principles:

- acknowledging that feelings of pain for our world are natural and healthy;
- being clear that this pain is only morbid if denied;
- understanding that information alone is not enough;
- being conscious that unblocking repressed feelings releases energy and clears the mind;

- recognising that unblocking our pain for the world reconnects us with the larger web of life.

(ibid.: 22–3)

In following Joanna Macy's principles, transformational training creates spaces that loosen such despair, enabling people to re-sense their wishes and dreams for a better world. In those loosening and enabling processes, people reclaim feeling, which is a key engine room for imaginative capacity.

Asserting response-ability through action

The final step in Yalom's proposition is that of reclaiming a sense of choice and responsibility. With a renewed trust of dreaming for a better world, people are then faced with the raw fact of responsibility. No social change can happen unless people choose to participate in the change process – that is, unless they have cultivated the will to participate. We are face to face with the stark reality of decision that we referred to as either 'transformation' or 'regression' in the earlier reflection.

Decision is the bridge between wishing and action – it is the test of willingness. However, as Macy has remarked, this is not a purely rational decision-making process, but often a hard choice infused with deep feeling. It is this infusion with feeling that can galvanise people to act, moving from a sense of moral responsibility towards an enthusiastic *response-ability*. There is energy within, acquired through this inner working of imagination and inspiration, that evokes, motivates and enables action.

This logic of wishing, willing and acting is woven into the transformative training processes we design in our community work practice. The modalities of thinking, feeling, infusing and enthusing are central to effective learning for social change. Imagining a new world is a creative place to begin. Wishing for a new world opens up the possibilities of change. However, action and response-ability actually make the change.

Summing up

This chapter has presented our vision for a cadre of change agents and organic intellectuals as possibilitators in every locality and community of interest. They will be the catalysts in transforming their communities. In this framework of dialogical community development, the training of such change agents is a central task.

The first reflection on *space to re-imagine* started with an observation that the failure of the imagination of modernity means that most people can no longer imagine a community or society based on anything other than what is. The mass media dominate people's dreams, and there is too little space to create a society in which people devise new ways to care for earth, politics, economies, the socio-cultural and the ordinary. In the light of this domination we reflected on the work of creating space for imaginative literacy, and creating spaces that support imaginative literacy.

The second reflection identified *stories* as a vital resource for education in re-imagination. Stories provide the models, images and pictures that ignite imagination, and provide a soulful counter to modern infotainment. Trainers need to provide soulful, alternative stories that engage the imaginative faculties of possibilitators. So we turn to contemporary storytellers who write with depth, integrity, passion and insight; thoughtful essayists who reflect in critical and imaginative ways on contemporary society; and author-activists who articulate the practice wisdom of the global traditions of community development. Imagination is also fired by living stories – both people's ordinary and extraordinary lived experiences, and those of groups and organisations that keep the dream alive and model the structuring of change.

The third reflection explored different models and methods of training – such as experiential, elicitive, the spiral and the participatory action and learning models, along with our own model of *deconstructive conversation*. The reflection focused on the social journey of deconstructive conversation, preferably shared by a cadre of collaborators, as the *mythos* of our social, cultural, ecological, economic and political worlds is destabilised. Mandate was then considered – a process ensuring that people freely enter into the process of a training dialogue with full awareness and consent.

The fourth reflection argued for a training focus on *inspiration* and *empowerment not information*. The fallacy that information is power was exposed. We argued that for people to experience empowerment they need to feel inspired to be involved in processes of change that relate to their real, lived experiences; and they need to believe that change can happen and that they can make it happen. We considered how empowerment-oriented training often involves particular kinds of capacity-building practices and potent trainers and also argued for more experimentation in embodied learning experiences, theatre and other performance-oriented training processes. Furthermore it becomes important to resist the seduction of content-focused technologies that are destroying the role of dialogue within any learning space.

The final reflection argued that the learning process is a failure if it does not inspire action. The journey from *wishing*, to *willing*, to *acting* involves regaining the ability to wish for a better world, unlocking willingness that is captive to despair and asserting *response-ability* through action.

Conclusion

As stated within the introductory chapter, this book is a story of one framework of community development, grounded in a social learning tradition, which puts the focal lens on dialogue. Reiterating Ife's (2002) comments about practitioners building their own framework (Westoby and Ingamells 2011), *dialogical community development* is one that has been constructed through reflection on our combined 50 years of practice, observation of what other practitioners are doing, and research into relevant case studies alongside engagement with theory. The lens of dialogue has also been applied to many orthodoxies of community development practice – such as place, participation, method, conflict, training, economics and so forth. In many ways it is up to the reader to discern how successful we have been in creating a framework that makes sense not only to us but also to other citizen and professional practitioners (you, the reader). To make this discernment task easier we would like to draw some of the threads together at this point, reminding the reader of the core ideas and articulating again what we have aimed to achieve in writing the book.

The first thread consists of the framework articulated within the Introduction. This framework rests on three cornerstones: dialogue, community and development. Each of these is discussed in the Introduction, with dialogue more thoroughly explored in Chapter 1, the 'Theoretical prelude'. Dialogue is explored as other-oriented, humanising attention to the kinds of relationship that enable creative transformation. Community is re-theorised as 'dialogue' and hospitality, as *communitas* and as ethical space, and finally as collective practice. Both dialogue and community were situated within a post-development imagination.

Holding these three cornerstones together is the idea of 'depth' – orienting the reader and practitioner to a philosophical approach to community development, one that provides enough substance to avoid being drawn into modernist, instrumental, technique-oriented approaches. Within the Introduction we argue that a Euro-centrist modernist paradigm is underpinned by an epistemological worldview that is reductionist, 'wilful' and instrumental. Within such a paradigm, solutions are reduced to the technical, and technique becomes the 'instrument' of social change. Such a worldview applied to community development constructs or frames practice in terms of interventions comprised of inputs, timelines, outputs, impacts and measurable indicators. The assumption is that the 'will' for intervention, supported by the technologies of modernity and markets (experts, money, technology, coordination and effective management), affects social change that benefits the marginalised. This Euro-centric modernist paradigm often accompanies colonial and neo-colonial processes of 'aid and development' or 'scaled-up programmes'. The assumption is that a supposed 'universal' model of community development technique, aligned to a universal model of development, can be imported and exported anywhere in the world – transferred through capacity-building initiatives, train-the-trainer courses and so forth. It is with such an analysis in mind that we were motivated to articulate an alternative dialogical approach to community development.

It is worth repeating in this conclusion that our critique of modernist community development is in no way meant to imply that techniques are unimportant. On the contrary, techniques are essential; but they must be put in their right context. Any use of technique must be informed by an understanding of the intellectual, methodological and geographically shaped traditions that provide a deeper reading of community development work (Westoby and Hope-Simpson 2010).

With the above analyses in mind we argue for a philosophical approach, one conscious of the depth of traditions that have informed community development theory and practice for many decades. A depth approach to dialogical community development invites workers to bring philosophy, theory and attentiveness to the practice. It challenges practitioners to learn how to observe and 'read' the complex patterns that both foreground and background complex social phenomena. It requires a resistance to the 'shallow-ing' of practice, the product of an age of speed, spin, quick fixes and amnesia. Instead it learns from the practice wisdom captured in mantras such as 'it takes time', 'slow down', 'first watch, and then listen and learn'. They invite a depth approach that opens up the possibilities of counter-cultural practice.

The rest of the dialogical framework consists of six other dimensions, each explored in detail within the Introduction:

- enfolding community development within a commitment to social solidarity;
- infusing practice with a soulful orientation;
- contextualising practice as vocational professionals;
- reconstituting community work as a social practice;
- reading our work with an ecological sensibility;
- opening ourselves up to deconstructive movements.

This framework as a whole provides a conceptual map or structure to community development practitioners, citizens or professionals, who wish to explore the transformative, progressive, playful, edgy, soulful approach we invite people to consider.

The second thread of this book focuses on dialogue theory and practice within community development and invites the reader to consider the relevance of the 'narrative' or 'dialogical' turn within applied social sciences. In the same way that Robert Chambers' work on participatory development paved the way for the 'participatory turn' in the 1980s, we observe that the groundwork for a narrative or dialogical turn is being put together within many social science disciplines, from psychology through to politics and sociology. This narrative and dialogical turn is of huge significance as community workers engage with people in the contexts of mass migration, post-colonialism and the spectre of increased conflict as ecological disaster approaches and social inequalities grow. Working with and among strangers, inviting people to work across difference, conflicting carefully, and engaging 'the other' will be the test of many citizens and practitioners. Dialogue as forms of communication and connecting, reaching out across difference, building a coherent understanding of the complex whole that constructs so many social problems, questioning hegemonic assumptions, and opposing dominating, ossifying forces and actors within historical processes, becomes more crucial than ever.

The third thread of this book considers the formation of dialogical community development as a theory-building exercise. In doing this readers are invited to contemplate the contribution of several theorists of dialogue to community development. These theorists offer ways of imagining dialogue that have then been diffused into the more orthodox practices of community development. While theorising dialogue for community development has been our core project we have also attempted to re-theorise concepts such as place-making and participation, method and analysis, and training and transformation, in the light of the core project. We have used dialogue to frame fresh ways of seeing these fundamental processes, weaving a tapestry of ideas that can inform reflective and reflexive practice, while holding dialogue as a lens for understanding the world and giving insight into the work.

The fourth thread of this book consists of an iterative process of moving between theory and stories of practice – ensuring that the 'theory-building' process is also grounded in the messy, swampy, complex realities of citizen or professional practice. We have avoided high-level theory, and instead prioritised attempts to make theoretical ideas accessible and applicable. We are hopeful that the reader experiences the interplay between theory and practice in the same way as musicians experience the playful riff in creating music. There is an easy to and fro, back and forth, each gifting the other. In such a dialectic relationship theory and practice should be experienced in harmony with one another.

The fifth thread of this book is an invitation to people to test our ideas. In many ways the framework has emerged from us testing the ideas of people before us – our teachers and mentors. For example, practitioners such as Anthony Kelly, Ann Ingamells and Dave Andrews each introduced us to traces of the dialogical and hospitality traditions of practice. They in turn acknowledge their many influences, such as Buber and Gandhi. We have built on their teaching – experimenting and exploring new theory, ideas and concepts. In doing this we extend the invitation to others to continue testing the theory. We have offered numerous practices and examples of dialogue, considered conditions that are crucial for dialogue, examined some of the limits of dialogue, and briefly delved into what weakens dialogue within community development. We see this as a platform to build upon. As authors it is easy to apply a deconstructive lens to our own writing, ever conscious of the cracks and silences. We are aware of the contribution of theorists removed from the text and practice stories we would love to have shared – that we have edited out in order to provide a more concise and balanced reading experience. Therefore, there are many gaps that should only feed an ongoing curiosity about the ideas pursued and ones missed.

A passion of not knowing

As a final word we also invite readers to consider this framework of dialogical community development through cultivating a 'passion of not knowing' (Caputo 1997b: 338). Modernist thinking loves to understand and explain, and then to provide the final word and sure solution. Some approaches to community development have become captive to such thinking, with the resultant 'cookbook approach'. To ensure that community practitioners do not become captive to this tendency, it is crucial to cultivate a passion of not knowing that keeps us searching for ongoing dialogue and depth.

We advocate a willingness to open up to mysteries and to unmask any illusions about a final word, employing what Paulo Freire (1997: 100) called 'epistemological curiosity'. Although such a willingness and curiosity could lead to potential chaos for some, it ensures that practitioners remain inquisitive, humble and open, regaining the ability to wish for a better world through losing a sense of security and assuredness. We are indebted to Henri Nouwen (1975) for the counter-intuitive insight that poverty of mind makes a good host. An expression of certainty can disempower the people community practitioners are working with. However, a hospitable expression of uncertainty shifts practitioners towards the other – into a shared space of mutual unsure-ness. Only 'we' in social solidarity with one another can work this out. So the onward journey is infused with ownership and mutuality, expressed through statements such as 'I'm not sure either, but I'm confident *we* can work through this together.'

The notion of hospitality has been a central theme of this book. Embedded within the idea of hospitality is a stance that constantly welcomes the stranger – in this case the unknown. If such an idea of hospitality is combined with the passion of not knowing, then the only possible trajectory for community development theorising and practice is more dialogue, opening up space for mystery, possibility and imagination.

Invitation to dialogue and dissent

As stated in the Introduction, we hope readers will engage with us in a dialogue. Here we reiterate this hope. Welcome to the dialogue. Any dissent is welcome.

Notes

Introduction: a practice framework

1 Recognising that even the notion of normative is historically constructed.
2 It also, conversely, opens up the possibility of illusion – thinking there is dialogue across difference, when there is in fact profound misunderstanding.
3 Albeit with a nuanced understanding of the collective as discussed in Chapter 2.
4 We are uncomfortable with the notion of the 'poor' as the word is inevitably read through an economic lens, whereas in many ways poverty is a political process.
5 We acknowledge a conversation with British colleague David Harding for this insight.
6 Note how the idea of reflexivity is used in a completely opposite way in some disciplines, for example referring to unconscious reactivity within various traditions of psychology.

1 Theoretical prelude: an introduction to dialogue for community development

1 It also, conversely opens up the possibility of illusion – thinking there is dialogue across difference, when there is in fact profound misunderstanding.
2 For this insight we acknowledge the conversation of 27 community practitioners, facilitated over three days by Allan Kaplan and Sue Davidoff during July 2012.

2 Re-imagining community practice

1 Australian Agency for International Development, the Australian Government's overseas aid programme.
2 'Not in my backyard'.

References

Ackerman, J.M. (2005) 'Human rights and social accountability', in *Social Development Papers: Participation and Civic Engagement*, Paper No. 86, Washington, DC: World Bank.
Agamben, G. (1993) *The Coming Community*, trans. M. Hardt, Minneapolis, MN: University of Minneapolis Press.
Alexander, C., Ishikawa, S. and Silverstein, M. (1977) *A Pattern Language: Towns, Buildings and Construction*, New York: Oxford University Press.
Alinsky, S. (1969) *Reveille for Radicals*, New York: Vintage Books.
Alinsky, S. (1971) *Rules for Radicals: A Practical Primer for Realistic Radicals*, New York: Random House.
Amin, A. (2009) *Social Economy: International Perspectives on Economic Solidarity*, London and New York: ZED Books.
Andrews, D. (1992) *Can You Hear the Heartbeat*, London, Sydney, Auckland and Toronto: Hodder & Stoughton.
Andrews, D. (2007) *Living Community*, Brisbane, Qld: Community Praxis Co-op and Tafina Press.
Andrews, D. (2012) *In-depth Community Work*, Preston, Vic.: Mosaic Press.
Appadurai, A. (1996) *Modernity at Large: Cultural Dimensions of Globalisation*, Minneapolis, MN: University of Minnesota Press.
Archer, D. and Cottingham, S. (2012) *Reflect Mother Manual: Regenerated Freirean Literacy through Empowering Community Techniques*, London: International Reflect Network.
Arnett, R., Fritz, J.M.H. and Bell, L.M. (2009) *Communication Ethics Literacy: Dialogue and Difference*, Los Angeles, CA: Sage Press.
Australia Institute (2008) 'Some crises are more equal than others', *Between the Lines*, 22 October, available online at http://nothing-new-under-the-sun.blogspot.co.uk/2008/10/some-crises-are-more-equal-than-others.html (accessed 25 January 2013).
Bachelard, G. (1994) *The Poetics Of Space*, Boston, MA: Beacon Press.
Baken, J. (2004) *The Corporation: The Pathological Pursuit of Profit and Power*, New York: Free Press.
Bakhtin, M.M. (1981) *The Dialogic Imagination: Four Essays*, Austin, TX: University of Texas Press.
Bakhtin, M.M. (1986) *Speech Genres and Other Late Essays*, trans. Vern W. McGee, Austin, TX: University of Texas Press.
Banerjee, V.A. and Duflo, E. (2011) *Poor Economics: A Radical Rethinking of the Way to Fight Global Poverty*, New York: Public Affairs.

Barringham, N. (2003) *Structuring Without Strangling: The Story of the Community Initiatives Resource Association 1993–2003 – An Experiment In Doing More With Less*, Brisbane, Qld: Community Initiatives Resource Association

Barrios, L. (2007) 'Gangs and spirituality of liberation', in *Gangs in the Global City: Alternatives to Traditional Criminology*, ed. J. Hagedorrn, Urbana and Chicago, IL: University of Illinois Press.

Batten, T.R. (1962) *Training For Community Development: A Critical Study of Method*, London: Oxford University Press.

Batten, T.R. and Batten, M. (1967) *The Non-Directive Approach in Group and Community Work*, London: Oxford University Press.

Bauman, Z. (1998) *Globalisation: The Human Consequences*, Cambridge: Polity Press.

Beavitt, R. (2012) *The Demands of Liminality: Community, Communitas, and Reflexivity*, Honours thesis, Murdoch University, Perth, WA.

Bell, B., Gaventa, J. and Peters, J. (eds) (1990) *We Make the Road by Walking: Conversations on Education and Social Change: Myles Horton and Paulo Freire*, Philadelphia, PA: Temple University Press.

Blaser, M., Feit, H.A. and McRae, G. (2004) *In the Way of Development: Indigenous Peoples, Life Projects and Globalization*, London: Zed Books.

Bleiker, R. (2000) *Popular Dissent, Human Agency and Global Politics*, Cambridge: Cambridge University Press.

Block, P. (2008) *Community: The Structure of Belonging*, San Francisco, CA: Berrett-Koehler.

Boal, A. (1979) *Theatre of the Oppressed*, London: Pluto Press.

Bohm, D. (1980) *Wholeness and the Implicate Order*, London: Routledge.

Bohm, D. (1994) *Thought as a System*, New York: Routledge.

Bohm, D. (1996) *On Dialogue*, New York: Routledge.

Bollier, D. and Helfrich, S. (eds) (2012) *The Wealth of the Commons: A World Beyond Market and State*, Amherst: Levellers Press.

Booth, W. (1993) *Households: On the Moral Architecture of the Economy*, Ithaca, NY: Cornell Press.

Botes, L. and Rensburg, D. (2000) 'Community participation in development: nine plagues and twelve commandments', *Community Development Journal*, 35(1): 41–58.

Boulet, J. (2010) 'Community economic development outside the capitalist square', *New Community Quarterly*, 8(1): 24–32.

Boulet, J., Krauss, J. and Oelschlaegel, D. (1980) *Gemeinwesenarbeit als Arbeitsprinzip: eine Grundlegung (Community Development as a Working Principle: A Foundation)*, Bielefeld: AJZ Verlag.

Bourdieu, P. (1984) *Distinction: A Social Critique of the Judgement of Taste*, Cambridge, MA: Harvard University Press.

Bourdieu, P. (1999) *The Weight of the World: Social Suffering in Contemporary Society*, Stanford, CA: Stanford University Press.

Brookfield, S.D. and Holst, J.D. (2010) *Radicalizing Learning: Adult Education for a Just World*, San Francisco, CA: John Wiley.

Brotherton, D. (2007) 'Towards the gang as a social movement', in *Gangs in the Global City: Alternatives to Traditional Criminology*, ed. J. Hagedorrn, Urbana and Chicago, IL: University of Illinois Press.

Brown, L. (2012) *How Much Will It Cost to Save Our Economy's Foundation?*, Washington, DC: Earth Policy Institute, available online at www.earth-policy.org/book_bytes/2012/wotech10_ss4 (accessed 19 May 2012).

References

Brown, W. (1995) *States of Injury: Power and Freedom in Late Modernity*, Princeton, NJ: Princeton University Press.
Brown, W. (2010) *Walled States, Waning Sovereignty*, New York: Zone Books.
Buber, M. (1947/2002) *Between Man and Man*, 2nd edn, London and New York: Routledge Classics.
Buber, M. (1958) *I and Thou*, New York: Charles Scribener's Sons.
Buckley, H. (2007) *The Development of a Community Cooperative on the Sunshine Coast: A Building Links Project*, Maleny, Qld: Community Praxis Co-op.
Burke, J. (2006) 'Gang wars shake Spain's Latin quarter', *The Guardian*, available online at www.guardian.co.uk/world/2006/oct/15/spain.jasonburke (accessed 24 July 2012).
Butcher. H., Banks, S., Henderson, P. and Robertson, J. (2007) *Critical Community Practice*, Bristol: Policy Press.
Calthorpe, P. (1993) *The Next American Metropolis: Ecology, Community, and the American Dream*, New York: Princeton Architectural Press.
Campfens, H. (ed.) (1997) *Community Development around the World: Practice, Theory, Research and Training*, London and Toronto: University of Toronto Press.
Capra, F. (1994) *Ecology and Community*, Berkeley, CA: Center for Ecoliteracy.
Caputo, J.D. (ed.) (1997a) *Deconstruction in a Nutshell: A Conversation with Jacques Derrida*, New York: Fordham University Press.
Caputo, J.D. (1997b) *The Prayers and Tears of Jacques Derrida: Religion Without Religion*, Bloomington and Indianapolis, IN: Indiana University Press.
Carmen, R. (1996) *Autonomous Development: Humanizing the Landscape*, London: Zed Books.
Casey, E. (2011) 'Strangers at the edge of hospitality', in *Phenomenologies of the Stranger: Between Hostility and Hospitality*, eds R. Kearney and K. Semonovitch, New York: Fordham University Press.
Chambers, R. (1997) *Whose Reality Counts? Putting the First Last*, London: ITDG Publishing.
Chambers, R. (2005) *Ideas for Development*, London: Earthscan.
Cohen, A. (1957) *Martin Buber*, London: Bowes & Bowes.
Cohen, A. (1985) *The Symbolic Construction of Community*, Chichester: Ellis Horwood.
Cohen, C., Varea, R.G. and Walker, P. (eds) (2012) *Acting Together: Performance and the Creative Transformation of Conflict: Volumes I and II*, Oakland, CA: New Village Press.
Congress for the New Urbanism (2001) *Charter of the New Urbanism*, Chicago, IL: Congress for the New Urbanism.
Connolly, W. (1999) *Why I Am Not a Secularist*, London and Minneapolis, MN: University of Minnesota Press.
Cooper Marcus, C. and Francis, C. (1998) *People Places: Design Guidelines for Urban Open Space*, 2nd edition, New York: John Wiley and Sons.
Cooper Marcus, C. and Sarkissian, W. (1988) *Housing As If People Mattered: Site Design Guidelines for Medium-density Family Housing*, Berkeley, CA: University of California Press.
Cornwall, A. (ed.) (2011) *The Participation Reader*, London and New York: Zed Books.
Cousineau, P. (1998) *The Art of Pilgrimage: The Seeker's Guide to Making Travel Sacred*, Boston, MA: Conari Press.
Craig, G. and Mayo, M. (1995) *Community Empowerment: A Reader in Participation and Development*, London: Zed Books.
Crapanzano, V. (1990) 'On dialogue', in *The Interpretation Of Dialogue*, ed. T. Maranhão, Chicago, IL, and London: University of Chicago Press.

References

Dasgupta, S. (1968) *Social Work and Social Change: A Case Study in Indian Village Development*, Boston, MA: Extending Horizons Books.

Daveson, C. (2000) 'From private concern to public action', *Culture Matters*, Issue 01: 38–41.

Day, C. (1990) *Places of the Soul: Architecture and Environmental Design as a Healing Art*, London: Thorsons.

de Botton, A. (2007) *The Architecture of Happiness*, London: Penguin Books.

de Tocqueville, A. (1835) *Democracy in America*, London: Penguin Books.

Deacon, E., Esser, C., Moore, C. and Coover, V. (eds) (1985) *Resource Manual for a Living Revolution: A Handbook of Skills and Tools for Social Change Activists*, Philadelphia, PA: New Society Publishers.

Deb, D. (2009) *Beyond Developmentality: Constructing Inclusive Freedom and Sustainability*, London: Earthscan.

Denborough, D. (2008) *Collective Narrative Practice: Responding to Individuals, Groups and Communities Who Have Experienced Trauma*, Adelaide, SA: Dulwich Centre Publications.

Denborough, D. (2010) *Kite of Life: From Intergenerational Conflict to Intergenerational Alliance*, Adelaide, SA: Dulwich Centre Foundation.

Derrida, J. (1997) *Politics of Friendship*, London and New York: Verso.

Derrida, J. (2001) *On Cosmopolitanism*, New York: Routledge.

Dethlefs, W. and Kelly, A. (1988) *Spinning the Web – the People Net that Works – a Participation Technology*, School of Social Work Community Development Working Paper Series, University of Queensland.

Devananda, A. (1986) *Mother Teresa: Contemplative at the Heart of the World*, New York: Fount.

Duany, A., Plater-Zyberk, E. and Speck, J. (2000) *Suburban Nation: The Rise of Sprawl and the Decline of the American Dream*, New York: North Point Press.

Eade, D. (1997) *Capacity Building: An Approach to People-centred Development*, Oxford: Oxfam.

Ellul, J. (1965) *The Technological Society*, London: Cape.

Escobar, A. (2010) 'Latin America at a crossroads', *Cultural Studies*, 24(1): 1–65.

Esposito, R. (2010) *Communitas: The Origin and Destiny of Community*, Stanford, CA: Stanford University Press.

Esteva, G. (1987) 'Regenerating people's space', *Alternatives*, 12(1): 125–52.

Everatt, D. and Gwagwa, L. (2005) *Community Driven Development in South Africa, 1990–2004*, Africa Region, Working Paper Series No. 92. Washington, DC: World Bank, available online at www.worldbank.org/afr/wps/wp92.htm (accessed 21 May 2012).

Falzon, C. (1998) *Foucault and Social Dialogue*, London and New York: Routledge.

Faubion, J. (1994) *Michel Foucault: Power – The Essential Works 3*, London: Penguin Group.

Feixa, C. (1998/2008) *De Jovenes, Bandas Y Tribus*, Barcelona: Barcelona Press.

Finch, J. (2007) 'Bonanza in British boardrooms', *The Guardian Weekly*, 29 August, available online at www.guardian.co.uk/business/2007/aug/29/executivepay2 (accessed 10 September 2012).

Flecha, R., Gomez, J. and Puigvert, L. (2003) *Contemporary Sociological Theory*, New York: Peter Lang.

Forester, J. (1999) *The Deliberative Practitioner: Encouraging Participatory Planning Processes*, Cambridge, MA: MIT Press.

Freeden, M. (2003) *Ideology: A Very Short Introduction*, Oxford: Oxford University Press.

Freire, P. (1972) *Pedagogy of the Oppressed*, London: Penguin Books.
Freire, P. (1974) *Education for Critical Consciousness*, New York: Continuum.
Freire, P. (1994) *Pedagogy of Hope: Reliving Pedagogy of the Oppressed*, New York: Continuum.
Freire, P. (1997) *Pedagogy of the Heart*, New York and London: Continuum.
Fromm, E. (1957) *The Art of Loving*, London: Thorsons, HarperCollins.
Furedi, F. (2004) *Therapy Culture: Cultivating Vulnerability in an Uncertain Age*, London and New York: Routledge.
Furedi, F. (2005) *Politics of Fear: Beyond Left and Right*, London and New York: Continuum.
Gadamer, H.G. (1975) *Truth and Method*, New York: The Seabury Press.
Gadamer, H.G. (1998) *Praise of Theory: Speeches and Essays*, New Haven, CT, and London: Yale University Press.
Gandhi, M. (1940) *An Autobiography: The Story of My Experiments with Truth*, Ahmedabad: Navajivan.
Gap Filler (2012) *Gap Filler*, available online at www.gapfiller.org.nz (accessed 1 June 2012).
Geoghegan, M. and Powell, F. (2009) 'Community development and the contested politics of the late modern agora: of, alongside or against neoliberalism', *Community Development Journal*, 44(4): 430–47.
Gergen, K. (2009) *Relational Being*, New York: Oxford University Press.
Gibney, P. (2003) *The Pragmatics of Therapeutic Practice*, Melbourne, Vic.: Psychoz Publications.
Gibson-Graham, J.K. (2006) *A Post-capitalist Politics*, Minneapolis, MN: University of Minnesota Press.
Giddens, A. (1984) *The Constitution of Society: Outline of a Theory of Structuration*, Cambridge: Polity Press.
Gilchrist, A. (2004) *The Well-connected Community: A Networking Approach to Community Development*, Bristol: Policy Press.
Glatzer, N. and Mendes-Flohr, P. (eds) (1991) *The Letters of Martin Buber: A Life of Dialogue*, New York: Schocken Books.
Gogatz, A. and Mondejar, R. (2005) *Business Creativity: Breaking the Invisible Barriers*, Basingstoke and New York: Palgrave Macmillan.
Green, D. (2008) *From Poverty to Power: How Active Citizens and Effective States Can Change the World*, Oxford: Oxfam International.
Groundviews (2012) *Groundviews*, available online at http://groundviews.org/about/ (accessed 1 September 2012).
Guardiola-Rivera, O. (2010) *What If Latin America Ruled the World? How the South Will Take the North through the 21st Century*, London, Berlin and New York: Bloomsbury.
Gupta, U.D. (ed.) (2006) *Rabindranath Tagore: My Life in My Words*, New Delhi: Penguin Books India.
Hage, G. (1998) *White Nation: Fantasies of White Supremacy in Multicultural Society*, Sydney: Pluto Press.
Hage, G. (2003) *Against Paranoid Nationalism: Searching for Hope in a Shrinking Society*, Sydney: Pluto Press.
Haines, N. (2012) 'Creativity and technique: a participatory approach to farmer education in Cambodia', in *Learning and Mobilising for Community Development: A Radical Tradition of Community-based Education and Training*, eds P. Westoby and L. Shevellar, Farnham: Ashgate.
Hamdi, N. (2010) *The Placemakers' Guide to Building Community*, London: Earthscan.

Hamdi, N. and Goethert, R. (1997) *Action Planning for Cities: A Guide to Community Practice*, Chichester: John Wiley.

Hamilton, C. (2005) *Affluenza*, Sydney: Allen & Unwin.

Harvey, D. (2011) *The Enigma of Capital and the Crisis of Capitalism*, London: Profile Books.

Healy, K. (2005) *Social Work Theories in Context: Creating Frameworks for Practice*, Basingstoke: Palgrave Macmillan.

Henderson, P. and Thomas, D. (2005) *Skills in Neighbourhood Work*, 3rd edition, London: Routledge Press.

Hickey, S. and Mohan, G. (eds) (2004) *Participation, from Tyranny to Transformation? Exploring New Approaches to Participation in Development*, London and New York: ZED Books.

Hicks, D. (2011) *Dignity: The Essential Role It Plays in Resolving Conflict*, New Haven, CT, and London: Yale University Press.

Hillman, J. (1983) *A Healing Fiction*, Woodstock: Spring Publications.

Hillman, J. and Ventura, M. (1993) *We've Had a Hundred Years of Psycho-therapy and the World's Getting Worse*, New York: HarperCollins.

Hollis, J. (2001) *Creating a Life: Finding Your Individual Path*, Toronto: Inner City Books.

Hollis, J. (2005) *Finding Meaning in the Second Half of Life*, New York: Gotham Books.

Homer-Dixon, T. (2006) *The Upside of Down: Catastrophe, Creativity and the Renewal of Civilization*, Melbourne, Vic.: The Text Publishing Company.

hooks, b. (1990) *Yearning: Race, Gender and Cultural Politics*, Boston, MA: South End Press.

hooks, b. (1994) *Teaching to Transgress: Education as the Practice of Freedom*, New York and London: Routledge.

hooks, b. (2003) *Teaching Community: A Pedagogy of Hope*, New York and London: Routledge.

Hope, A. and Timmel, S. (1984) *Training for Transformation: A Handbook for Community Workers, Volumes 1–3*, Harare: Mambo Press.

Hope, R. (2005) *Creativity: Theory, History, Practice*, London and New York: Routledge.

Horton, M. and Freire, P. with Bell, B., Gaventa, J. and Peters, J. (eds) (1990) *We Make the Road by Walking: Conversations on Education and Social Change*, Philadelphia, PA: Temple University Press.

Hustvedt, S. (2012) *Living, Thinking, Looking*, London: Sceptre Books.

Hutchinson, V. (2012) 'Learning communities', in *How Communities Heal: Stories of Social Innovation and Social Change*, ed. V. Hutchinson, Auckland: New Zealand Social Entrepreneur Fellowship.

Ife, J. (2002) *Community Development: Community Based Alternatives in an Age of Globalisation*, 2nd edition, Melbourne, Vic.: Pearson Education.

Ife, J. (2009) *Human Rights from Below: Achieving Rights through Community Development*, Cambridge: Cambridge University Press.

Ife, J. (2012) 'The future of community development', *New Community Quarterly*, 10(1): 4–10.

Illich, I. (1977) *Disabling Professions*, London: Salem & Boyars.

Ingamells, A., Lathouras, A., Wiseman, R., Westoby, P. and Caniglia, F. (eds) (2010) *Community Development Practice: Stories, Meaning and Method*, Champaign, IL: Common Ground.

Inspiring Communities (2010) *What We Are Learning about Community-led Development in Aotearoa New Zealand*, Wellington: Inspiring Communities Trust.

Isaacs, P. (1993) *Obligations of the Profession*, Brisbane, Qld: Queensland University of Technology.

Jameson, F. (1983) *The Political Unconscious: Narrative as a Socially Symbolic Act*, London and New York: Routledge.
Jha, C., Prasai, S., Hobley, M. and Bennett, L. (2009) *Citizen Mobilisation in Nepal: Building on Nepal's Tradition of Social Mobilisation To Make Local Governance More Inclusive and Accountable*, available online at www.gsdrc.org/docs/open/VA1.pdf (accessed 1 June 2012).
Kaplan, A. (1996) *The Development Practitioners' Handbook*, Chicago, IL, and London: Pluto Press.
Kaplan, A. (2002) *Development Practitioners and Social Process: Artists of the Invisible*, Chicago, IL, and London: Pluto Press.
Kaplan, A. (2005) 'Emerging out of Goethe: conversation as a form of social inquiry', *Janus Head*, 8(1): 311–34.
Kapuscinski, R. (2008) *The Other*, London and New York: Verso.
Kearney, R. and Semonovitch, K. (eds) (2011) *Phenomenologies of the Stranger: Between Hostility and Hospitality*, New York: Fordham University Press.
Keen, A. (2012) *Digital Vertigo: How Today's Online Social Revolution Is Dividing, Diminishing and Disorienting Us*, London: Constable.
Kelly, A. (2008) *People Centred Development: Development Method*, Brisbane, Qld: The Centre for Social Response.
Kelly, A. (forthcoming) *With Love and a Sense of Necessity*.
Kelly, A. and Burkett, I. (2008) *People Centred Development: Building the People Centred Approach*, Brisbane, Qld: The Centre for Social Response.
Kelly, A. and Sewell, S. (eds) (1986) *People Working Together: Volume II*, Brisbane, Qld: Boolarong Publications.
Kelly, A. and Sewell, S. (1988) *With Head, Heart and Hand: Dimensions of Community Building*, Brisbane, Qld: Boolarong Publications.
Kelly, A., Morgan, A. and Coghlan, D. (1997) *People Working Together, Volume III: Traditions and Best Practice*, Brisbane, Qld: Boolarong Press.
Kolb, D.A. (1984) *Experiential Learning: Experience as the Source of Learning and Development*, Englewood Cliffs, NJ: Prentice Hall.
Korten, D. (1995) *When Corporations Rule the World*, West Hartford, CT: Kumarian Press.
Korten, D. (2000) *The Post-corporate World: Life after Capitalism*, Melbourne, Vic.: Pluto Press.
Kretzmann, J. and McKnight, J. (1993) *Building Communities from the Inside Out: A Path toward Finding and Mobilizing a Community's Assets*, Chicago, IL: ACTA Publications.
Kropotkin, P. (1902) *Mutual Aid: A Factor of Evolution*, London: Heinemann.
Kumar, S. (2002) *Methods for Community Participation: A Complete Guide for Practitioners*, London: ITDG Publishing.
Kurlansky, M. (2006) *Non-violence: A History of a Dangerous Idea*, London: Jonathan Cape.
Lakey, G. (2010) *Facilitating Group Learning: Strategies for Success with Diverse Adult Learners*, San Francisco, CA: Jossey Bass.
Land, C. (2011) 'Decolonising activism/deactivating colonialism', *Action Learning and Action Research Journal*, 17(2): 42–62.
Lederach, J.P. (1995) *Preparing for Peace: Conflict Transformation across Cultures*, New York: Syracuse University Press.
Lederach, J.P. (2005) *The Moral Imagination: The Art and Soul of Building Peace*, Oxford: Oxford University Press.

Ledwith, M. (2005) *Community Development: A Critical Approach*, Bristol: Policy Press.
Leunig, M. (2001) *The Curly Pyjama Letters*, Camberwell: Penguin Books Australia.
Levinas, E. (1999) *Alterity and Transcendence*, London: Athlone Press.
Liebersohn, H. (2011) *The Return of the Gift: European History of a Global Idea*, New York: Cambridge University Press.
MacIntyre, A. (1984) *After Virtue*, 2nd edition, Notre Dame, IN: University of Notre Dame Press.
McKibben M. (2007) *Deep Economy: Economics As If the World Mattered*, Oxford: OneWorld Oxford.
Mackie, G. (2000) 'Female genital cutting: the beginning of the end', in *Female 'Circumcision' in Africa: Culture, Controversy, and Change*, eds B. Shell-Duncan and Y Hernlund, New York: Lynne Rienner.
McKnight, J. (1995) *The Careless Society: Community and its Counterfeits*, New York: Basic Books.
McLuhan, M. (1964) *Understanding Media: The Extensions of Man*, New York: Mentor.
McMichael, P. (ed.) (2010) *Contesting Development: Critical Struggles for Social Change*, New York: Routledge.
McMichael, P. (2012) *Development and Social Change: A Global Perspective*, Los Angeles, London, New Delhi, Singapore and Washington, DC: Sage.
Macy, J. (1983) *Despair and Personal Power in the Nuclear Age*, Philadelphia, PA: New Society Publishers.
Macy, J. and Brown, M.Y. (1998) *Coming Back to Life: Practices to Reconnect Our Lives, Our World*, Gabriola Island, BC: New Society Publishers.
Madeley, J. (2008) *Big Business, Poor Peoples*, London and New York: Zed Books.
Malkki, L. (1995) 'Refugees and exile: from "Refugee Studies" to the national order of things', *Annual Review of Anthropology*, 24: 495–523.
Mann, A.T. (2010) *Sacred Landscapes: The Threshold between Worlds*, New York: Sterling Publishing.
Maranhão, T. (ed.) (1990) *The Interpretation of Dialogue*, Chicago, IL, and London: University of Chicago Press.
Masters, L.A. and Wallace, H.R. (2011) *Personal Development for Life and Work*, 10th edition, Mason, OH: Cengage Learning.
Mathie, A. and Cunningham, G.D. (eds) (2008) *From Clients to Citizens: Communities Changing the Course of Their Own Development*, Manchester: Practical Action Publishing.
Mauss, M. (1925/1990) *The Gift: Forms and Functions of Exchange in Archaic Societies*, New York: Norton.
Max-Neef, M. (1991) *Human Scale Development: Conception, Application and Further Reflections*, New York and London: The Apex Press.
Max-Neef, M. (1992) *From the Outside Looking In: Experiences in Barefoot Economics*, London and New York: Zed Books.
Mayo, P. (1999) *Gramsci, Freire and Adult Education: Possibilities for Transformative Action*, London: Zed Books.
Mega, V. (1999) *The Participatory City: Innovations in the European Union*, MOST Programme for Urban Development Discussion Paper No. 32, Paris: UNESCO.
Menon, G. (2010) 'Recoveries of space and subjectivity in the shadows of violence: the clandestine politics of pavement dwellers in Mumbai', in *Contesting Development: Critical Struggles for Social Change*, ed. P. McMichael, New York: Routledge.
Midgley, G. (2000) *Systemic Intervention: Philosophy, Methodology, and Practice*, New York, Boston, Dordrecht, London and Moscow: Kluwer Academic/Plenum Publishers.

Monbiot, G. (2007) *Heat: How To Stop the Planet Burning*, London: Allen Lane.
Moore, T. (1992) *Care of the Soul: How To Add Depth and Meaning to Your Everyday Life*, London: Judy Piatkus.
Moore, T. (1996) *The Re-enchantment of Everyday Life*, Sydney: Hodder & Stoughton.
Mouffe, C. (2005) *On the Political: Thinking in Action*, London and New York: Routledge.
Nancy, J.L. (1991) *The Inoperative Community*, Minneapolis, MN: University of Minnesota Press.
Nelson Mandela Foundation (2010a) *Dialogue for Social Changes: Social Cohesion*, Johannesburg: Nelson Mandela Foundation.
Nelson Mandela Foundation (2010b) *Community Conversations: HIV/AIDS Programme Findings & Lessons*, Johannesburg: Nelson Mandela Foundation.
Norberg-Hodge, H. (2009) *Ancient Futures: Learning from Ladakh*, Melbourne, Vic.: Random House.
Nouwen, H.J.M. (1975) *Reaching Out: The Three Movements of the Spiritual Life*, New York: Doubleday.
Nussbaum, M. (2010) *Not for Profit: Why Democracy Needs the Humanities*, Princeton, NJ, and New York: Princeton University Press.
O'Leary, T., Burkett, I. and Braithwaite, K. (2011) *Appreciating Assets: Report of the International Association of Community Development & The Carnegie UK Trust*, Fife: Carnegie UK Trust.
Owen, J. (2009) *A History of the Moral Economy: Markets, Custom and the Philosophy of Popular Entitlement*, Melbourne, Vic.: Australian Scholarly Publishing.
Owen, J. and Westoby, P. (2012) 'The structure of dialogue within developmental practice', *Community Development*, 43(3): 306–19.
Parenti, C. (2011) *Tropic of Chaos: Climate Change and the New Geography of Violence*, New York: Nation Books.
Patel, R. (2009) *The Value of Nothing: How To Reshape Market Society and Redefine Democracy*, Melbourne, Vic.: Black.
Patel, R. (2010) 'Cities without citizens: a perspective on the struggle of Abahlali base Mjondolo, the Durban shackdweller movement', in *Contesting Development: Critical Struggles for Social Change*, ed. P. McMichael, New York: Routledge.
Patkar, A. (2006) *Master the Mind Monkey: Experience your Excellence*, Mumbai: Jaico.
Pawar, M. (2010) *Community Development in Asia and the Pacific*, New York and London: Routledge.
Peacemaker (2004) *Annual Report 2004*, Oldham: Peacemaker.
Peacemaker (2006) *Annual Report 2006*, Oldham: Peacemaker.
Peacemaker (2012) *Peacemaker*, available online at www.peace-maker.co.uk/ (accessed 26 July 2012).
Peile, C. (1990) 'Networking', in *Working with Departmental Clients and Their Families in a Community Context*, Brisbane, Qld: Department of Family Services.
Peile, C. (1994) *The Creative Paradigm: Insight, Synthesis and Knowledge Development*, Sydney: Avebury.
Pettit, J. (2010) 'Multiple faces of power and learning', *IDS Bulletin*, 41(3): 25–35.
Polanyi, K. (1944) *The Great Transformation*, Boston, MA: Beacon Press.
Poteete, A., Janssen, M. and Ostrom, E. (2010) *Working Together: Collective Action, the Commons, and Multiple Methods in Practice*, Princeton, NJ, and Oxford: Princeton University Press.
Pretty, J.N., Guijt, I., Scoones, I. and Thompson, J. (1995) *A Trainer's Guide for Participatory Learning and Action*, London: International Institute for Environment and Development.

Princen, T. (2010) *Treading Softly: Paths to Ecological Order*, Cambridge, MA, and London: MIT Press.

Proudhon, P.J. (1902) *What Is Property? An Inquiry into the Principle of Right and of Government*, London: W. Reeves.

Pupavac, V. (2004) 'War on the couch: the emotionology of the new international security paradigm', *European Journal of Social Theory*, 7(2): 149–70.

Rahnema, M. (2010) 'Participation', in *The Development Dictionary*, ed. W. Sachs, London and New York: Zed Books.

Rawsthorne, A. and Howard, A. (2011) *Working with Communities: Critical Perspectives*, Champaign, IL: Common Ground Publishing.

Rayfield, A. and Morello, R. (2012) 'Bikin Kacau [untuk kebaikan]: solidarity education for civil resistance in West Papua' in *Learning and Mobilising for Community Development: A Radical Tradition of Community-based Education and Training*, eds P. Westoby and L. Shevellar, Farnham: Ashgate.

Restakis, J. (2010) *Humanizing the Economy: Co-operatives in the Age of Capital*, Gabriola Island, BC: New Society Publishers.

Rihani, S. (2002) *Complex Systems Theory and Development Practice*, London: Zed Books.

Rist, G. (2011) *The History of Development: From Western Origins to Global Faith*, London and New York: ZED Books.

Rose, D.B. (2011) *Wild Dog Dreaming: Love and Extinction*, Charlottesville, VA, and London: University of Virginia Press.

Rose, D.B., D'Amico, S., Daiyi, N., Deveraux, K., Daiyi, M., Ford, L. and Bright, A. (2002) *Country of the Heart: An Indigenous Australian Homeland*, Canberra, ACT: Aboriginal Studies Press.

Rose, N. (1999) *Powers of Freedom: Reframing Political Thought*, Cambridge: Cambridge University Press.

Roy, Arundhati (2011) *Broken Republic: Three Essays*, London: Penguin Books.

Sandercock, L. (2003) *Cosmopolis II: Mongrel Cities in the 21st Century*, London: Continuum.

Sarkissian, W. and Hurford, D. (2010) *Creative Community Planning: Transformative Engagement Methods for Working at the Edge*, London: Earthscan.

Schumacher, E.F. (1974) *Small is Beautiful: A Study of Economics as if People Mattered*, London: Abacus.

Schutzman, M. and Cohen-Cruz, J. (eds) (1994) *Playing Boal: Theatre, Therapy, Activism*, London: Routledge.

Sen, A. (1999) *Development as Freedom*, Oxford: Oxford University Press.

Senge, P. (1990) *The Fifth Discipline: The Art and Practice of the Learning Organisation*, London: Random House.

Sennett, R. (2003) *Respect: The Formation of Character in an Age of Inequality*, London: Penguin Books.

Sennett, R. (2012) *Together: The Rituals, Pleasures and Politics of Cooperation*, London: Allan Lane/Penguin Books.

Shiva, V. (2005) *Earth Democracy: Justice, Sustainability and Peace*, London: Zed Books.

Shuman, M. (2007) *The Small-Mart Revolution: How Local Businesses are Beating the Global Competition*, San Francisco, CA: BK Publishers.

Slade, G. (2012) *The Big Disconnect: The Study of Technology and Loneliness*, Amherst, NY: Prometheus Books.

Smith, J. (2005) *Jacques Derrida: Live Theory*, New York and London: Continuum.
Spretnak, C. (2011) *Relational Reality: New Discoveries of Interrelatedness That Are Transforming the Modern World*, Topsham: Green Horizon Books.
Storey, D., Muhidin, S. and Westoby, P. (2010) 'Planning for social inclusion amidst growth', *Australian Planner*, 47(3): 142–51.
Swan, J. and Swan, R. (eds) (1996) *Dialogues with the Living Earth: New Ideas on the Spirit of Place from Designers, Architects and Innovators*, Wheaton, IL: Theosophical Publishing House.
Szeman, I. (2000) 'Genocide, after all is an exercise in community building', *Other Voices, Journal of Cultural Criticism*, 2(1).
Taylor, C. (2002) 'Gadamer on the human sciences', in *The Cambridge Companion to Gadamer*, ed. D. Dostal, Cambridge: Cambridge University Press.
Tennyson, A. (1850) *In Memoriam*, London: Edward Moxon.
Thayer-Bacon, B. (2003) *Relational 'Epistemologies'*, New York: Peter Lang.
Thomas, P. and Bromley, M. (2010) *An Introduction to Communication and Social Change*, St Lucia: University of Queensland Press.
Thompson, T. (2011) 'Circles of change', *Stanford Social Innovation Review*, Fall 2011.
Turner, V. (1969) *The Ritual Process: Structure and Anti-structure*, London: Routledge and Kegan Paul.
Turton, D. (2005) 'The meaning of place in a world of movement: lessons from long-term field research in southern Ethiopia', *Journal of Refugee Studies*, 18(3): 258–80.
Twelvetrees, A. (2008) *Community Work*, 4th edition, London and New York: Palgrave Macmillan.
Ubels, J., Acquaye-Baddoo, N. and Fowler, A (eds) (2010) *Capacity Development in Practice*, London: Earthscan.
United Nations General Assembly (2007) *Cooperatives in Social Development: Report of the Secretary-General*, New York: United Nations.
Vanier, J. (1979) *Community and Growth*, Sydney: St Paul Publications.
von Hoffman, N. (2010) *A Portrait of Saul Alinsky*, Radical: Nation Books.
Vonnegut, K. (2005) *A Man Without Country*, New York, London, Melbourne and Toronto: Seven Stories Press.
Walker, P. (2012) 'Strengthening governance through storians: an elicitive approach to peace-building in Vanuatu', in *Learning and Mobilising for Community Development: A Radical Tradition of Community-based Education and Training*, eds P. Westoby and L. Shevellar, Farnham: Ashgate.
Wals, A.E.J. and Heymann, F. (2004) 'Learning on the edge: exploring the change potential of conflict in social learning for sustainable living', in *Educating for a Culture of Social and Ecological Peace*, ed. A. Wenden, New York: State University of New York Press.
Wates, N. (ed.) (2000) *The Community Planning Handbook: How People Can Shape Their Cities, Towns and Villages in Any Part of the World*, London: Earthscan.
Wates, N. and Knevitt, C. (1987) *Community Architecture: How People Are Creating Their Own Environment*, London: Penguin Books.
Watkins, M. and Shulman, H. (2008) *Toward Psychologies of Liberation*, Basingstoke and New York: Palgrave Macmillan.
Westoby, P. (1997) *A Soulful Approach to Community Development*, Durban: OLIVE Publications.
Westoby, P. (2010) 'Dialogue and disentanglement: navigating tensions for sustainable community economic development within Vanuatu', *International Journal of Environmental, Cultural, Economic and Social Sustainability*, 6(1): 81–92.

170 References

Westoby, P. and Brown, A. (2007) 'Peaceful community development in Vanuatu: a reflection on the Vanuatu kastom governance partnership', *Journal of Peace-building and Development*, 3(3): 77–81.

Westoby, P. and Dowling, G. (2009) *Dialogical Community Development: With Depth, Solidarity and Hospitality*, London and Brisbane, Qld: Tafina Press.

Westoby, P. and Hope-Simpson (2010) 'Re-thinking "tradition" and community development practice: integrating Derrida's "trace" and Peile's "creative synthesis" into a reconceptualising of "traditions" and community development practice', *European Journal of Social Work*, 14(2): 213–28.

Westoby, P. and Ingamells, A. (2011) 'Teaching community development personal practice frameworks', *Social Work Education*, 31(3): 383–96.

Westoby, P. and Morris, K. (2011) '"Community as dialogue" and "dialogical community development" with/in schools', in *Schools, Communities and Social Inclusion*, eds D. Bottrell and S. Goodwin, South Yarra, Vic.: Palgrave Macmillan.

Westoby, P. and Owen, J. (2010) 'The sociality and geometry of community development practice', *Community Development Journal*, 45(1): 58–74.

Westoby, P. and Shevellar, L. (eds) (2012) *Learning and Mobilising for Community Development: A Radical Tradition of Community-based Education and Training*, Farnham: Ashgate.

Westoby, P. and Sokhela, S. (2012) 'The "craft" of community-based education and training: the South African National Council of YMCAs and youth empowerment', in *Learning and Mobilising for Community Development: A Radical Tradition of Community-based Education and Training*, eds P. Westoby, and L. Shevellar, Farnham: Ashgate.

Westoby, P., Owen, J. and Hope-Simpson, G. (2009) 'Stability without strangling: the ongoing story of the Community Initiatives Resource Association, 2003–2008', *New Community Quarterly*, 7(2): 21–5.

Wheatley, M. and Frieze, D. (2011) *Walk Out Walk On: A Journey into Communities Daring to Live the Future Now*, San Francisco, CA: Berrett-Koehler.

Wicks, J. (2004) *Good Morning Beautiful Business: Twenty-Fourth Annual E.F. Schumacher Lectures*, Great Barrington, MA: E.F. Schumacher Society.

Wicks, J. and Klause, V.K. (1998) *White Dog Café Cookbook: Multicultural Recipes and Tales of Adventure from Philadelphia's Revolutionary Restaurant*, Philadelphia, PA: Running Press.

Wilkinson, R. (2005) *The Impact of Inequality: How To Make Sick Societies Healthier*, London and New York: Routledge.

Wilkinson, R. and Pickett, K. (2009) *The Spirit Level: Why More Equal Societies Almost Always Do Better*, London: Penguin Books.

Wink, W. (1992) *Engaging the Powers: Discernment and Resistance in a World of Domination*, Minneapolis, MN: Fortress Press.

Yalom, I.D. (1980) *Existential Psychotherapy*, New York: Basic Books.

Yeats, W.B. (2000) *The Collected Poems of W.B. Yeats*, Ware: Wordsworth Editions.

Young, I.M. (1990) 'The ideal of community and the politics of difference', in *Feminism/Postmodernism*, ed. L. Nicholson, New York: Routledge.

Young, J. (1999) *The Exclusive Society: Social Exclusion, Crime and Difference in Late Modernity*, Newbury Park, CA: Sage Press.

Yunus, M. (1999) *Banker to the Poor: The Story of the Grameen Bank*, London: Aurum Press.

Zizek, S. (2011) *Living in the End Times*, London and New York: Verso.

Index

action learning 39, 146, 149
action research 39, 51, 146
agency
  social 15, 39, 94, 95
  structure dilemma 113
agenda
  common 25
  hidden 114
  hold lightly 24, 62, 147
  practitioner 24, 62, 81
  shared 26
agonistic
  engagement 116, 117
  politics 93, 116, 117, 125
agora 112–16, 122, 123, 127
agreement
  joint 71
  mutual 25
  shared 28
agreement generation 71, 72
Alexander, C. 50
Alinsky, S. 2, 3, 63, 79, 135
Alinskian 79
alterity 17, 53
analysis
  building 44, 59, 70–1, 72, 68, 86 140
  collective 140
  community 59, 61, 64, 71, 73, 75, 76, 85, 86, 89
  critical 9, 27, 31
  dialogical *see* dialogic/dialogical
  group 61, 62–3, 68, 70–3, 75, 80, 89
  'needs' 85
  practitioner 16, 68, 69, 70, 71, 89, 99
  shared 44, 59, 86
  widening 68–70, 89
Andrews, D. vii, 1, 3, 5, 55, 61, 74, 112, 156
antagonistic
  engagement 116
  politics 20, 80, 117, 127
anti-hospitality 34
antithesis 25, 36, 100
antithetical 75, 117
assets based community development approach (ABCD) 3

associationism 12, 106
attentive/attentiveness viii, 11, 13, 29, 49, 50, 51, 55, 59, 148, 155
Australia Institute 121–2
author–activists 135, 153

Barringham, N. viii, 84, 85
Bakhtin, M. M. 27, 28, 30, 31
banding 61, 62, 64
Batten, R. 3, 146
Bauman, Z. 112
'becoming' 10, 40, 48–9
belonging 48–9
Better Life Options Programme (BLP) 145
Bohm, D. 4, 15, 22, 25, 26, 31, 76, 133
bonding 61, 62, 64
Bourdieu, P. 96, 97
Brazil 13, 40, 128
brokering 51
bridging 61, 63, 86
Brown, A. ix, 67
Brown, W. 97, 120
Buber, M. xiii, 1, 4, 6, 14, 19, 22, 23, 24, 26, 28, 29, 31, 34, 35, 50, 129, 135, 156
building
  analysis *see* analysis
  bridges 58
  community *see* community
  capacity 3, 11, 146–7, 150, 153
  economies 87, 104, 105, 126
  fences 34
  gated communities 34
  the other 73–5
  peace *see* peace
  relationship/s 24, 35, 57, 81, 87, 88
  'social capital' 15
  trust 67–8
  understanding 5, 21, 22, 68, 69, 70, 87, 130, 156
  walls 120
bureaucratised mind 40
Burkett, I. ix, 24, 111

Cambodia 141, 149
Caniglia, F. 113

Index

capacity building *see* building
capital
  global 49
  social 15
capitalist
  logics 96
  non-capitalist 103, 110
  post-capitalist 10
care xiv, 18, 24, 44, 50, 59, 72, 83, 86, 95, 99, 107, 111, 115, 118, 127, 152
careful conflict *see* conflict
caring 18, 99–127, 130
Carmen, R. 109
Capra, F. 118
Chambers, R. 3, 39, 73, 140, 146, 147, 155
circles 124, 132, 133, 137, 138, 150
citizen, project 1, 9
Community Praxis Co-operative vii, 3, 105, 149
conviviality 95, 100
co-operative/s 12, 13, 63, 83, 104–5, 124, 128, 137
code, Freirean 5, 21, 134
collective
  action 8, 16, 30, 36, 41, 62, 95, 97, 129
  analysis *see* analysis
  coherence 25, 26, 31
  framework 4, 8, 12, 18, 20, 32, 99, 128, 152, 155, 156–7
  narrative practice 72
  pledge 71
  practice 4, 5, 8, 17, 22, 154
  practice, ethical 30
commons 8, 9, 49, 126
communication 23, 24, 27, 52, 86, 87, 156
  horizontal 86
  technologies 113
  vertical 86
communion xii, 23, 24, 154
communitas 4, 5, 6, 7, 8, 17
communities of resistance 48–9, 72
community
  building 3, 6, 9, 43, 100–1, 119
  as dialogue 5, 6, 17, 23–5, 31, 33, 34, 38, 91, 92, 100, 111, 118, 120, 154
  'of enquiry' 76
  as an ethical space 4, 5, 7, 17, 154
  as hospitality 5–7, 17, 34, 38, 44, 50, 59, 86, 92, 100, 117, 118, 120, 154
  as a paradigmatic site 117
Community Capacity Enhancement (CCE) 71–2
complex system/s i, 16, 121, 125
complexity
  flourishes 28
co-motion 6, 16, 35, 39, 43, 67
conflict 68, 78, 79, 81, 82
  careful 61, 77, 80, 81, 89, 153
  intracultural 75
  resolution 96
consciousness, participatory 25, 26, 31
contemplation 17, 133

contestation 15
'contextualised evaluation' 139
conversation
  in-context 5, 21
  deconstructive 138, 141, 142, 144, 145, 153
creative
  action 5, 21
  energies 47, 57
  potential 52
  process 1, 40, 49, 50, 51, 56
  transformation xiii, 4, 149
'creative transgression' 30
creativity 35, 38, 39–43, 45, 52, 56, 59, 129, 141

data generation 71–2
decolonising 9
deconstructive
  conversation 138, 142, 144–5, 151, 153
  movements 12, 16–17, 65, 97, 111, 155
decontextualised definition 4, 21
'delicate relationship' 27, 64
de-humanisation 30
democratisation 111–13, 115
democratising 83, 104, 113, 115
Denborough, D. 3, 7, 72, 73
depth i, x, xi, xiii, 4, 21, 36, 53, 59, 101, 130, 134, 153, 154, 157
  approach xiv, 11–12, 17, 155
  embracing 11
  restoring 10–12
  psychologist/s 29, 94
  and soul/soulfulness 10, 12, 13, 18, 32, 45, 55, 56
Derrida, J. 2, 5, 6, 7, 17, 53, 117, 118, 129
Derridean 6, 111
despair 138, 151, 152, 153
destabilise 16, 17, 30, 34, 59, 60, 82, 106, 108, 111, 119, 132, 136, 142, 144, 153
de Tocqueville, A. 112
dialectic xiii, 23, 25, 27, 67, 93, 156
dialogic/dialogical
  analysis 73, 74, 75, 76
  approach xiv, 1, 3, 6, 11, 12, 15, 23, 34, 36, 38, 49, 53, 54, 56, 57, 59, 61, 64, 66, 74, 77, 78, 82, 97, 99, 108, 110, 111, 120, 128
  challenges 35, 91, 93, 97–155
  commitment 12, 14, 19, 24, 34, 35, 74, 81, 82, 89, 93, 94, 155
  logics 25
  method/s 17, 39, 61–8 , 89, 138
  muscles 25, 95, 97
  politics 20, 80
  practice/s 14, 17, 26, 67, 72, 89, 93, 138
  process/es 14, 15, 25, 43, 49, 50–1, 75, 95, 110, 141
  turn 4, 22–3, 26, 126, 155
  relations 96
dialogue
  arrested 144
  attitudes 23–4, 30
  as community *see* community

context 4, 5, 20, 24, 27–8, 127
  'of class struggle' 30
  embodied 24, 29
  faculties 29
  forces for 30
  fresh 130
  genre 21, 27, 28, 31, 42
  orientation 141
  responsive dance 18, 28, 29, 31, 64
  rules of 28
  skills 7, 29, 138
  strategic 23–5, 31
  sub-text 24
  technical 23–4
  text 24
  'thin' 29
  weaken/ing 18, 91–8, 99, 156
disruptive 5, 17, 21
diversity 118–20, 127
domination 5, 14, 21, 30, 31, 67
'double stories' 72
dramaturgical 20
Dulwich Centre 3, 7, 72, 137

Earth Policy Institute 121, 122
ecological 16, 18, 97, 102, 106, 108, 110, 120, 122, 124, 125, 156
  impact 123, 127
  objectives 104, 126
  sensibility 12, 15, 17, 155
  spheres 19, 99, 131
  sustainability 31, 103
  worlds 142, 144, 153
economic, rationalism xii
economy
  Buddhist 102
  caring for 102–10
  community 102–4, 106, 108
  death 102
  diverse 103, 109
  human-scale 102, 104, 108, 109, 110, 122
  living 102, 104, 105, 106
  market 48, 103, 106
  moral 102, 104, 105, 106
  relational 103–5, 106, 108, 110, 122
  social 102, 104
  solidarity 102
Ecuador 77–8, 86, 125
Ellul, J. 10, 135
Elos Institute 40–1
embodiment 23
emplacement 45–8, 85
empowerment xiii, 35, 81, 130, 139, 145–7, 150, 153
episteme 10, 39
eros 36–7, 59
Escobar, A. 9, 10
Esposito, R. 6
Esteva, G. 5, 6
ethical
  'to be' 120

'dividend' 105
imperative 13, 21, 106
practice 14, 29–30
space 4, 5, 7, 17, 21, 29, 30, 154
experiment xv, 40, 44, 52, 89, 104, 105, 106
Expo '88 65, 74, 101

Falzon, C. 29, 30
Feixa, C. 54
feminist/s 7, 92, 112
focalised, view 54
Forester, J. 41, 51, 76
Foresters Community Finance 105
Foucault, M. 4, 29, 30, 31, 52, 53
fourth sector 106
framework/s:
  assets-based 3, 104
  community-driven 2
  dialogical *see* dialogic/dialogical
  people-centred 3
  practice xi, 1–19
  rights-based 3
  sustainable-livelihoods 3, 104
Freire, P. 1, 4, 5, 8, 12, 15, 19, 22, 26, 27, 28, 31, 32, 33, 36, 38, 40, 43, 54, 69, 86, 111, 130, 134, 135, 147
friendship 6, 95, 100
Fromm, E. 33, 36
fundamentalism 91–2
Furedi, F. 94, 97

Gadamer, Hans-Georg 4, 10, 17, 22, 23, 26, 28, 29, 31, 33
Gandhi, M. 1, 4, 19, 79, 100, 135, 156
Gandhian 19, 40, 79, 108
Gap Filler 52
genre 1, 21, 27, 28, 31, 42, 67, 113
gentling 61–4, 89, 151
Gibson-Graham, J. K. 7, 103, 109
Gilchrist, A. 3
Gramsci, A. 129
Gram Vikas 65
Groundviews 113
GROW group 58

Haines, N. 141
Hamdi, N. 51, 52
Hamilton, C. 107, 135
Harris, V. 71
Hermeneutical 17
Highlander Folk School 128
Hicks, D. 96, 97
Hillman, J. 94, 142
Hollis, J. 29, 42, 92, 151
holistically, thinking 26, 54
hooks, b. 48, 49, 135
Hope, A. 3, 26, 128
Hope, R. 39
'horizons' 22
Horton, M. 63, 130, 135

Index

humanising xiii, 4, 8, 14, 23, 24, 33, 34, 35, 154
   dehumanising 26, 48
hydro-fracking 125

ideology 76, 91, 92, 93, 97, 162
ideologues 91–3
Ife, Jim 2, 3, 45, 154
Illich, I. 10, 109
imaginative literacy 131–5, 143, 144, 153
India 32, 48, 79, 92, 100, 125, 137
inequalities
   growing 91, 95–7, 106, 156
indigenous 7, 9, 28, 34, 42, 50, 54, 61, 67, 77, 79, 109, 114, 119, 125–6, 137, 139
industrial 9, 105, 110, 123
Ingamells, A. 1, 61, 154, 156
Innovative
   social change 30
   structures 83–5
innovation, social dialogue 133
inspiration 130, 133, 135, 145–9, 150, 152, 153
instrumental 6, 10, 11, 14, 30, 39, 96, 99, 112, 118, 154
intervention 6, 11, 39, 45, 51, 53, 55, 56, 59, 67, 94–5, 97, 99, 148, 154
intimacy 13, 43–4, 67

Jameson, F. 30
jazzy exchange 28

Kaplan, A. 3, 9, 11, 15, 16, 54, 124, 158 (n)
'Kate's Cuppa' 44
Kelly, A. 1, 3, 15, 16, 23, 24, 25, 61, 64, 67, 79, 111, 156
Kite of Life 72
Korten, D. 102
Knitta 49

Lakey, G. 132, 144
Lathouras, A. 67
La Via Campesina movement 87
leadership
learning 63, 87, 128
   action *see* action
   community 133
   embodied 147–9, 150, 153
   experiential 138–9, 140, 149
   horizontal 146
   local-level 146
   participatory 138, 140–1, 153
   peer-oriented 146
   social 2, 154
   space/s 136, 141, 150, 153
   transformative 51
   transformational 142
Lederach, J. P. 16, 81, 139, 149
Ledwith, M. 3, 26, 129
life-project/s 1, 6, 10, 109, 110
linguistic-structural 20
listening 12, 24, 26, 35, 50, 75, 76, 111, 120, 133, 142, 145

literary imagination 43
living wage 106
love 32–8, 40, 44, 50, 55, 59, 79, 100–1, 120, 126
'lurking with intent' 67

MacIntyre, A. 27
McLuhan, M. 150
McMichael, P. 8, 19, 20, 87
Macy, J. 123, 124, 125, 135, 151, 152
mandate 26, 67–8, 70, 89, 114, 124–5, 153
Mathie, A. 104
Max-Neef, M. 3, 11, 86, 102, 109, 135
Menon, G. 48
metaphor 4, 9, 11, 16, 29, 73, 132, 145
method
   community development 61–8
   dialogical *see* dialogic/dialogical
   invitation 66–7
   micro 61, 62, 64, 68, 72, 89
   mezzo 61, 68, 89
   macro 61, 63, 86, 89
   meta 61, 63, 86, 89
methodology, Community Capacity Enhancement 71–2
model
   elicitive 138, 139–40, 149, 153
   experiential 138–9, 149, 153
   participatory learning and action 138, 140–1, 153
   spiral 138, 140, 153
Monbiot, G. 108, 123, 135
monologue 91
Moore, T. 13, 37
Moorooka 47
Mouffe, C. 93, 116,
movements 24, 40, 63, 73, 74, 123, 129, 136
   deconstructive 12, 16–17, 65, 155

narrative
   approach 3
   shifting 111
   thread 25, 41, 54, 93
Nelson Mandela Foundation 71–2
Nepal 115
neo-liberalism xii, 92
'new urbanism' 51
New Zealand Social Entrepreneur Fellowship 133
non-violence 79
normative
   framework 14
   ideal 4
   perspective 20, 22
normatively 5, 21
Nouwen, H. 5, 92, 135, 157
Nundah Community Enterprises Co-op 105
Nungeena Indigenous Women's Healing 42

O'Connor, M. 1, 64
Oasis Game 40, 42

objectivity 1
objectivised 2
ordinary 19, 36–8, 44, 59, 100–2, 112, 121, 125, 126, 145, 152, 153
'organic intellectuals' 129, 130, 152
orientation
 dialogue *see* dialogue
 hospitality 116
 mystical 23
 other 4, 22, 26, 31, 33, 36, 59, 154
 philosophical 11
 service 89
 soulful 12, 13, 17, 37, 53, 93, 97, 155
Ostrom, E. 8
other-oriented *see* orientation
'Out of the Shadows' 75–7

Palmer, D. 28
Papua New Guinea (PNG) ix, 54, 66, 132, 136
paradigm/s 9, 10, 11, 15, 16, 39, 51, 53, 76, 85, 99, 117, 154
paradigmatic 117–18
paradox 23–5, 31, 36, 109
Parenti, C. 122, 123
participation 32, 35, 38, 45
 deepening 39–44, 59, 67, 72, 111, 115, 139, 154
 disembedded 39, 40
 'economically appealing proposition' 39
 'politically attractive slogan' 39
 and story-ing 41
 and resonance 41–3
 widening 44–5
participatory action research 39
participatory consciousness 25, 26, 31
Patel, R. 49, 87, 102, 126
patterns 11, 16, 30, 40, 50, 82, 97, 99, 108, 123, 151, 155
peace-building 113, 149
Peacemaker 121
performance 20, 38, 75, 149, 150
performative 20
phenomenological 20, 22
philosopher 5, 6, 7, 11, 12, 22, 23, 29, 52, 96, 123
philosophical xiv, 1, 3, 11, 17, 154, 155
Peile, C. 16, 17
place-making 45–52, 59, 156
poetic 43–4
'Politics in the Pub' 113, 124
positionality 28–9, 31
'possibilitator' 129–33, 136–8, 143, 145–7, 152, 153
post-capitalist 2, 10
post-development 4, 6, 10, 154
post-structural 10
practice/s
 dialogical *see* dialogic/dialogical
 geometry of 65
 reflective 2, 18, 156
 reflexive 2, 12, 18, 156

practitioner, analysis *see* analysis
principle, working xv
professional, project 1, 9, 14
provisional, mutual understanding 22–3

QPASTT 88–9, 137
questioning, mutual critical 27, 28

radical xiii, 3, 9, 79, 125, 128
rationalisation 14, 106, 107, 108
rebuilding 36, 105, 109, 110
reductionist xiii, 10, 15, 26, 53, 141, 154
re-humanisation 24, 30, 31
REFLECT groups 27
reflective/ively xiii, 1, 2, 18, 27, 62, 64, 94, 146, 149, 156
 non-reflective 93
 questions 64
reflexive/ively 2, 12, 18, 36, 156
 non-reflexive 93, 97
refugees 47, 48, 49, 72, 88, 89, 95, 119, 122, 135, 136, 137, 143
Refugee Learning Circles 80
relational, practices xiii, xiv
Resource Association 3, 84, 85, 86, 137
resistance xiii, xiv, 9, 11, 24, 30, 48, 49, 72, 74, 78, 94, 96, 101, 109, 110, 125, 127, 149, 155
responsibilities 75, 82, 83, 147
responsive dance 18, 28–9, 31, 64
Restakis, J. 83, 104
Reverse Garbage 105
rights, human xiv, 88, 89, 113
 'from below' 3
Rist, G. 9
Rose, D. B. 7, 11, 36, 37, 50
Rose, N. 53
Roy, A. 79, 126

scaling
 across 63, 124
 up 63, 146
Sen, A. 39
Senge, P. 14, 133
Senegal 70
Sennett, R. 12, 13, 25, 27, 28, 64, 67, 76, 95, 96, 97
Shack Dwellers International movement 87
shadow
 as potential 2, 52, 57, 59
 as gift 58, 59
shallow i, 21, 32, 33, 34, 43, 53, 55, 141
shallowing 11, 155
Shiva, V. 49, 102
Shulman, H. 27, 49
Shuman, M. 104
skilful practice 18, 25, 28
social
 change 8, 9, 11, 18, 30, 33, 38, 40, 56, 61, 65, 71, 74, 89, 98, 113, 115, 129, 130, 146, 152, 154, 155
 forces 5, 21, 30, 70

pain 97
distress 97
practice 6, 12, 15, 16, 17, 49, 67, 81, 97, 118, 128, 155
  processes 18, 46, 49, 50, 94, 97, 124
  solidarity 12–13, 15, 64, 78, 97, 155, 157
solidarity
  political 13, 64
  social *see* social
  worker 97
soul 6, 10, 13, 14, 37, 38, 55, 59, 116, 134, 143
soulful xiv, 12–14, 17, 18, 32, 33, 36, 37, 38, 44, 45, 49, 50, 51, 53, 55, 56, 57, 59, 61, 77, 89, 93, 95, 97, 130, 134, 136, 153, 155
South Africa ix, 3, 55, 71, 87, 100, 107, 112, 125, 128, 136, 137, 145, 147
South East Queensland Intercultural Cities Forum 75
Sri Lanka 113
state of responsivity 29
stories, living 135–6
structure
  of thought 25
  agency dilemma 113
structural, transformation 26
structuring 61, 63, 64, 82–9, 137, 138, 141, 153
sub-text 24
Sudanese 47, 119
Sunshine Coast Community Co-op 88
Swan, J. & R. 50
synthesis 2, 25, 76, 82

Tagore, R. 13, 14, 43
Tampa 80
Taylor, C. 22
technique, oriented 11, 15, 17, 154
technology/ies 11, 72, 108, 110, 113, 123, 125, 150, 153, 154, 155
territorialisation 53
text 1, 19, 21, 24, 130, 134, 135, 157
theatre
  applied 147–8
  forum 147–8
theoretical, attitude 11, 17, 18
theorist 5, 7, 20, 21, 27, 29, 156, 157
theory x, xv, 1, 4, 5, 8, 9, 11, 17–20, 23, 25, 29, 31, 91, 128, 131, 138, 140, 141, 154, 155, 156
theory-building 156
therapeutic, culture 91, 94–8
thesis 25, 50, 52, 96
third space 23
Timmel, S. 3, 26, 128
tradition/s
  anarchist 2
  associationism 12

conflicting 79–80, 89
communitarian 2
critical 2, 12
intellectual 2, 11, 155
methodological 2, 155
Nova-Scotia 2
geographical 2, 11, 155
Settlement House 2, 12
social learning 2, 128, 154
social mobilisation 2
social guidance 2
train-the-trainer 11, 155
training
  for transformation 3, 19, 26, 128–53
  transformational 129, 130, 131, 138, 139, 143, 144, 146, 147, 148, 150, 151, 152
transformation xiii, xiv, 4, 5, 19, 21, 26–7, 30, 36–8, 50, 55, 57, 58, 59, 99, 106, 111, 115, 117, 121, 128–53, 154, 156
Turner, V. 7–8
Turton, D. 45

Ubels, J. 146
uncertainty 11, 22, 23, 29, 30, 93, 144, 157
UK 2, 3, 107, 117, 121, 124, 137
unity, in-diversity 8
USA 51, 92, 111, 136, 137, 149

Vancouver 72
Vanier, J. 5, 135
Vanuatu x, 9, 10, 49, 50, 67, 68, 69, 70, 107, 108, 109, 110, 112, 132, 136, 139, 140, 148, 149, 150
Vietnam 34, 42
vocational xvi, 12, 14, 17, 128, 155
voice 1, 27, 43–4, 50, 73, 111, 113, 115
Vonnegut, K. 46–7

Walker, P. 67, 149
Watkins, M. 27, 49
Wates, N. 51
web 16, 50, 56, 62, 86, 100, 120, 127, 138, 152
West End 58, 61, 74, 83, 84, 101, 103, 114, 136
West Papua 78–9
Wheatley, M. 6, 15, 16, 40, 55, 56, 63
Wicks, J. 87, 105
Wilkinson, R. 97, 98, 106

Yalom, D. 33, 129, 150, 151, 152
Yeats 93
Yunus, M. 105

Zizek, S. 96